Foreword

Dear students,

Welcome to the Collins Cambridge IGCSE® English as a Second Language Student Book! We hope it will enable you to take charge of your learning on the IGCSE English as a Second Language course and to develop an independent, thoughtful approach to your English language studies. You are perhaps already fluent in one or more other languages, so we hope this book becomes an effective guide to the requirements of this fast-paced, practical English course.

The skills and vocabulary covered in the book revolve around a number of interesting topics and world issues that will help you become much more fluent, clear and confident in your responses, both oral and written. It provides you with key skills in reading, writing, speaking and listening that will help make you a better communicator in all situations and give you a basis for further study in English. These skills include skimming and scanning, note-taking, summarising and shaping your writing for different audiences.

The Student Book builds on your understanding of how languages work and offers you a variety of useful tips and strategies to improve the quality and accuracy of your spoken and written communication. Most importantly, this book gives you lots to think about and talk about while developing your reading, writing and listening skills in an international context. It uses a number of fun activities and current genres like emails, blogs, websites, news reports and magazine articles.

Each chapter begins with a set of fascinating 'Big pictures' to get you thinking around the topic and working out what you already know about it. You might discuss some of this in your first language, but make sure you record your responses in a handy journal to keep track of your growing knowledge and vocabulary in English. Once you have worked through a series of interactive reading, writing, speaking and listening tasks, you have the opportunity to work on a 'Big task' with your classmates, which allows you to showcase your skills and vocabulary in a real-world context. You could set up an exciting competition around each task and get your friends and teachers to assess this.

You could use this book to cover a series of key examination skills which you wish to focus on, or as a topic-based textbook that you work through in class. It is helpful if you work with a friend or classmates to make the most of all aspects of the book, and not just the speaking and listening parts.

Good luck with your English studies and the language of global communication!

Shubha Koshy,

Hong Kong

Contents

How to use this book

Section 1: The coursebook section

Your Cambridge IGCSE English as a Second Language Student Book is divided into two main sections. The first section (pages 8–247) is your coursebook. This contains 12 chapters based on topics such as technology, exploration and the environment.

Each of these chapters starts with a 'big picture' feature and ends with a 'big task' – you can find out more about these on page 3. The chapter is then split into four parts, each focusing on one skill: reading, writing, speaking or listening.

The skills you will explore and practise are all assessment objectives in the Cambridge IGCSE English as a Second Language syllabuses (0510 and 0511). You can find out more about these assessment objectives, as well as more information on the questions you will face in each paper and the marks available, at http://www.cie.org.uk/qualifications/academic/middlesec/igcse/subject?assdef_id=854

The coursebook chapters end with a 'Check your progress' feature. For each of the reading, writing, speaking and listening skills you have explored in the chapter, think about how you would place yourself in a table: higher (very good understanding), middle (okay understanding) or lower (need to improve). This is a great way for you to take responsibility for your own development.

Here are some more features you will see in the coursebook section:

This tells you which assessment objectives in the Cambridge IGCSE English as a Second Language syllabus are covered in this part of the chapter.

'Language boosters' help you improve your understanding of English grammar and vocabulary.

This symbol means that there is an audio track on the Student Book CD-ROM. You will need to listen to this track to answer the questions. You will also find transcripts (written-out versions of the track) on the CD-ROM.

You will see the same headings in each of Chapters 1–12: *Getting started, Exploring the skills, Developing the skills, Going further*. Each one builds your understanding of specific skills.

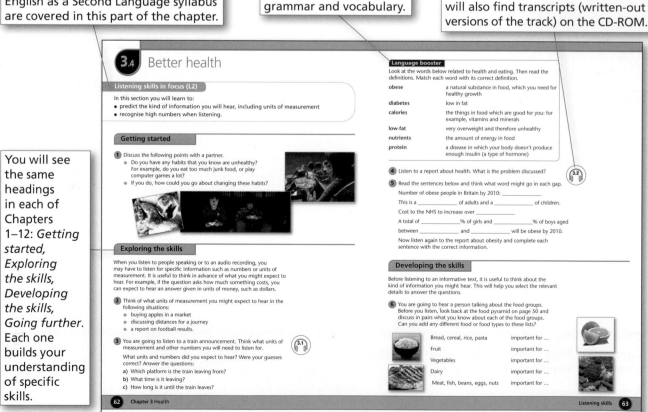

Section 2: The exam guidance section

The second section of the Student Book (pages 248 to the end of the book) helps you prepare for your Cambridge IGCSE English as a Second Language exam. Chapters 13–20 show you the different types of question you will find on your Cambridge IGCSE exam papers:

- Reading questions on short texts
- Reading questions on longer texts
- Information transfer questions
- Note-making questions
- Summary-writing questions
- Long writing questions to explain or describe
- Long writing questions including opinion or argument
- Listening questions
- Oral (speaking) assessment.

In each of Chapters 13–20, you will find out what different types of question look like, the skills you need, and a step-by-step guide to approaching and answering these questions. In each chapter there is also an exam-style question or questions for you to answer.

In Chapter 21 there are example answers to each of the exam-style questions in Chapters 13–20. There are generally two example answers, at different levels, for each question, together with our marker's marks and comments.

Reading through these marks and comments will help you understand the total marks each question is given, and how to avoid common mistakes. You could try covering up the marks and comments first, and think about what mark you would have given the answer. Then check your marks against our marker's. You can do this on your own or with a partner.

Cambridge International Examinations have a webpage for Cambridge IGCSE English as a Second Language students, including past papers and a learner guide. Go to: http://www.cambridgestudents.org.uk/subjectpages/english/igcsesl

Here are some features you will see in the exam guidance section:

This tells you which skills and questions are for Extended-level students only. This **C** means the question is for Core-level students only.

These appear in all chapters of the book and give extra advice. Another common feature is a glossary box, which explains words you may not already know.

In the exam guidance section, these checklists are a summary of what you need to do when approaching different types of exam question.

You can practise exam-style questions in Chapters 13–20 and look at example answers and comments in Chapter 21.

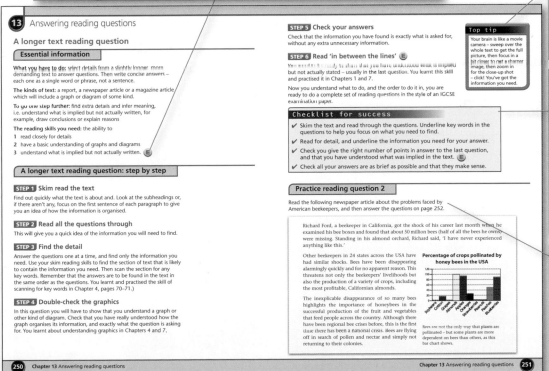

The big picture

In this chapter you are going to think about technology and how it is rapidly changing the world we live in. You will:

- read about the origins of some of the technology we take for granted today

- think about the effects that it has on us

- research, think, talk and write about what you consider to be the greatest technological inventions of our times.

Thinking big

1 On your own, pick any two pictures from the collage that you find interesting.
   - Looking carefully at each picture, note down what you think each one is saying about technology.
   - Make notes ready for a discussion.

2 In pairs:
   - Explain to your partner why you chose these two pictures. Discuss your ideas and see how far you agree or disagree.
   - Note down any interesting words or ideas from this conversation.

3 On your own, note answers to the following questions:
   - What examples of technology have you used since you got out of bed this morning?
   - Which of these items would you consider to be essential?
   - Which of these items would you consider to be non-essential?
   - How would you define technology? Write your own definition of what you consider to be 'technology'.

Chapter 1

Technology

The evolution of technology

In this section you will learn to:
- skim and scan different kinds of texts for facts and details
- understand what is implied but not actually written in an advertisement.

Getting started

1 What is technology and how is it used?
  a) As a class or in groups, share the ideas that you wrote about in 'Thinking big'.
  b) What were the earliest forms of technology and what did they help people to do?
  c) Discuss examples of technology that have changed in your lifetime and what they help you to do.

Exploring the skills

When there is too much text to read, or you are short of time, you do not need to read every single word on the page. Skimming and scanning are two techniques that will help you find quickly the information you need.

Skimming involves moving your eyes quickly over a text to get a general sense of it. It helps you get the 'gist' – the overall meaning – of the writing, without having to read it all carefully. You can then decide which parts you need to read more closely.

To find out quickly what a text is about:
- read the title first and then the subheadings
- look at any pictures to see what hints they give
- read the beginning and end of each paragraph
- let your eyes skim over the text and look out for key words.

2 Skim read the text below and to find out what it is about.

A Computing then and now
The 20th century was definitely the age of computers, although they were only invented around the middle of the century. The early machines were **unwieldy** and could only perform basic tasks.

Yet today, tiny handheld devices are used for complicated purposes, such as word processing, storage and delivery of images and music. Electronic **devices pervade** every aspect of our lives today and we are definitely part of an exciting Computer Age. Here are some of the highlights.

B 1958 Integrated circuit invented
Jack Kilby of Texas Instruments and Robert Noyce of Fairchild Semiconductor independently invent the integrated circuit – an electronic system essential for computers.

C 1968 The computer mouse makes its public debut
The computer mouse is demonstrated at a computer conference in San Francisco. Its inventor, Douglas Engelbart of the Stanford Research Institute, receives the **patent** for the mouse 2 years later.

D 1977 Apple II is released
Electronics hobbyists Steve Jobs and Steve Wozniak release the Apple II, a desktop personal computer for the mass market.

E 1992 Personal Digital Assistant
Apple chairman John Sculley coins the term 'personal digital assistant' (PDA) to refer to handheld computers. One of the first on the market is Apple's Newton, which has a liquid crystal display operated with a **stylus**.

Extract from www.greatachievements.org

Which of the following statements explains what the text is about?
a) It gives the reasons why you should have computers.
b) It tells you the bad things about computers.
c) It tells you the history of computers.
d) It is from a story about computers.

3 With a partner, discuss how you could tell which statement in task 2 was correct, and which it could not be.

Once you have skimmed a text to get an overall sense of its meaning, you might need to find a specific detail. This is called **scanning** – looking over a text to find the exact information you want.

4 Now scan the text above to find which paragraph (A, B, C, D or E) contains the answer to each of these questions.
a) What is another name given to the time period of the late 20th century?
b) When was the computer mouse first seen by the general public?
c) Which was the first personal computer?

5 Scan the text above again and answer these questions.
a) Who invented the integrated circuit?
b) Who invented the computer mouse?

Glossary

unwieldy – large and awkward to use or handle
device – an tool invented for a particular purpose
pervade – are all around, everywhere
patent – official right given to an inventor to make or sell an invention, without being copied
stylus – an electronic pen

Top tip

When you scanned for details, you probably used the subheadings to help you. You can also look for key words in the questions. For example, 'When?' will need a date or a time. 'Who?' will probably need a name. Underline these key 'question words' to help you narrow down what you're looking for.

Developing the skills

You can also use your skimming and scanning skills to find facts and details when looking at pictures and diagrams in text. For example, you can:

- look at what the pictures show
- look at any captions that go with the pictures
- see if the pictures have any labels explaining more about them.

6 Read the advertisement opposite. It is from the 1980s. Skim and scan the advertisement, looking at the images and headings, to answer the following questions.

a) Which company designed, produced and distributed the BBC Microcomputer System?

b) What are the six ways you can use the BBC Microcomputer?

c) Which two pieces of equipment do you need to use this computer?

Now scan for these details:

d) How much does the BBC Microcomputer cost?

e) Where is it available?

f) What information is contained in the 'Welcome' **cassette**?

> ### Glossary
>
> **cassette** – magnetic tape used to record audio or video to play on a cassette player

Going further

To understand the purpose of a text, we have to use our reading skills. Sometimes when reading we have to understand what is **implied** but not actually written down.

Language booster

When a meaning is **implied**, the writer does not say openly what he or she means, but the reader can work it out. For example, the meaning of a sign that says 'No smoking!' is not implied, it is clearly stated.

However, the meaning of a sign saying 'Thank you for keeping this area smoke free' implies that the reader should not smoke!

7 Look again at the advertisement. In pairs, reread the first four paragraphs ('Above ...' to '... those above'), then answer questions i) and ii)..

i) *Above are just some of the ways you could use a BBC Micro computer* means:

   A There are very few ways to use the computer.

   B It is really hard to know how to use the computer.

   C There are many ways you could use the computer.

ii) *you don't have to be a technical wizard to use a micro* means:

   A The computer works like magic.

   B The computer is really hi-tech.

   C The computer is really easy to use.

These sentences give information in a subtle way. The text expects you to 'read between the lines' and understand more than is actually written. For example, *just some of the ways you could use a BBC Micro computer* suggests that there are others. So the answer to i) is C. Now write an explanation for the answer you gave for ii) and then read the rest of the advertisement and answer iii).

iii) Which of these best completes the sentence?

The main purpose of this text is …

A to advise us how to use this computer.

B to tell a story about someone and this computer.

C to persuade us to buy a particular computer.

THE BOOK-KEEPER.

THE COOK.

THE CHILD-MINDER.

Meet the ultimate home-help.

THE GARDENER.

THE TEACHER.

THE SECRETARY.

Above are just some of the ways you could use a BBC Micro computer.

And we say 'you' advisedly. For, contrary to popular misconceptions, you don't have to be a technical wizard to use a micro – especially a BBC Micro. Nor do you need any complex equipment.

All you need is an ordinary TV set and a cassette player.

Then with a few basic instructions you can run programs like those above.

There is a huge range of these programs available for the BBC Micro covering games, education and business applications as well as those closer to home.

But, of course, the more you get used to the computer and its language, the more you can get out of it.

To help you do just that, you will receive a step by step User Guide which explains the full capabilities of your micro and shows you how to construct useful programs of your own.

You will also receive a free "Welcome" cassette which contains different programs for you to experiment with, ranging from Music and graphics, to games like Kingdom and Bat 'n Ball.

The BBC Micro is at the heart of the BBC's massive Computer Literacy Project; it is also the most popular and successful machine being ordered by British schools, under the current DOI scheme.

So it is the ideal micro to introduce you – and the family – to home computing. (Although if you have children at school you may find them ahead of you already.)

The BBC Micro costs less than the average video – only £399. It is available from WH Smith Computer Shops, Boots, John Lewis and local Acorn stockists.

However, if you would like to order one with your credit card, or if you want the address of your nearest supplier just phone 01-200 0200.

The BBC Microcomputer System.

Designed, produced and distributed by Acorn Computers Limited.

33

1.2 Cell phones on the brain

In this section you will learn to:
- collect and organise ideas before writing to explain or inform
- communicate your ideas clearly and accurately through writing
- use exactly the right word to express your ideas precisely.

Getting started

1 Cell phones, or mobile phones, are so convenient that they are everywhere and nearly everyone uses them. Note down some ideas about mobile phones, using these prompts to help.
- How often do you use a cell phone?
- In what ways do you find cell phones useful?

Exploring the skills

Whenever you write you need to have a clear idea of what the purpose of your writing is. For example, if you are giving someone information about mobile phones, you would not need to include a description of your own feelings about mobiles. Just keep to the facts and be really clear.

2 Imagine you have been asked to write a school magazine article about the advantages and disadvantages of mobile phones. You have done some brainstorming and produced a list of points:

Cell phones
- used to send and receive text messages, emails, photos and video
- used to access the internet, play games, listen to music, and more
- unfortunately, used by students to cheat in tests or to bully their classmates
- used to carry around useful contacts in your pocket
- used for word processing and emails
- used for web surfing, mobile banking, calendars, reminders, alarms, memos
- used to keep in touch with friends around the world through social networking
- can be a disturbance at meetings, funerals, music shows or the cinema
- can be a dangerous distraction while driving

Before you write, organise your the points into a concept map based on the advantages and disadvantages of mobile phones. Make sure you have only ONE new idea per box. Add related ideas in smaller boxes linked to the main idea.

Copy the diagram below and add more points into the related boxes.

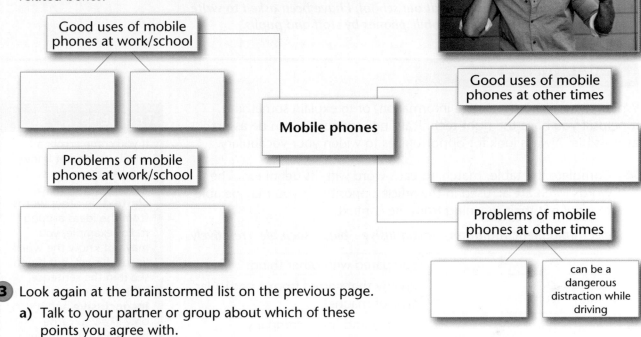

3   Look again at the brainstormed list on the previous page.

a) Talk to your partner or group about which of these points you agree with.

b) Note down:
   ● any interesting words that came up in your discussion
   ● the main points that were raised in your discussion.

Developing the skills

Remember that when you are explaining something to someone you need to be very clear and keep to the facts.

4   Imagine that your school or college needs to decide on its policy about mobile phones. You have been asked to produce a report for the management team. This **report** needs to **explain**:
   ● how mobile phones are used by staff and students during the working day
   ● the benefits and drawbacks of allowing mobile phones at school.

At this point the management is not asking for your opinion – they want to know the current situation.

Draw a new concept map to organise your ideas. You might like to include the following headings in your boxes:
   ● How staff use phones and the benefits to them and others
   ● How students use phones and the benefits to them and others
   ● Possible problems for staff
   ● Possible problems for students.

5 Now write the report for your school or college management team. Write about 200 words.

You could start like this:

As a student representative at our school, I have been asked to write a report about the use of mobile phones by staff and pupils.

Going further

When you are writing to give information, or to explain something, it helps if you have the right technical language so you can be as precise as possible. Always look for opportunities to widen your vocabulary.

6 Complete the table, matching each word with its definition. The words listed are all used in the article opposite, so you may be able to work out their meaning from the context.

electromagnetic radiation   inconclusive   bias   sociable   relatively

	compared with other things
	energy that comes from a particular type of magnet
	friendly and good company
	not giving a definite answer
	leaning towards one particular opinion without good reason

7 Now read the article opposite.
- You are going to send an email of about 150 words to the management team of your school/college/workplace drawing attention to the issues it raises.
  - As you are giving information, you must be clear, accurate and concise. Using the correct technical words will help you.
  - As before, brainstorm your ideas first and put them in a concept map to help you plan your email.

> **Top tip**
>
> If you come across a word you do not know, you can often guess its meaning from its **context**: in other words, from the ideas around it. For example, you may not know the word 'inconclusive', but if you see it in the sentence, 'If the evidence is **inconclusive** and it's only *likely* to cause harm', you should be able to guess that it means 'not definite'.

Should I limit my child's mobile phone use?

ALTHOUGH THERE IS no evidence at the moment that mobile phones cause brain damage, some people think they might. To be on the safe side, encourage your children to text rather than call, and to use them hands-free.

The problem

If you have a child of 10 years old or more, they probably have a mobile phone. Maybe you gave it to them to keep safe, so you would know where they are, but mobile phones are not without their own risks. Not only can your children waste an enormous amount of time texting their friends instead of doing their homework, but mobile phones emit a form of **electromagnetic radiation** that is absorbed by the brain. Last month the World Health Organisation said that mobile phones could 'possibly' be harmful. Children, who will not have finished developing and therefore have thinner skulls, could absorb more of this kind of radiation than adults and be at a greater risk of brain damage.

The dilemma

Should you rip your child's BlackBerry from his or her hands, mid instant-message session? Or, if the evidence is **inconclusive** and the WHO says it's only *likely* to cause as much harm as coffee, maybe mobile phones are **relatively** safe.

The WHO spent a week reviewing the evidence from 14 countries. Very little research exists on the effects of mobile phones on children. The largest study found no evidence that mobile use increased the risk for brain tumours. However, a small proportion of people in the study who spent the most time on mobile phones did have a small increase in a kind of tumour called 'gliomas', reporting them to be on the same side of their head as they used their phones. However, this could have been due to reporting **bias**, i.e. people may have mistaken which side of the head they held their phone against.

The solution

Given that using mobile phones excessively can cause problems for your child – preventing them from sleeping, doing their homework and being **sociable** in the house – it makes sense to try to limit their use.

Extract from 'Dr Dillner's health dilemmas: should I limit my child's mobile phone use?'
By Louisa Dillner, Guardian.co.uk 15 August 2001

1.3 Where in the world is the internet?

In this section you will learn to:
- communicate your ideas clearly, accurately and appropriately
- keep a conversation going by developing ideas with details and examples.

Getting started

Note down some thoughts on the questions below. Write down everything you think about, without worrying about whether it is correct or not.

1 What happens when you send an email? Where does it actually go?

2 Why do you think the **metaphors** 'net', 'web' and 'cloud' are used to refer to the internet?

3 Has the internet made our lives better? Why or why not?

> **Language booster**
>
> A **metaphor** is a comparison that makes something easier to visualise or understand.

Exploring the skills

Conversations are all about communicating your ideas clearly and appropriately. What makes for a good conversation in class?

It takes two to have a conversation, so both people need to:
- offer ideas
- listen carefully to the other person and respond properly
- not dominate the conversation
- find ways to keep the conversation going, for example by asking questions, sympathising, giving a personal example, asking for an opinion.

4 In pairs, have a conversation about what you think the internet is, using the notes you made earlier.

To 'respond properly' to your partner, make sure that you:

✔ Maintain eye contact. Keep your body language open and interested – lean forward, nod, smile. Don't cross your arms or look away.

✔ Ask clarifying questions, such as 'When you say … do you mean … or … ?'

✔ Respond to answers:
   'Oh yes, I see, you meant … when …'
   'How interesting. Now what about … ?'
   'How did you feel? I know I would have felt …'
   'I think … What do you think?'

5 On a sheet of paper, with your partner, create a concept map of your ideas about what the internet is.

6 Read the following information about the internet.

> The World Wide Web is the collection of linked pages that are accessed using the internet and a web browser.

> The internet is a huge network of networks that links computers together all over the world using a range of wires and wireless technologies.

> Social networking websites such as Facebook, MySpace and Twitter are very popular.

> The popularity of the web has exploded over the last 10 years.

> Website addresses such as http://www.sciencekids.co.nz are known by the term Uniform Resource Locater (URL).

> The internet is used for applications like email, file sharing, online chat, phone and video calls, online gaming and more.

> English physicist Tim Berners-Lee is regarded as having invented the World Wide Web in 1989.

> The web is now used for online shopping, social networking, games, news and much more.

> People are often unaware of the potential risks they take when uploading confidential data, passwords and personal information into various websites. Viruses and spam emails also frequently cause disruptions for web users.

> One of the best and most common ways of finding information on the web is through the use of search engines such as Google, Live and Yahoo.

Extracts from www.sciencekids.co.nz

In pairs, discuss:
- any of the ideas that were new to you
- any of the ideas that might be hard to understand
- how you would explain the following technical words to someone who had never used a computer before: web browser, URL, social networking, search engines, spam emails, viruses.

7 Think back to your conversation in task 6 and give each other feedback on how well you both communicated with one another. Look at the checklist above to help you.

Developing the skills

Whether you are chatting to a friend or giving a formal talk to a group of people, and whether you are the speaker or the listener, you still have a responsibility to help communication. Think about eye contact, looking interested and asking questions at the right moment.

8 You are going to listen to an advertisement. It is for a product called an 'eBackpack'. However, before you listen, jot down your ideas on the answers to these questions:

a) What is a backpack normally used for?

b) How is a backpack particularly useful for school students?

c) What might an eBackpack be used for? What other words use 'e' at the beginning like this, and what does the 'e' stand for?

d) Here are some words used in the advertisement:

Dropbox   e-portfolio   collaboration   assign a task   digital copies

What do you think they mean? Look up the meaning of any you don't understand.

9 Talk together in pairs, comparing your notes. Then listen to the advertisement.

10 Listen again and, this time, make a note of any positive words or persuasive phrases the speaker uses.

Listen a third time and make notes summarising the information on eBackpack.

11 Imagine you are a sales person trying to sell eBackpack. Prepare a short pitch – a persuasive talk – to give to your class. Explain why 'cloud storage' is considered a safe way of storing data online. Include the benefits of using this method. Practise with a partner.

12 Listen to some of your class's pitches. Are you persuaded?

Going further

When you are talking with another person, you have to be willing to keep the conversation going. We've already looked at some ways of doing this. Another way to keep a conversation going is to develop it, to move it on further, by giving examples and explaining them a little.

13 Read the advertisements on page 21 and then, in pairs, discuss task 14.

Averting disaster

Dropbox offers you **2GB** of free storage that you can expand to a full 16GB by referring others to the service. Because Dropbox also **syncs** files to your other computers and makes your files easily accessible on your mobile devices, it's a good candidate for your primary work files.

SugarSync offers 5GB of free storage and syncs files just like Dropbox. SugarSync is especially good at handling media files and photos.

Memopal offers 3GB of free cloud storage and gives you more space through referrals in the same manner as Dropbox. It's capable of automatic backup.

ADrive offers 50GB of storage for free. You won't get any sync or auto-backup options, so it'll make for a better file archive than anything, but it's still 50GB of free online storage and you can access your folders via a browser or an android smart-phone or tablet app, or apple iPhone or iPad app. ADrive also has premium plans that include file transfer and back up options such a desktop, webDav or FTP client.

14 An adult you know has had an IT disaster. Their home computer has crashed, losing all their important documents. They do not have any up-to-date back-ups, and you have decided to help them be more organised in the future. Prepare for a conversation where you will discuss their use of the computer and explain some ways they could back up their files.

Use the information above and the table below to make notes for your conversation.

Name of application	Storage capacity in GB	How it works	Back up or synchronise options	Cost	Notes/Ranking 1–5 (1 = best, 5 = worst)

15 Now, with your partner, take turns to role-play the adult. When you are discussing the issue of backing-up files, remember:
- if you are role-playing the adult, ask questions and encourage the younger person
- if you are playing yourself, give examples and be ready to offer further details (you should have plenty to say after preparing the chart above).

Listening skills in focus (L1 and L4)

In this section you will learn to:

- listen for details and answer questions on a spoken text
- listen out for, and use, key question words
- listen for what is implied but not actually said in a more formal conversation.

Getting started

1 Brainstorm some questions that you might ask your teachers, parents or grandparents about technology in their youth. For example:

How did your grandparents communicate with friends, family and the rest of the world?

What equipment did your parents and grandparents use to listen to music?

What were some of the advantages and disadvantages of these methods?

2 Look at the pictures below. Considering each one in turn, discuss the following questions with your group.

a) What form of communication does the picture show? Describe it.

b) Which of these traditional methods of communication are still relevant? Why?

c) Under what circumstances might these methods of communication become relevant again?

Exploring the skills

Being a good listener is just as important as being a good speaker. There are many situations where you have to listen carefully to people talking and make sense of what they are saying. In your exam you will have to answer some specific questions. So what do you do? Try the following:

- Always skim read the questions first so that you know what you are listening for.
- Sometimes words in the questions will give you a clue. Questions starting with 'when', for example, will expect a date or a day or a time. You should underline these question words before you hear the recordings.
- Listen carefully to the details of what is said.
- Listen out for factual information like dates, names of places, opening times, prices, names of people.

3 The questions below are general questions – the specific answer is not spoken, so you have to guess from the clues, or understand the gist (get a general overview). Before you hear the recording you should underline the question words that give you a clue about the sort of answer to give. For example, *Where* in a) suggests it will be a place.

Listen to the conversation that your teacher will play for you, and quickly write down answers to the following.

a) Where do you think the parents are as they speak?

b) Where do you think Edmond is at the start of the recording?

c) What are they talking about?

4 Listen to the recording for a second time to answer the following questions. This time you will be listening closely for details.

a) Why is Mrs Chan calling out to Edmond?

b) What makes Mr Chan cross?

c) What are two of Edmond's excuses for being online?

d) Why does Mr Chan not believe him?

e) What is one of the comments on Edmond's report card?

f) What is Edmond's excuse for this?

g) What's for dinner at the Chan household?

Developing the skills

Remember to read the questions and make sure you understand them before you hear the recording for the first time. Underline any words in the question that will help you focus your mind and listen out for the answer.

5 Read through the questions below.

a) What is the problem with Edmond's performance at school? Give at least two concerns that Ms Burroughs has.

b) How much of the final English mark is made up by coursework?

c) What is happening in January?

d) What grades is Edmond getting now? What grades did he get in the past?

e) What is Mr Chan's complaint about the school's use of computers?

f) What are the suggestions offered by Ms Burroughs for Edmond's use of the internet at home? Which of them is the most extreme?

g) What are the benefits of the internet to teaching and learning, according to Ms Burroughs?

h) What has been agreed between the Chans and Ms Burroughs?

Now listen to the conversation between the Chans and Ms Burroughs, Edmond's English teacher. It is taking place during a teacher–parent meeting at the school. Then listen to the recording again to gather the information you need to answer the questions.

Going further

Sometimes you have to work out from the clues what the speaker is thinking or feeling – what is being implied. We don't always say exactly what we mean, especially when we are in a sensitive situation. We don't want to be rude or cause upset.

6 Most schools hold meetings where parents meet with their children's teachers to discuss how they are getting on at school. Do you think parents and teachers speak differently at these meetings when the student is there, compared with when they stay at home? Spend a few minutes noting down your thoughts. Consider your own experiences of parent–teacher meetings , if you have been to any. Then copy and complete this table of 'teacher phrases' and what they might really mean, adding some more that you may have heard yourself:

Teacher phrase with **implicit** meaning	Possible **inference**
Edmond is often distracted in class.	Edmond does not listen to me and wastes his time.
Edmond could make more of an effort.	Edmond has been lazy. He needs to start working harder.
This is a little dangerous for an exam course.	
Pop in to see how Edmond is getting on.	

7 Now listen to the recording again.
  a) What does Mrs Chan want to find out in this conversation?
  b) What are the three individuals' attitudes to internet use by young people? Write one sentence each about:
    i) Mr Chan
    ii) Mrs Chan
    iii) the teacher.
  c) Find an example where you can tell what each person means, even though they are not saying it openly or **explicitly**.

8 In groups of three, role-play Mr and Mrs Chan's conversation with Edmond after the parent–teacher meeting. What do you think his reactions might be?

Make sure you keep the parents true to their characters from what you have heard. You will be showing that you understand what is implied as you take on the personality of each character. You have more freedom with Edmond to decide how he might react.

Glossary

implicit – suggested but not clearly stated; related to implied meaning
infer – coming to a conclusion or answer using various connected facts or ideas
explicit – giving a clear and definite meaning

The big task

You are about to organise and take part in a very important competition, called *Techno Greats*, in which your group of four has to choose and present a case for one of the following:

- the most influential technological invention *before* the 20th century
- the most influential technological invention of the 20th century
- the most influential technological invention of the 21st century (so far).

Independent judges will adjudicate the competition.

In your presentation you must **explain**:

- who invented your chosen technology, where and why
- the purpose of the invention
- how it benefited and improved lives
- how it changed the way we work, live or entertain ourselves
- who it benefited most
- the future of this invention in the 21st century – what improvements are possible to make it bigger and better, or smaller and sharper, or more intelligent
- any possible drawbacks/problems and how you would overcome them.

Each team has to research their inventions and decide how they are going to present the information. Consider some of the following options:

- Bring in the object or invention, or a picture of it, to explain how it works/worked and what is/was remarkable about it.
- Find posters, labelled diagrams and pictures.
- Create a short documentary explaining how the invention worked or what life would be like without this invention.

The judges must decide which group has the strongest case based on their choice of inventions and their unique method of presentation.

Check your progress

Here are the Reading, Writing, Speaking and Listening skills you learnt about in Chapter 1.

Use this table to decide how good you are at the different skills, and make a note of what you need to do in order to move up a level.

READING	I can ...
Higher	usually pick out the details I need from most kinds of texts, including difficult ones usually understand what is implied but not written
Middle	pick out many details correctly from different kinds of texts understand some of what is implied but not written when given some help
Lower	pick out a few details correctly from straightforward texts understand how to skim read and scan a text

WRITING	I can ...
Higher	organise most of my ideas clearly before I start writing write complicated information and detailed explanations clearly and with few mistakes use a good range of vocabulary precisely, including subject-specific words
Middle	organise some of my ideas before I start writing write clear information and explanations and only make mistakes when I try to use hard words or phrases use a fair range of vocabulary and sometimes try to use more subject-specific words
Lower	understand how to collect ideas before I start writing write down simple ideas and explanations but make mistakes use a basic range of vocabulary to express some ideas

SPEAKING	I can ...
Higher	express most of my ideas clearly and accurately interact with other people in a conversation and help move the conversation forward by developing and adding ideas
Middle	express many ideas clearly respond at some length to other people in a conversation, giving details and examples
Lower	express simple ideas so that they are understood respond to other people in a conversation and answer straightforward questions

LISTENING	I can ...
Higher	understand most kinds of listening texts, including difficult ones use the key words in questions to answer questions in full detail correctly usually understand what is implied but not actually said
Middle	understand different kinds of listening texts listen out for key words in questions to answer questions in some detail understand some of what is implied but not actually said
Lower	understand straightforward listening texts understand how to listen out for key words in questions

The big picture

In this chapter you will:

● think about exploration – how important it is for discovery, how exciting it can be and how it has shaped and changed our lives

● read, think, talk and write about the value of exploration and what inspired explorers past and present

● discuss what frontiers remain to be explored in the future.

Thinking big

1 Choose two images that you find interesting. Decide who looks the bravest and what makes you think that. Note down your ideas. Make notes ready for a discussion.

2 In pairs:

● Explain your choice of photos to your partner. Say why you think they are interesting.

● Respond to your partner. Do you agree with your partner's explanation for why someone looks brave?

● Which expedition would you have most liked to go on? Explain why.

3 Discuss your choice with another pair.

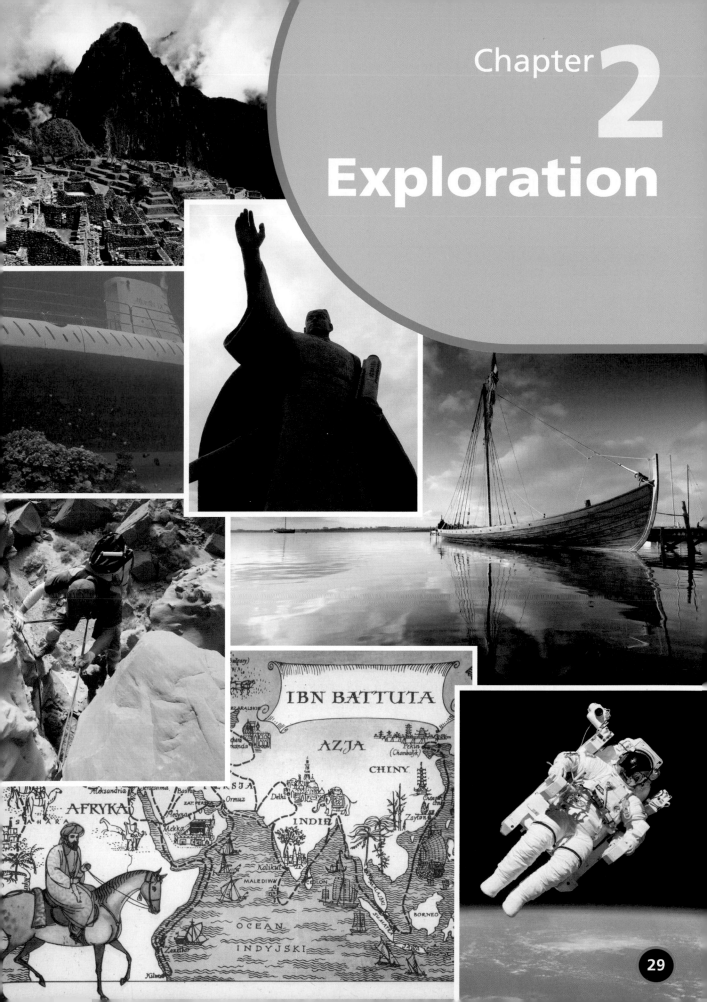

Chapter **2**

Exploration

IBN BATTUTA

AZJA

CHINY

AFRYKA

INDIE

OCEAN INDYJSKI

Reading skills in focus (R2)

In this section you will learn to:
- understand and pick out details from what you read in order to make notes or fill in forms.

Getting started

1. In pairs, brainstorm all the explorers you can think of. Then answer the following questions, writing short notes.
   - Which explorers do you think have made the most dangerous journeys?
   - What discoveries did they make?
   - What dangers do you think they faced?
   - What do you think the people back home thought about their travels?

2. Read the quotations below from explorers explaining their reasons for their expeditions. In pairs, discuss the following questions for each quote.
   - What qualities do you think this explorer had?
   - What do you think made them want to do these things?

> ❝ *I seemed to **vow** to myself that some day I would go to the region of ice and snow and go on and on till I came to one of the poles of the earth …* ❞
> Ernest Shackleton, 1874–1922

> ❝ *When I was but a little child, I had already a strong desire to see the world. Whenever I met a **travelling-carriage**, I would stop **involuntarily** and gaze after it until it had disappeared.* ❞
> Ida Pfeiffer, 1797–1858
> from 'A Visit to Iceland and the Scandinavian North'

> ❝ *But in truth, should I meet with gold or spices in great quantity, I shall remain till I collect as much as possible, and for this purpose I am proceeding in **quest** of them.* ❞
> Christopher Columbus, 1451–1506

> ❝ *Never, if possible, cover any road a second time.* ❞
> Ibn Battuta, 1303–1365

> ❝ *All adventures, especially into new territory, are scary.* ❞
> Sally Ride, 1951– astronaut

Ida Pfeiffer

Glossary

vow – promise
travelling-carriage – coach pulled by horses
involuntarily – without meaning to
quest – search

Exploring the skills

Often, in order to do a particular task when you read, you need to pick out only the relevant details or information. Remember:

- If you have to answer a question, read it carefully.
- Read headings carefully.
- Identify key words and information.

3 You are going to read a passage about a great Chinese explorer who set off on a series of amazing expeditions from the year 1405 to 1433.

Read the text quickly and look at the picture. Which paragraph would you read to find out about the following?

- the ships used for the voyages
- the aims of the exploration
- where Zheng He went

A Chinese armada

Six centuries ago a mighty armada of Chinese ships crossed the China Sea, then ventured west to Arabia and East Africa. The fleet consisted of up to 300 giant ships, escorted by dozens of supply ships, water tankers, ships to transport cavalry horses, and patrol boats. The **armada's** crew totalled more than 27 000 sailors and soldiers.

Reasons for the voyages

The object of the voyages was to display the glory and might of the Chinese Ming **dynasty**. Loaded with Chinese silk, porcelain and lacquerware, the **junks** visited ports around the Indian Ocean from East Africa to Indonesia to trade. Here, Arab and African merchants exchanged the spices, ivory, medicines, rare woods and pearls so eagerly sought by the Chinese imperial court.

Details of Zheng He's voyages

On his first trip in 1405, Zheng He visited Vietnam and reached the port of Calicut, India. On his return, he battled pirates.

Zheng He's fourth and most ambitious voyage in 1414 went to the Persian Gulf and brought back a giraffe from the Kingdom of Bengal as a gift to the emperor.

He then went to eastern Africa where he loaded lions, leopards, 'camel-birds' (ostriches), 'celestial horses' (zebras) and a 'celestial stag' (oryx) onto his ships. Back in China officials bowed low in **awe** before the **divine** creatures.

4 Reread the text under the second heading and complete the table.

Date of voyage	Where voyage went	Details of voyage

5 In pairs, discuss the following.

- Which voyage you would like to have made? Explain why.
- Do you think the voyages displayed *the glory and might of the Chinese Ming dynasty?* Explain your answer.

Developing the skills

In the exam you often need to pick out information to complete a table or fill in a form.

6 Eva wants to go on an expedition. She needs to complete an application form.

a) Read the application form carefully first. Then read the text about Eva.

b) Pick out the information you will need to complete the application form.

c) Select the expedition you think Eva will choose based on her interests and experience.

Top tip

If you have to complete a form using information from another text it is a good idea to **read the form first** and make sure you understand what is needed.

Eva Ramirez is a tenth grade student at Santa Maria High School in Concepcion, Chile. She lives with her family at 24/6 Calle Cortez. Their home telephone number is 00 (1) 345 28761. Eva is 17 and her hobbies are skiing, snowboarding, rock climbing, hiking in the mountains and camping. She loves being outside and exploring new places.

Eva's favourite subjects at school are Geography and Science. When she graduates from High School she wants to study Environmental Sciences at university and specialise in the biodiversity of polar regions.

Last year, Eva went on a two-week school trip to Tierra del Fuego where they studied the effects of climate change on wildlife. Eva enjoyed it so much that she has been saving up to go on an expedition in her school vacation with an organisation called Science Exploration Worldwide. She won't be able to save up all the money, so her father has agreed to pay 50% of the total fee.

Expedition choice   (please tick the box)

South Georgia	Monitoring changing weather patterns and penguin population	☐
Bahamas	Observing dolphin behaviour and breeding patterns	☐
Panama	Assessing affects of deforestation on plant and animal species	☐

Full name: _____

Home address: _____

Age: _____   Home telephone number: _____

Previous field study experience   Yes/No (please delete one)

Where did you go? _____

Purpose of trip: _____

Future plans

University course: _____   Other: _____

Please write one sentence giving the reason for your choice of trip.

_____

Please write two sentences giving reasons why we should choose you for this trip.

_____
_____

Fee $1850 Who will pay this?   (please circle)

Self   Sponsor   School   Other

Going further

Making brief notes from a text is a good way to identify the key points. Usually, notes are not sentences, just key words and phrases. They do not contain descriptive details, emotional comments or opinions unless these are specifically required.

7 Many explorers in the past tried to get to the North Pole or South Pole – regions which were so remote and cold that it was very difficult to get there. Nowadays, it is possible for us all to visit.

You need to answer the following question:

What has made a trip to the North Pole possible for many people today?

a) Read the text and identify the information you will need to answer the question. Ignore details you don't need, such as personal opinions.

b) Make some brief notes.

Few places have stirred the hearts and minds of explorers more than the North Pole. I imagined the icy north as being a distant land. However, as I found out, it is now very accessible. This distant land is now explorable, thanks to modern transport, satellite and computer technology. This technology has really changed things and now there are lots of opportunities to go to the North Pole.

Prior to my trip I found out all I could about the North Pole using the internet. In the end I flew to Spitzbergen – an island off the north coast of Norway. I then took a pre-arranged 10-day trip on board an ice cutter – that is a type of ship built specially to cut through ice. On the trip I stayed in a well-heated two-berth cabin. The ship was equipped with a helicopter, satellite maps and mobile phones. All of these items made the trip seem less hazardous and quite comfortable.

However, if the North Pole no longer seemed mysterious, it did not stop the beating of my heart as I experienced the once-in-a-lifetime thrill of standing on the top of the world looking around at the astonishing arctic landscape.

8 In pairs, compare your notes. Talk about any similarities and differences you find. Discuss ways in which you might be able to improve your notes.

Space exploration

Writing skills in focus (W2)

In this section you will learn to:
- collect and organise ideas and be ready to write for or against a point of view
- include your own ideas when writing to argue a point.

Getting started

1 Look at the photos and take five minutes to note down your ideas about the following questions.

a) What do I know about space exploration?

b) What would I like to know about space exploration?

Exploring the skills

When writing it is a good idea to collect relevant information about your topic and organise it before you start.

One way of doing this is to use a **KWL** table (the highlighted words in the table show you why it has this name). KWL tables help you focus on what you need to find out in order to write or talk about something.

What do I KNOW about space exploration?	What I WANT to know about space exploration?	What I have LEARNT about space exploration
There have been unmanned missions to Mars.	How much does space exploration cost? What…? When…? Where…? Why…? How ?	

2 Copy the table and complete the first column.

3 In pairs, discuss what you know and what you would like to know about space exploration. Add your questions to the second column.

4 Now try and find answers to your questions. Decide together on good places to look for this information.

5 In pairs, read the sentences opposite and organise them using the instructions a) to d) to help you.

  a) Identify one sentence that is irrelevant to the topic of space exploration.

  b) Organise the sentences into two groups: advantages and disadvantages of space exploration.

  c) Add any facts that you found out from your KWL research.

  d) Decide on your three most important reasons/facts from each group of sentences.

6 Space exploration inspires many people to dream of becoming an astronaut. This passage from an internet site talks about why we explore space.

Read the text quickly and, in pairs, identify ideas about the following questions.

  a) What are the benefits of exploring space?

  b) What is the writer's **point of view**?

- Mobile phones rely on satellite technology.
- America, China and Russia only use space exploration to monitor other countries' army and defence capabilities.
- At night I gaze at the stars and wonder.
- Very few women are involved in space exploration.
- Most studies estimate that China's space program costs $1.5 to $2 billion per year, but NASA gets $17.7 billion per year.

Language booster

A person's **point of view** is the attitude they take or the position from which they think, talk or write about something.

Joint Space Agency JSA

Search [   ]

| Home | News | Missions | Media | Resources |

- ► Space science
- ► Multimedia
- ► Media centre
- ► Science missions
- ► Subscribe
- ► Why explore space?

Why should we explore space? Why should money, time and effort be spent researching something with apparently so few benefits? Why should resources be spent on space rather than on conditions and people on Earth?

Perhaps the best answer lies in our history. Nearly all successful civilisations have been willing to explore. In exploring, the dangers of surrounding areas may be identified and prepared for. Without knowledge, these dangers have the ability to harm us. With knowledge, their effects may be lessened.

While many resources are spent on what seems a small return, evidence shows that knowledge or techniques acquired in exploring nearly always filter from the developers to the general population. Techniques may be medical applications, such as new drugs or ways of living to increase the quantity or the quality of time lived.

Why Explore Space? From www.esa.int

Language booster

7 Look at the phrases in the box below. Classify them according to the strength of opinion they show.

> I am certain that …   It is undeniably true that …
>
> I am absolutely convinced that …   I would argue that …
>
> It is possible that …   I would like to suggest that …
>
> I don't think we need to…

Developing the skills

Mind maps, webs and KWL tables like the one on page 34, help you **plan** your writing.

8 Complete Column 3 of your KWL table with the answers to your questions in Column 2.

9 Plan a speech for a debate on either the advantages or the disadvantages of space exploration.

- Write down three questions you would like to investigate about the advantages or disadvantages of space exploration.
- In groups of four, combine your ideas and make a web like the one below to note your ideas and questions.

Web diagram with central node "DISADVANTAGES OF SPACE EXPLORATION" connected to: "Who …?", "When …?", "Where …?", "Why …?", "How much money is spent on space exploration?", "What else could this money be spent on?"

Decide together which are your best three ideas.

10 Now, on your own, write the first draft of the speech on either the advantages or disadvantages of space exploration. Write between 100 and 150 words. Follow the pattern of the bullet list on page 37 and think about using phrases like the ones in the 'Language booster' above.

- Introductory paragraph: say whether you are arguing for the advantages or disadvantages of space exploration.
- Paragraph 2: state your first idea.
- Paragraph 3: state your second idea.
- Paragraph 4: state your third idea.
- Closing paragraph: summarise what you have said.

Going further

Often there are different views about an issue. You need to show that you have considered different opinions before you give your own view on the issue. Read the following text and identify the phrase(s) used to introduce opinion(s).

> *It is undeniably true that budgets for space exploration run to the billions; however, we must take into consideration that the benefits to mankind are also great.*

11 Respond to the strong statements listed below using the phrase, 'It is undeniably true that …'. Then, either use one of the phrases in the 'Language booster' on page 36 or use your own words to write another sentence. Use your own ideas.

Example: *It is undeniably true that space exploration can bring peace to the world. However, I would like to suggest that most of the information is used by the world's superpowers (such as the USA, Russia, China) to monitor each other's armies.*

- Space exploration can bring peace to the world.
- Space is the most exciting place left to discover.
- Going to the Science Museum is boring.
- Neil Armstrong was the greatest astronaut of all time.
- There may be life on Mars.
- Astronauts must be male.

Language booster

Use a **semicolon** to contrast two sentences or ideas that are closely related. Each sentence should contain a **verb**.
Example: *He knew everything about space; I knew nothing.*

12 Can a semicolon be used to separate each pair of ideas below? The first two are answered for you.

a) Mars is red… rusty and red. *No, no verb in second part.*

b) Mars is red … no one knows why it looks red. *Yes.*

c) I wish I could be an astronaut … so glamorous and exciting.

d) I wish I could be an astronaut … it seems so glamorous and exciting.

e) The Chinese Shenzhou space capsule returned to earth recently … the mission was declared a success.

f) The Chinese Shenzhou space capsule returned to earth recently … China works with Russia on its space mission.

2.3 Oil exploration

In this section you will learn to:

- research and organise ideas for giving a talk or presentation
- plan an effective, individual opening to a talk or presentation.

Getting started

1 Below are some photographs of oil exploration. Choose one photo. Write notes answering the following questions:

- What does the image show?
- Where is the photo taken or from?
- How does the photo or image make you feel?

Exploring the skills

When giving a talk, you need to express your ideas clearly to make sure your listeners understand. People find it hard to follow if you jumble together lots of different ideas. To express your ideas clearly, you have to know what you are going to say. You need to **organise** your thoughts and words.

2 Give a 30-second talk about the photograph you chose on page 38. Think about what you are going to say.

- First say what you are going to talk about.
- Then say what the image shows.
- Next say how the image makes you feel.
- In your final sentence, thank your partner for listening.

3 Colour coding can help you organise your ideas. Linking a colour to an idea makes it clearer. Imagine you are a member of a fishing village and a well-known oil company has been visiting your village to test for oil reserves. Read the sentences below. In groups, decide on which coloured sheet of paper each one should go.

- Let us agree to block the request from the oil company – whatever they try to bribe us with.
- The revenues from oil are great and the oil company has promised to build a school and a health centre for us if we agree to let them drill here.
- At the moment there are always electricity power cuts because we don't have enough oil to generate enough electricity.
- However, the environmental impact from oil drilling is also great – with dangerous gas flares and real possibilities for oil spills. The oil spills will kill the fish in the rivers and we depend on the fish for our livelihood.
- We all know that oil is necessary for industry and we all need petrol to put into our cars.

> The needs of people for oil

> The experiences of people with oil

> The advantages of oil exploration

> The disadvantages of oil exploration

> The way forward

Developing the skills

Remember that to help others understand, you need to express your ideas clearly and organise your thoughts and words into a sensible order.

Language booster

Match the words and phrases with the definitions.

a) fumes   **A** the building or structure used to get oil or gas out of the ground
b) gas flares   **B** the amount of oil/gas/electricity that people want
c) oil rig/well   **C** for example, electricity that is made from the Sun's energy
d) offshore   **D** gas that is burnt off at an oil rig
e) demand for energy   **E** harm
f) damage   **F** gases which are harmful
g) renewable energy   **G** in the sea

4 You have been given the information below about oil exploration, but it is not in a logical order. In groups of four:

a) Silently read the information on oil exploration.

b) Copy each idea onto separate pieces of paper.

c) Decide how to organise the ideas into paragraphs/themes. Write the title of each paragraph/theme on a piece of coloured A4 paper.

d) Discard any ideas that are not useful.

e) Decide which theme each idea belongs to and place it on the relevant coloured paper.

f) Add your own ideas to the relevant coloured paper.

Information on oil exploration

- The demand for energy keeps increasing due to a rising population.
- Advances in technology mean that it is easier to find and drill for oil.
- The Middle East has 56% of the world's oil.
- Oil drilling exposes people to risks such as explosions and oil leaks, which destroy the environment.
- Companies identify either onshore (on land) or offshore (in the ocean) sites.
- The United Nations thinks it will take 30 years to clean up the damage to the environment in the Niger Delta.
- Gas flares are illegal because they produce so many poisonous fumes.
- It is better to invest in renewable energy such as solar energy or wind energy.
- Until recently unwanted gas was burnt off at the oil well. These are called gas flares.
- In China demand for energy is expected to increase by 75% by 2035.
- Offshore sites are thought to be much riskier than onshore sites.

5 In pairs, take turns to play both parts in the following role-play:

Person A: You work for an oil exploration company trying to convince a village it is worth looking for oil in their region.

Person B: You represent the village and you don't want the oil company to drill there.

Going further

Try using a strong opening when you give a talk or presentation, so that it grabs your listeners' attention. Add ideas and stories of your own to make it more interesting.

Checklist for success

Successful openings to presentations often do one or more of the following:

✔ Greet the audience.

✔ State what the person is going to speak about.

✔ Use **rhetorical questions**.

✔ Use the personal pronoun 'we' to connect with the audience.

✔ Use facts and statistics.

✔ Use an anecdote (personal story).

> **Language booster**
>
> A **rhetorical question** is a question used for effect. It does not require an answer.

6 Read the following openings to two presentations.
- Which features from the 'Checklist' are used in each opening?
- In pairs, discuss which features work the best. Say why.

❝ *Good morning everybody. We have come together today to discuss oil exploration in our country. As we all know, there is an increasing demand for energy. Statistics show that worldwide energy consumption is projected to increase by 36 per cent by 2035. But how can we meet the world's increasing demand for oil?* ❞

❝ *We all know that oil companies are bad, right? Wrong! When I was a little girl an oil company wanted to drill just outside our village. This company trained the men and women of my village to work on the oil well; this company invested heavily in the local school; this company was not 'bad'.* ❞

7 In groups, give a presentation to the rest of your class about an aspect of oil exploration that interests you. Your talk is only four minutes long.
- Give each person in your group a section of the presentation:
  - the opening
  - the first point
  - the second point
  - the closing.
- Use an anecdote to show independence of thought.
- Practise giving your part of the presentation to the rest of your group.

Listening skills in focus (L2)

In this section you will learn to:
- understand and pick out facts when listening to short spoken texts
- understand and pick out facts when listening to a longer and more difficult text
- listen carefully and understand complicated instructions.

Getting started

1 Did you know that a lot of the Earth's deep ocean remains unexplored? Look at the photos on this page and page 43.

a) Think of five questions you would like to ask about underwater exploration.

b) In groups of four:
- share and make a list of all your questions
- sort the questions into themes or ideas.

Exploring the skills

A fact is something that can be proved to be true, for example, *The Mariana Trench is the deepest part of the ocean*. It is useful to be able to select facts when you are listening to information.

2 Look at the two advertisements below, then listen to each radio advertisement. What is each one advertising?

!FRIDAY SALE!

Joe Diver Equipment

We are the underwater specialist.

2.1

DEEP BLUE DIVER TRAINING COURSES

Only $25 per hour for those aged 16 to 18.

2.2

3 You are now going to hear some phrases from the first advertisement again. Note down the letters (a), b), c), etc.) as you hear the facts.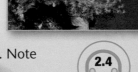

   a) We are the underwater specialist.

   b) Well known for their superb comfort.

   c) This special offer is our best price ever!

   d) That's an amazing $13 saving.

   e) And don't forget, there's free shipping with orders over $100.

4 Listen again to some phrases from the second advertisement. Note down the letters as you hear the facts.

   a) We believe that all courses should be fun.

   b) Our 'Discover scuba diving' course is for ages 16 and above.

   c) An hour in the beautiful azure sea accompanied by your instructor.

   d) Our prices are very reasonable.

   e) If you are aged between 16 and 18, it is $25 per hour.

   f) Prices include all equipment hire.

5 Which advertisement gives more facts than opinions?

Developing the skills

In the exam, you might be asked to listen for particular words to fill in gaps. Read the questions through carefully before you listen to the recording, to give you an idea of the sort of information you should listen for. Afterwards, check that the answer makes sense – especially the grammar.

Language booster

All these words come from an interview with a deep-sea diver that you will hear. Match the word to the correct definition.

a) cannot stand the pressure	**A** dangerous
b) device	**B** a small amount of something
c) irreplaceable	**C** difficult or impossible to get to
d) on board	**D** on a ship
e) mesmerising	**E** not strong enough to bear the force
f) inaccessible	**F** very valuable
g) sample	**G** machine
h) hazardous	**H** so fascinating you cannot take your eyes off it

6 Listen twice to the interview with a diver about deep-sea exploration. Then answer the questions.

   a) What has Nadima done for the last 10 years?

   b) What is amazing for Nadima?

   c) Where is Nadima today?

   d) What is a hydrothermal vent?

7 Listen again to the interview and then complete the form below with the relevant details. Each answer will be between one and four words.

DEEP-SEA EXPLORATION

<u>**Equipment used:**</u> the equipment used for deep-sea exploration is called an .... vehicle.

<u>**How it works:**</u> they are .... to a ship on the sea. Someone on board the ship can look at a .... and .... the vehicle where to go.

<u>**What the arm does:**</u> it can collect ....

<u>**Advantages of vehicles:**</u> they can stand .... in the very deep sea.

They can dive much deeper than we can.

They .... of underwater exploration.

They .... the risk of diving in hazardous areas.

<u>**Where discoveries are made:**</u> in the .... depths

<u>**Discoveries recently made:**</u> new ideas about the beginnings of life on earth.

Plants and minerals that scientists think could be used for ....

Mineral deposits have been found that they think could be twice as large ....

<u>**How discoveries are made:**</u> discoveries are made ....

Going further

You need to listen particularly carefully for facts and details when you are being given instructions.

(8) In pairs, look at the instructions below for how to make a boat out of paper (origami).

(9) Take turns to read aloud the instructions. The other person listens carefully and makes the boat. See if the person making the boat can do it without looking at the diagrams.

> **Language booster**
>
> Instructions use the **imperative** form of the verb. This is the root of the verb, e.g. 'to fold' →
> 'fold' (root) →
> 'Fold the paper in half.'

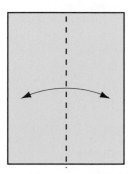

Start with a rectangular piece of paper. If you have coloured paper, it should be coloured side up. Fold in half, then open.

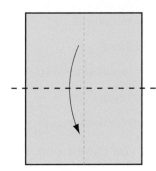

Fold in half downwards.

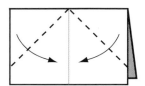

Bring the top corners in to the centre fold line.

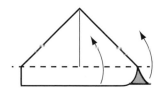

Fold the bottom flat edge upwards and do the same to the back. Crease well.

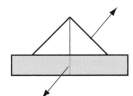

Pull the sides out and flatten.

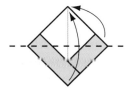

Fold front layer up to top and do the same at the back.

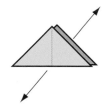

Pull the side apart and flatten.

Gently pull the top parts of the model outwards, making a boat shape.

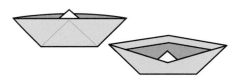

Flatten well to crease all folds. Then open out slightly, forming a boat shape.

www.origami-fun.com/origami-boat.html

(10) Make up instructions to make something else out of paper.

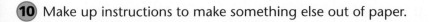

The big task

Imagine that you live in a country which has a hundred million dollars and wants to invest money in exploration. You are going to give a presentation to win the money for your chosen exploration project.

- Project A: exploring for oil offshore
- Project B: exploring for possible valuable shipwrecks in the sea
- Project C: exploring the planet Mars
- Project D: an exploration project of your choice

Work in groups of four. Three of you choose one of the projects each. You are going to put forward reasons to invest in that project. The fourth person will be the decision maker.

First, brainstorm for your presentation.

- In silence, write five questions you would like to explore about your chosen project.
- Join together with other people in your class who are working on the same project and combine your ideas and make a concept map or web to note down your ideas.
- Decision makers, think of three questions you would like to ask each person about their project.
- Decision makers, join together and produce a list of questions you would like to ask each person about their project.

Now research more information for your presentation.

- Each person uses the internet or the library to find out more information.
- Skim the information. You cannot use all of it.
- Make notes of five facts that you think are interesting or you can use to support your project.
- Now report back to other people supporting your project. Share ideas. Decision makers do likewise.

Next, organise your information.

- Organise the information into themes for reasons why the country should invest in your project. Use colour to help you.
- Use only your best ideas. Discard any facts or ideas that you don't need.

Now prepare the first draft of your presentation. Your presentation can only last two minutes.

Here are the Reading, Writing, Speaking and Listening skills you learnt about in Chapter 2.

Use this table to decide how good you are at the different skills, and make a note of what you need to be able to do in order to move up a level.

READING	
I can …	
Higher	usually understand and pick out all the details I need to complete notes and fill in forms
Middle ⬆	pick out many details correctly to complete notes and fill in forms
Lower ⬆	pick out a few details correctly to complete notes and fill in forms

WRITING	
I can …	
Higher	organise most of my ideas clearly before writing for or against a point of view
	confidently include several of my own ideas or examples when writing to argue a point
Middle ⬆	organise some of my ideas before I start writing for or against a point of view
	sometimes include a few of my own ideas or examples
Lower ⬆	understand how to collect ideas before I start writing for or against a point of view
	make use of ideas given to me and try to include one or two of my own examples

SPEAKING	
I can …	
Higher	research efficiently and then organise a good range of relevant ideas for a talk or presentation
	prepare an effective opening for a talk, using my own ideas
Middle ⬆	research and then organise some relevant ideas for a talk or presentation
	plan a suitable opening for a talk, trying to use a few of my own ideas
Lower ⬆	research and prepare some simple ideas for a talk or presentation
	try to prepare an opening to a talk, using the ideas I have found or been given

LISTENING	
I can …	
Higher	understand most kinds of listening texts, including longer and more difficult ones, and can usually pick out all the facts I need
	listen thoughtfully and closely, and follow complicated instructions successfully
Middle ⬆	understand different kinds of listening texts and pick out many of the facts I need
	listen very closely and can follow quite complicated instructions with some success
Lower ⬆	understand straightforward listening texts
	pick out some of the facts I need
	listen closely and can follow straightforward instructions

The big picture

In this chapter you will:

- consider health – what it means to be healthy, and why it is important to stay as healthy as possible
- think about healthy food, and about exercise
- research, think, talk and write about the most important ways to stay healthy.

Thinking big

1 Look at the images.
  - Make notes about the different aspects of health shown in the photos.
  - Which of the activities do you think are the healthiest?
  - Which of these activities do you do? Which ones don't you do?
  - Which things shown in the photos can cause health problems? Which ones can prevent problems?
  - In your experience, are there any challenges to staying healthy? Describe these.

2 In pairs, look at the photos with your partner.
  - Discuss what you know about each of the types of exercise or food shown.
  - Ask your partner questions about what they like and dislike in the photos, and what they do to stay healthy.

3 On your own, jot down ideas about the following:
  - What advantages and disadvantages can you think of for some of the activities shown?
  - Do you think you are healthy? Why, or why not? What do you do that makes you healthy, or what could you do to improve?
  - Why is it important to be healthy?

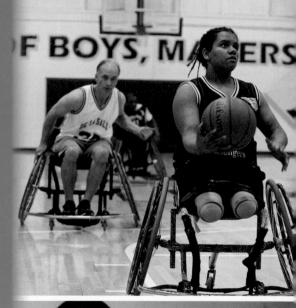

Chapter **3**

Health

Healthy eating

In this section you will learn to:

- select facts and details accurately from a written text
- understand the importance of units of measurement
- understand phrases about time
- use key question words to help find answers.

Getting started

1 Read the questions below and discuss your ideas about them with a partner.

- What is your favourite food?
- What kind of food is healthy?
- It is easy to have a healthy **diet**?
- Do you think you have a healthy diet?
- The diagram below shows advice for a healthy diet. Study the different **food groups**. How does this compare with what you discussed with your partner on page 48? How often do you eat food from these different groups?

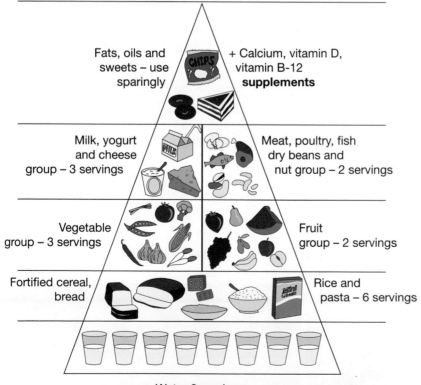

Fats, oils and sweets – use sparingly

+ Calcium, vitamin D, vitamin B-12 **supplements**

Milk, yogurt and cheese group – 3 servings

Meat, poultry, fish dry beans and nut group – 2 servings

Vegetable group – 3 servings

Fruit group – 2 servings

Fortified cereal, bread

Rice and pasta – 6 servings

Water 8 servings

Glossary

diet – the type and range of food that you eat regularly

food group – types of food that have something important in common

supplements – pills or liquids you take which contain the vitamins and minerals your body needs

Exploring the skills

When you read a text you will often have to select facts, as these contain the important information you need to know. For instance, you may need to use numbers and measurements in order to be able to follow instructions. Always remember to include or check the units of measurement being used – there is big difference between a teaspoon of chilli powder and a tablespoon of chilli powder!

2 Read the following recipe. Do you think you would like this meal?

Moroccan chicken with saffron honey

Ingredients

1 tbsp olive oil

1 × 1.5 kg chicken, cut into 8 pieces

1 large onion, chopped

3 cloves garlic, crushed

A good chunk of fresh ginger

2 tsp of ground coriander

2 tsp of ground cumin

½ tsp of ground fenugreek

1 tsp of turmeric

2½ tsp ground cinnamon

500g tomatoes, chopped

100ml chicken stock or water

4 tbsp of yogurt

Small bunch coriander, chopped couscous to serve

Raisins (optional for the couscous)

Method

1. Heat 1 tablespoon of olive oil in a pan. Fry the chicken. Put the chicken aside and fry the onion in the same pan until soft. Stir in the ginger, garlic, cinnamon, cumin, coriander, turmeric and fenugreek and cook for about a minute. Add the tomatoes, mix everything together well, reduce the heat, and cook for 15 minutes, stirring occasionally.

2. Boil the water or stock. Add this liquid and bring everything up to the boil. Place the chicken pieces on top, lower the heat, cover and cook until the chicken is tender – it should take about 30 minutes.

3. Stir in the yogurt and serve with a sprinkling of chopped coriander on a bed of couscous.

4. Raisins can be added to the couscous for extra Moroccan sweetness.

Language booster

Abbreviations for measurements are often used in factual writing such as recipes:

g = gram
kg = kilogram
tsp = teaspoon
tbsp = tablespoon
ml = millilitre

3 Read the recipe again and answer the questions.

a) How much chicken do you need?

b) How many onions do you need?

c) How much chicken stock or water do you need?

d) How many tomatoes do you need?

e) How long do you cook the ingredients in the first stage?

f) How long do you cook the dish in the second stage?

(4) Underline the units of measurement (e.g. teaspoons) in your answers to the last question. Check that you have chosen the correct kind of measurement. Add to your answers, writing out the measurements in full and in their abbreviated form, if there is one.

(5) Do you think this is a healthy recipe? Why? Look back at the healthy food pyramid on page 50. Think about which food groups the recipe contains and which groups it doesn't.

Developing the skills

Information about timings is very important in texts like these. You can easily pick out numbers in a factual text, but also look out for words used with them, such as *about* or *up to* – these show that the times may not be exact.

(6) Underline the expressions in these phrases which show that the time is not exact:

a) I've been a vegetarian for <u>about</u> a year.

b) You can cook this dish for up to an hour in the oven at a low heat.

c) It doesn't take long to prepare; just five or six minutes.

d) This recipe will serve more than four people.

e) You don't need a lot of honey; only a spoonful.

Read the sentences again. In pairs, write similar sentences using these expressions.

Language booster

Factual texts need to be very clear in presenting information and instructions. In the recipe there are some **technical terms** related to cooking, such as *brown*, *season* and *simmer*. Look up the meaning of these and other words from the recipe. Make a list of these words and their definitions.

Going further

You may have to answer questions about longer texts. Read the questions first to find key words. These will give you clues about what you need to look out for. For example, if the question starts with 'When' you must look for a time or date. If a question asks 'Who?' you will look for the name of a person, or 'Where?' you will look for the name of a place.

7 Here are some questions. Read them carefully and underline the key question words. In pairs, discuss what sort of answer you might expect.

a) Where were the large, flat breads first baked?

b) When did people start to sell pizzas in Italy?

c) When did Queen Margherita go on a tour of Italy?

d) Who cooked her a special pizza?

e) Why did American and European soldiers eat pizza?

f) What happened when the soldiers went back to their countries?

8 Now read the text and answer the questions above.

Pizza is now an international dish. You may think that pizza is an Italian creation, but there is evidence to suggest that it was the early Greeks who first baked large, round, flat breads which they flavoured with oil, herbs, spices and dates.

The idea came to Italy in the 18th century, when flat breads called 'pizzas' were sold on the streets. They didn't have any of the toppings we expect today. They were cheap, tasty and filling, and they were eaten by poorer people.

In about 1889, Queen Margherita of Italy went on a tour of her country. During her travels she saw many people eating this large, flat bread. She was curious and wanted to try one. She loved it, and invited Chef Rafaelle Esposito to come from to the royal palace and make a selection of pizzas for her.

Rafaelle decided to make a special pizza for the queen. He topped it with tomatoes, mozzarella cheese and fresh basil, to represent the colours of the Italian flag: red, white and green. This became the queen's favourite pizza and the Pizza Margherita is now famous all over the world.

Pizza spread to America, France, England and Spain, but it didn't become popular until after World War II. Many American and European soldiers tasted it for the first time when they were in Italy during the war. When they returned home, it became a popular meal in their countries.

Adapted from 'pizza history' from www.inmamaskitchen.com

Healthy body

Writing skills in focus (W3)

In this section you will learn to:
- use a range of different kinds of sentences in your writing
- use simple, compound and complex sentences correctly
- include noun phrases to add detail and variety.

Getting started

1 Read the questions below and discuss them with a partner.
- What kind of exercise do you do?
- Do you exercise for fun, or because you want to be healthy?
- What are the benefits of exercise?
- Do you think that people you know do enough exercise, or should they do more?

2 Read the following comment from an article about exercise. Does this information surprise you? Discuss your ideas with a partner.

> ❝ *Running can slow the effects of ageing and give older people a new lease of life. The health benefits of exercise are greater than we thought.* ❞

Exploring the skills

Remember that a sentence always starts with a capital letter and ends with a full stop, question mark or exclamation mark.

Using a clear and accurate sentence structure is a basic part of writing. It is important to be able to use different types of sentences. This gives your writing more effect and impact. Two of the main types of sentence are called simple sentences and compound sentences.

Sentences contain a **subject** and a **verb**. Short sentences that contain one main idea are called **simple sentences**. For example:

subject   **verb**

I cycled to school.

Simple sentences are useful for giving clear explanations and instructions. They can be used to give advice, or when you are writing for younger readers. They can also add more drama to writing, or give emphasis to a particular point.

Read the following extract from a book about running:

> You will do most of your running on an athletics track. At school, this may be marked out on grass. In stadiums, tracks are made of a special surface which provides grip. Outdoor tracks are 400m long. Different races have different starting points. These are marked out on the track.
>
> From *Tell me about sport: Running*

This uses a series of simple sentences to present the information in a clear way.

Compound sentences contain two or more ideas that are equally important. These are joined together using connectives such as 'or', 'and' or 'but'. For example:

We walked to school, <u>but</u> it was raining <u>and</u> we got wet!

Read a second extract from the same book:

> 66 *You may not break a world record but you can record a personal best.* 99

Here, the writer joins ideas with 'but' to explain the idea in more detail.

3 Read the text below. Decide whether each numbered sentence is simple or compound.

[1]Running is a good form of exercise. [2]It is cheap and easy to do. [3]You can run on your own or you can run with other people. [4]I usually run three times a week but sometimes I run more often. [5]It is a great way to get fit.

4 Choose a sport you know about. Imagine you are writing for a young reader and write instructions explaining how to do it. Use a combination of simple and compound sentences for different effects.
  ● To explain the sport and how to do it, use simple sentences.
  ● To give more information about why the sport is good for you, or why it is fun, use compound sentences.

Developing the skills

Using lots of simple sentences will get your ideas across but it may not be very interesting for the reader. Joining your ideas together in to compound and complex sentences is a more fluent way to write and it interests the reader more.

Complex sentences add further information, using other connectives such as 'when', 'after' and 'because'.

> *I often go to the sports centre <u>because</u> I go swimming and see my friends there.*

5 Read the following text and answer the questions below.

> *My friend does karate. He trains three times a week. Sometimes he trains four times. He does it at the sports centre. He's in a team there. It makes him healthy. It is also fun.*

a) Is the information easy to understand?

b) Is the text interesting to read?

Read another version of this text.

> *My friend does karate and trains three or four times a week at the sports centre. It makes him healthy and it is also fun.*

In this version, the connected ideas are joined together in compound sentences.

6 Now read another text and write a better version of it. Work with a partner. Decide which ideas are connected and could be linked together into compound or complex sentences. Use the connectives in the box.

> *Football is a popular sport. Lots of people watch football. Lots of people play it. There are football teams in most towns. There are matches between different teams.*

| and   when   but   after   or   because |

7 Now write your own paragraph about a sport you enjoy doing or watching, or one you know about. Use simple and compound sentences to express your ideas in different ways, as described above. Use compound sentences to join and explain your ideas. Use simple sentences to add effect and impact.

Going further

Another way to make your writing more interesting is by using noun phrases in your sentences. Look at the following examples.

We went on a bike ride.

We went on a long bike ride along the river and into the woods.

The second sentence tells us more about the bike ride. The noun 'bike ride' has been extended to 'long bike ride' by adding the adjective 'long'. This is called a **noun phrase**. Now we know that the writer travelled a long way on the bike and that he or she was next to a river.

You can also use noun phrases in persuasive writing, because you can use adjectives to support your arguments:

I think skiing is a dangerous sport. Lots of people get terrible injuries every year. It's hard to take them to hospital because they are on high mountains that are miles away from any large hospitals.

Here the writer uses *dangerous sport*, *terrible injuries*, *high mountains* and *large hospitals* to make their writing more persuasive.

8 Read the following sentences. Fill the gaps using the words in the box to make the sentences more interesting or persuasive.

> cold   three-kilometre   amazing   difficult   long

a) I really enjoy going for _____ walks in the country.

b) Josef is going on a _____ run on Saturday.

c) We had a _____ journey back down the mountain, but we got home safely in the end.

d) They went for a swim in the _____ sea after the race.

e) Don't you think she's an _____ athlete? She's set a new world record.

9 In pairs, discuss which sports you enjoy doing, and which sports you do not enjoy. Make notes about how you could describe the sports in interesting ways.

10 Now work individually to write a magazine article for young people about one of the sports you discussed. Remember to:
- use simple sentences to explain how the sport works and to give instructions
- use compound and complex sentences to join your ideas more fluently
- add information with noun phrases to persuade your reader that this is a good (or a bad!) sport.

Health around the world

In this section you will learn to:

- use a variety of structures when you are speaking
- speak using abstract nouns and noun phrases to give variety to your sentences.

Getting started

1 Around the world, there are major problems which cause sickness and poor health in large numbers of people. Read the questions below and discuss them with a partner.

- What causes can you think of that give people around the world problems with their health?
- What can be done to prevent these problems, or reduce their effects?

Exploring the skills

You can use a range of sentence structures accurately to add interest to your spoken communication just as you can to your written work

The connectives 'and', 'but', 'or' and 'so' can all be used to explain your ideas in more detail and to give your reasons. This is useful when you need to explain your ideas clearly and during discussions where you need to support your arguments.

Read the following sentences and the notes:

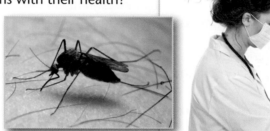

People say that medicine is very advanced, (*but*) *not everyone has access to the best treatment.* —— 'but' is used to introduce an idea which is different from the first idea

Not everyone has access to clean water (*or*) *is able to visit a doctor when they ill.* —— 'or' is used to give more possibilities than the first idea

More vaccines are being used, (*so*) *fewer people are becoming ill.* —— 'so' is used to show the result of the first idea

We need to improve education (*and*) *access to health care around the world.* —— 'and' is used to join similar ideas

These show how ideas can be joined or extended using a variety of connectives.

2 In pairs, think of a topic related to an important health issue you know about. One person says the beginning of a sentence and the other person completes it, using connectives. The ending can agree or disagree with the first idea in the sentence.

For example:

A *It's important to do exercise ...*

B *... and eat the right food to stay healthy.*

Here are some sentences you could start with:

You can do yoga ...

I don't like sport, ...

It's best not to eat a lot of chocolate ...

3 Look at the photos on page 58. Think about the words you need to describe what you see. Refer to a dictionary to check on any vocabulary you need.

4 Read the following comments:

> *I think the development of a malaria vaccine is the most important thing we need to do to improve healthcare around the world. It would save a lot of lives.*

> *For me, the most important issue is clean water. Dirty water can cause a lot of illness.*

With a partner, make notes about both of these comments. Try to think of at least three arguments to support each one. You could use some of the following phrases.

*I think that... I believe that... In my opinion...
I don't think that... I disagree with the idea...*

5 In your pairs, discuss which of these world health problems it is most important to solve. Choose a role and develop your notes from task 4. Try to use a mixture of simple and compound sentences.

6 Record your conversation and listen back to it. How did you develop your ideas using simple and compound sentences?

7 In groups, discuss your ideas about the newspaper stories below. You can argue for another health issue if you think something else is more important.

Report back to the class on what your group thought.

> New figures from the UN have revealed that between 1990 and 2010 over 2 billion people were provided with an improved water source.

> Millions of lives could be saved if the new vaccine is successful. It's important that it is available to everyone and isn't sold at a high price to make money for the developers.

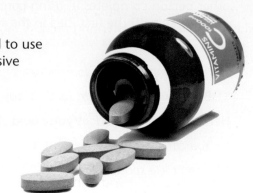

Developing the skills

When presenting your point of view in spoken form, you need to use compound sentences to give your reasons and make a persuasive argument – just as you do in persuasive writing.

8 Read the following comments and answer the questions.

> *I think vitamin supplements are a good thing. You can eat anything you like and get the vitamins you need from tablets. It's easy to be healthy with supplements.*

> *In my opinion, having a healthy, happy mind is more important than what you do or what you eat. Your mind is the most important thing.*

a) Does the first person think that a healthy diet is important?

b) Does the second person think that physical activity is as important as how happy you are?

c) Do you agree with either of these opinions?

8 Imagine you are a young person discussing health with a parent. Discuss what you think it means to be healthy. Work in pairs.

Student A: You are the teenager. You don't think it is important to have a healthy diet, and you don't understand why your mum or dad doesn't agree. You think it is more important to be happy. Think of reasons to support your point of view.

Student B: You are the parent. You think it is more important to eat well and exercise. Think of reasons to support your point of view.

Spend a few minutes preparing your ideas individually. You can make notes to help you remember your main points.

10 Now carry out the role-play in pairs. Record your conversation and play it back to check that you have used a variety of sentence types.

Checklist for success

When speaking:

✔ You can use simple sentences for more impact.

✔ Remember to use 'and', 'but', 'or' and 'so' to explain your ideas in more detail.

✔ Remember that it is quite normal in a conversation to have pauses, or to say *er...* or *um...* while you think.

Going further

Having as wide a vocabulary as possible will help you express your ideas when speaking. In the writing section earlier in this chapter, we looked at using noun phrases. Here are some examples of noun phrases you could use when talking about health and diet:

a balanced diet   fizzy drinks   clean water
junk food   active lifestyle   a healthy breakfast

11 Working with a partner, copy the table below and put the phrases above into it. Find more examples for each column from earlier in the chapter. Can you think of examples of your own to go in each column?

Phrases about food	Phrases about sport and exercise	Phrases about health and happiness
organic food	regular exercise	positive state of mind

Language booster

You can also use **abstract nouns** (nouns that name things that cannot be touched) to add interest to what you say. Read the following definitions and match them to the words in the box.

a) the feeling of being enthusiastic and anticipating something
b) not having enough strength to complete a task
c) being very tired, often because of exercise
d) wanting or having more of a thing than you need

> excitement   fatigue   weakness   greed

12 In pairs, take it in turns to use two of the abstract nouns above in a sentence about health.

13 Work with a partner. Discuss your ideas about the following points.
- What is your preferred method of staying healthy – having a healthy diet, or doing lots of exercise?
- Do you think it is easy to have a healthy diet?
- Is the lifestyle in your country generally healthy or unhealthy?
- What problems can be caused if many people in a society are unhealthy? For example, if lots of people smoke or eat too much junk food, what effect does this have?
- Do people all over the world have the same concerns about health? If not, how do they differ?

3.4 Better health

Listening skills in focus (L2)

In this section you will learn to:
- predict the kind of information you will hear, including units of measurement
- recognise high numbers when listening.

Getting started

1 Discuss the following points with a partner.
- Do you have any habits that you know are unhealthy? For example, do you eat too much junk food, or play computer games a lot?
- If you do, how could you go about changing these habits?

Exploring the skills

When you listen to people speaking or to an audio recording, you may have to listen for specific information such as numbers or units of measurement. It is useful to think in advance of what you might expect to hear. For example, if the question asks how much something costs, you can expect to hear an answer given in units of money, such as dollars.

2 Think of what units of measurement you might expect to hear in the following situations:
- buying apples in a market
- discussing distances for a journey
- a report on football results.

3 You are going to listen to a train announcement. Think what units of measurement and other numbers you will need to listen for.

What units and numbers did you expect to hear? Were your guesses correct? Answer the questions:

a) Which platform is the train leaving from?

b) What time is it leaving?

c) How long is it until the train leaves?

Language booster

Look at the words below related to health and eating. Then read the definitions. Match each word with its correct definition.

obese	a natural substance in food, which you need for healthy growth
diabetes	low in fat
calories	the things in food which are good for you: for example, vitamins and minerals
low-fat	very overweight and therefore unhealthy
nutrients	the amount of energy in food
protein	a disease in which your body doesn't produce enough insulin (a type of hormone)

4 Listen to a report about health. What is the problem discussed?

5 Read the sentences below and think what word might go in each gap.

Number of obese people in Britain by 2010: _____

This is a _____ of adults and a _____ of children.

Cost to the NHS to increase over _____

A total of _____% of girls and _____% of boys aged

between _____ and _____ will be obese by 2010.

Now listen again to the report about obesity and complete each sentence with the correct information.

Developing the skills

Before listening to an informative text, it is useful to think about the kind of information you might hear. This will help you select the relevant details to answer the questions.

6 You are going to hear a person talking about the food groups. Before you listen, look back at the food pyramid on page 50 and discuss in pairs what you know about each of the food groups. Can you add any different food or food types to these lists?

Bread, cereal, rice, pasta	important for …
Fruit	important for …
Vegetables	important for …
Dairy	important for …
Meat, fish, beans, eggs, nuts	important for …

8 Make notes of the figures you hear to complete the table below.

3.3

Food group	Number of servings
Bread, cereal, rice, pasta	
Fruit	
Vegetables	
Dairy	
Meat, fish, beans, eggs, nuts	

9 Read the extract below and complete the notes.

> I thought I ate quite healthy food, but I was surprised when
> I listened to information about the food pyramid. I only have one
> serving of vegetables and two of fruit a day – that isn't enough.
> I have four servings of food from the protein group, including
> meat and eggs, and that could be too much. I usually eat about
> seven servings of food from the bread and pasta group, so that's ok.

a) The writer should eat more _____.

b) She should eat less food from the _____.

c) She eats the right amount of _____.

10 Read the text below. What does it say about the diet of young
women in Britain? Discuss your ideas with a partner.

Nutritionists have discovered that a diet of
pizza, sweets, and sugary drinks is taking a
severe toll on the health of young women,
which is having implications as they get
older.

A study has concluded that teenage girls
are shunning fruit, vegetables and oily
fish, leading to almost half of teenage girls
being dangerously low in key nutrients,
such as iron, magnesium and selenium.

Iron, found in products such as red
meat and green vegetables, is vital for
the production of healthy red blood
cells and helps to keep the brain healthy.
Magnesium from shellfish helps keep
bones strong while selenium is beneficial
to the immune system.

Research has concluded that one in
ten girls is dangerously low in calcium,
putting them at risk of brittle bones and
falls and fractures in old age.

One in six is severely short of iodine, a
mineral key to brain development in the
womb.

The researchers, Carrie Ruxton, an
independent nutritionist, and Emma
Derbyshire, a Manchester University
nutritionist, believe that teenagers' diets
are particularly bad because they are at
a stage in life where they start feeding
themselves and skip meals.

Dr Ruxton said, 'While things like heart
disease and cancer affect people in their
40s, 50s and 60s, the very early stages
happen several decades before.'

She added that it was very important
that teenagers lay down a balanced diet
for the rest of their lives.

From 'Teenage girls' junk food diet leaves them starved
of vitamins' by Fiona MacRae, *Daily Mail* 9/7/2011

Look at this list of nutrients from the text. Research in your own language what they do, and write three foods which are a good source of each one.

| iron | magnesium | selenium | calcium | iodine |

11 Read the text again and answer the questions.

  a) According to the text, what do some teenage girls eat too much of?

  b) What should they eat more of? Give three examples.

  c) Why do you think this age group is affected by poor diet?

  d) Why is it important to have a healthy diet when you are a teenager?

12 Now listen to two friends discussing this article. Do they agree or disagree with it? Give reasons for your answers.

13 Working in groups, discuss whether you think you have a healthy diet. Give your reasons, in the same way as the girls in the dialogue did. Do more girls or boys eat well in your group?

Going further

You may have to distinguish and understand high numbers when you are listening. It is important to learn how high numbers are spoken and how they are written in numerals.

14 Practise reading aloud the numbers in the table below with a partner.

Number	Word
1000	One thousand
10 000	Ten thousand
100 000	One hundred thousand
1 000 000	One million
10 000 000	Ten million
100 000 000	One hundred million
1 000 000 000	One billion

15 Listen to some sentences containing more high numbers. For each one, choose the correct answer.

1 a) 120 400   b) 12 400   c) 1 240 000

2 a) 1 560 110   b) 15 110   c) 150 110

3 a) 3 075 000   b) 30 750   c) 3075

16 Write some high numbers of your own and think about how to say them. Swap your numbers with a partner and read out each other's numbers.

The big task

You are each going to prepare a web page about health for young people in your school. For example, it could be about ways to stay healthy and why it is important to stay healthy. Your aim is to inform young people about how to have a healthier lifestyle and to show them that it doesn't have to be difficult to eat healthily and exercise.

1. Working in groups, talk about your ideas and make notes.

2. Remember that a website needs to have a clear structure. It usually has a home page, which introduces the topic and gives an overview. Think of this page as an introduction. You can then have different headings to organise your work into different areas, such as Food, Exercise. These would make up different pages of the website.

3. In your groups, decide who is going to provide information for each web page. You can work individually to research information, then discuss it as a group and decide what to include.

4. Remember to present your ideas using a variety of sentence types. Use simple sentences for clear instructions, and compound and complex sentences for joining ideas and giving detail or reasons.

   Try to use noun phrases as well, to make your writing more interesting and persuasive, and include abstract nouns if possible.

5. When you present numbers and measurements to support your ideas, make sure you use the right abbreviations where necessary. Check that you know how to say any high numbers you are using.

6. You can also look for suitable images to accompany your work.

7. As a group, present your web pages to the rest of the class.

Check your progress

Here are the Reading, Writing, Speaking and Listening skills you learnt about in Chapter 3.

Use this table to decide how good you are at the different skills, and make a note of what you need to be able to do in order to move up a level.

READING I can …		WRITING I can …	
Higher	usually understand and pick out all the details I need make effective use of key question words to find all the information I need	**Higher**	use simple, compound and complex sentences correctly and securely, and can vary my sentence structures for clarity and effect use noun phrases securely and confidently to add variety
⬆ **Middle**	often understand and pick out many of the details I need make use of many key question words to find most of the information I need	⬆ **Middle**	use simple and compound sentences correctly and securely, and try to use complex sentences to vary my sentence structures sometimes use noun phrases to add variety
⬆ **Lower**	sometimes understand and pick out a few of the details I need recognise some key question words	⬆ **Lower**	use simple sentences correctly, and try to use compound or complex sentences to vary my sentence structures occasionally use simple noun phrases

SPEAKING I can …		LISTENING I can …	
Higher	confidently use a good variety of structures when speaking make confident use of abstract nouns and noun phrases to give accuracy and variety	**Higher**	understand and pick out exactly the details I need, including all numbers, when listening to longer and more complicated texts confidently predict the type of information I need by understanding the clues in the questions securely recognise and understand all numbers
⬆ **Middle**	use some variety of structures when speaking, though I may falter use abstract nouns or noun phrases to add some variety	⬆ **Middle**	understand and pick out many of the details I need, including most numbers, when listening to longer or more difficult texts often predict the type of information I need by understanding the clues in the questions
⬆ **Lower**	use a limited range of structures when speaking, and may hesitate or search for words identify abstract nouns and noun phrases	⬆ **Lower**	sometimes understand and pick out some of the details I need, including some numbers, when listening to straightforward texts sometimes predict the type of information I need by looking at the clues in the questions

The big picture

In this chapter you will:

- think about your amazing brain and the role it plays in your education, both formal and informal

- read about schools in ancient times and compare them with schools today and think about schools in the future

- listen to others talk about education and what needs to change.

Thinking big

1   Look carefully at the images about learning. Choose one image that you like most. Then be ready to explain why to a partner.

2   On your own, fast-write a response to the following questions using the pictures as a prompt for your thinking.

- How do you learn to do something?

- How did you learn to read or write? Did someone teach you?

- Think about a time when you enjoyed learning something. How did it feel?

- Think about a time when learning was hard. What were the reasons?

3   In pairs:

- Discuss what you have found in common. What are the differences? Start with the image you chose.

- Decide in what ways your partner's learning experiences differ from yours.

- Note down any interesting ideas that emerge from your conversation.

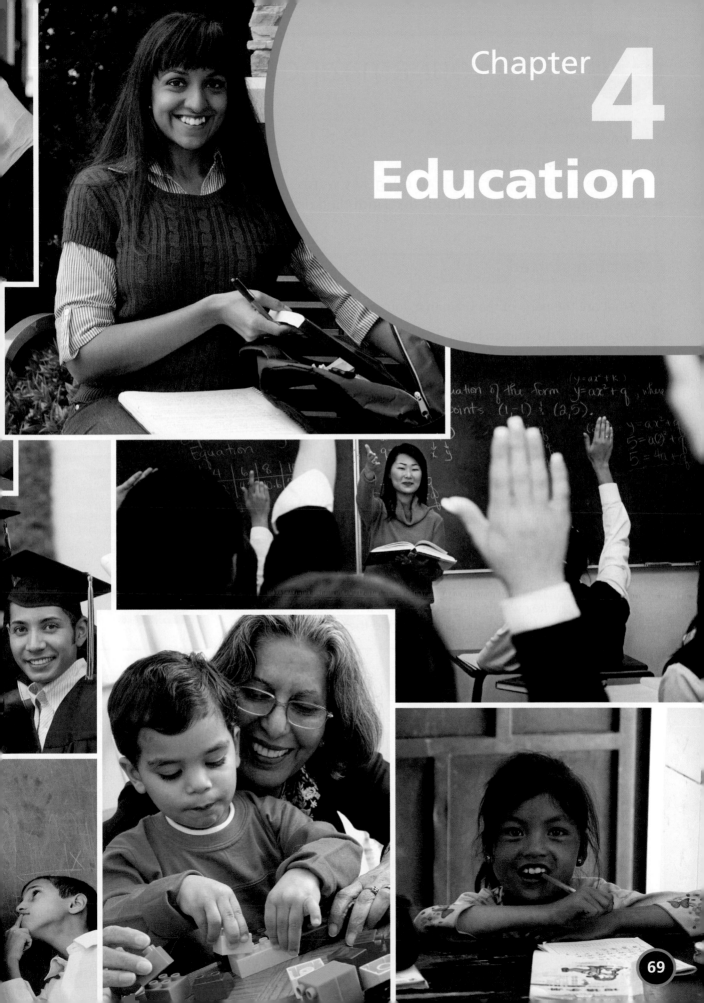

Chapter 4

Education

4.1 How your amazing brain works

In this section you will learn to:
- select details to answer questions using 'key words'
- select details from more difficult texts including diagrams and charts.

Getting started

1 What are the parts of the brain that you can actually name?

2 What makes the human brain so different from the brains of other mammals?

Note down some thoughts that might answer these questions before you proceed.

Exploring the skills

When you read for detail and information, you need to know exactly what you are looking for.

It can help to read the text in chunks. Stop and think what each section means. Then try to put the ideas into your own words.

If you have to answer questions, check that you understand them, look for key words in the questions and then scan for them in the text.

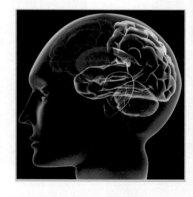

3 Look at the text below and answer the questions that follow. Underline the key words in the questions, as has been done in question a), and then scan the text to find them.

Brain facts

Did you know that the brain is made up of about 75% water and weighs around 3 pounds? Strangely, there are absolutely no pain receptors – nerve endings – in the brain. This means that although you may think you are experiencing pain in the brain, the brain itself can feel no pain.

Memory is formed by associations, so to promote memory when studying we should create associations – linking one idea with another. 'A for apple' is an example of an association that we learn early on in life when we begin to learn our ABC. We learn to link together the word 'apple' with the letter 'A' and probably a picture of an apple. This can be done in any language: children who learn letters, characters or symbols in their own language will make similar links and associations. Remarkably, children who learn two languages before the age of five have a different brain structure from children who learn only one language.

Adapted from, from 'Brain Facts' by Pamelia Brown, www.associatesdegree.com

---

a) What is the approximate <u>weight</u> of the human <u>brain</u>?

b) What is the brain largely made of?

c) Why does the brain not feel pain?

d) What helps us remember the alphabet?

e) What is remarkable about children who learn two languages before the age of five?

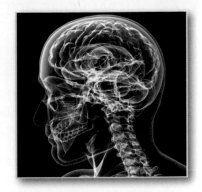

Developing the skills

Sometimes you have to look for another word or phrase which means the same as the key word. For example in d) above *alphabet* and *ABC* mean the same thing.

5 Read the article below twice, then write five questions that can be answered by it.

How your brain works with languages

Neurobiologists have recently found that being bilingual has some distinct advantages. Their research has shown that being able to speak and use more than one language before the age of five significantly improves a child's ability to concentrate and could delay or reduce the risks of diseases like **dementia**.

In the past, and even today, some parents and teachers have felt that children who are exposed to more than one language could become very confused. They even believed that it could delay their **intellectual** growth! This is clearly incorrect as most bilingual children reach the same language targets as their monolingual classmates and don't show any evidence of being confused. On the contrary, the latest research shows that most bilingual students are able to focus better on their tasks and are less **distracted**. They are also able to pick out more easily the information that is most relevant to their task and ignore **irrelevant** material.

Some scientists feel that being bilingual increases the supply of oxygen and blood flow to the brain. This keeps nerve connections healthy and keeps away diseases like dementia. It can also delay **Alzheimer's** by up to four years.

Glossary

dementia – a serious mental illness that usually affects older people's memory
intellectual – related to thought, ideas and understanding
distracted – having your attention taken away from what you are doing
irrelevant – not about the subject which is being focused on
Alzheimer's – a type of dementia

Going further

Reading texts that include charts and diagrams can be more challenging. When you have to answer questions about them, you still need to identify the key words in the text.

6 Read the following texts of Howard Gardner's view on Multiple Intelligences and then answer the questions on page 73.

Multiple intelligences

The Theory of Multiple Intelligences (MI) was proposed by Howard Gardner, a professor at Harvard University, in 1983. According to this theory, intelligence is not a single thing that can be measured as a number such as an IQ. Instead, there are nine types of intelligence, which everyone has in a different and unique combination.

Existential
To exhibit a tendency to pose and ponder questions about life, death and ultimate realities

Verbal/Linguistic
The capacity to use language to express what's on your mind and to understand other people.

Intrapersonal
Having an understanding of yourself, of knowing who you are, what you can do, etc.

Logical/Mathematical
The ability to understand the underlying principles of some kind of system of cause and effect.

Interpersonal
The ability to understand other people.

Multiple Intelligences

Visual/Spatial
The ability to present the spatial world internally in your mind.

Naturalist
The ability to tell the diffference between among living things as well as sensitivity to other features of the natural world.

Bodily/Kinaesthetic
The capacity to use your whole or parts of your body, to solve a problem, make something, or put on a production.

Musical/Rhythmic
The capacity to think in music, to be able to hear patterns, recognize them, and perhaps play with and move them around.

Multiple intelligences chart

Type of intelligence	What learners like to do
Linguistic (word smart)	Write articles, read books, tell stories, do word puzzles, learn rhymes, memorise facts, tell jokes, debate, learn song lyrics.
Mathematical-logical (logic smart)	Solve problems, do Sudoku, calculate quickly, play strategy games, reason things out, explore patterns and timelines, analyse statistics.
Spatial (picture smart)	Do art and design activities, draw, build and create models, read maps and charts easily, think in visuals, do jigsaw puzzles, make cartoons, charts, posters and floor plans, enjoy photography, art and design.
Bodily-kinaesthetic (body smart)	Move around, act things out, do hands-on learning, do craft, touch things to see how they work, dance, do sport and exercise.
Musical (music smart)	Sing and hum, remember melodies and rhythms, play instruments, keep time, rap, create jingles.
Intrapersonal (self smart)	Work alone, be independent, set ambitious personal goals, reflect and think, go after own interests, be individual at all times, keep diaries or journals, start independent research and inquiry projects.
Interpersonal (people smart)	Be with others and socialise, lead and organise groups, resolve conflicts, empathise with others, co-operate with others, organise and go to parties often.
Existential	Pose and ponder questions about life and death. Ask questions about who we are and our purpose in life. Read religious texts and philosophy in search of answers.
Naturalist (nature smart)	Learn about nature, love animals and birds, know about the natural world and how it works, show concern for the environment, enjoy being outdoors, can name plants and animals.

a) At which university did Dr Howard Gardner develop his Theory of Multiple Intelligences? In which year did he do this?

b) How many intelligences are listed here in total?

c) What other word describes people who are *body smart*?

d) What do those with a high naturalist intelligence like to do? What might their hobbies be?

e) What activities do *picture smart* people enjoy? Why?

f) If you like to play strategy games and explore patterns, which intelligence might you have more of?

g) Which intelligence encourages rewriting stories and learning poems?

h) List two qualities of those who have a high *interpersonal* intelligence.

i) What do those with high *existential* intelligence like to do?

Glossary

existential – to do with life and death

7 Rate yourself on a scale of 1 to 5, with 5 being the highest, on each of the areas of intelligence listed.

- Make sure you read the descriptors carefully before making your choice.
- Notice in which intelligences you rated yourself higher than 3.
- Talk to a partner about your highest intelligence scores and see if you match the descriptions.

In this section you will learn to:
- use appropriate vocabulary when writing to inform or explain
- use a wide range of vocabulary for variety and clarity.

Getting started

1 Think about the following ideas or discuss them with a partner. Note down your ideas.
- What kind of school do you go to today? Was it always this way?
- What is the history of schooling in your country or region?
- What did school look like for your ancestors 100 to 500 years ago?

2 Now look at the images above of an old-fashioned school in England. Talk to your partner about what has changed, considering the following:
- what the school building looked like
- what people thought of girls going to school
- what was taught as part of the curriculum
- what the teachers were like
- what the students wore
- how they were punished for bad behaviour.

Exploring the skills

In order to write effectively about a particular topic, you need to build up a bank of vocabulary that is associated with that topic. Start gathering words now from your discussion.

Building an effective vocabulary is a bit like a game. You need to complete the process below before you can 'win' and make the word your own.

Until this circle is complete, words can bounce into your brain and right out again without becoming a part of your vocabulary!

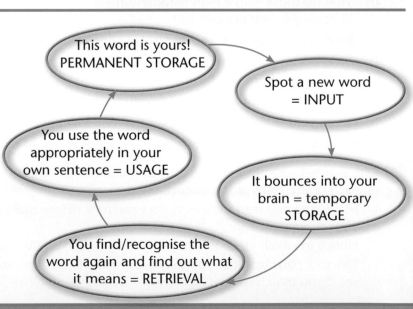

This word is yours! PERMANENT STORAGE

Spot a new word = INPUT

You use the word appropriately in your own sentence = USAGE

It bounces into your brain = temporary STORAGE

You find/recognise the word again and find out what it means = RETRIEVAL

3. Find out how accurately you can use words about education. How many of the words or phrases in the box below can you define? Group them under the following headings once you decide what they mean:

Behaviour   **Building**   **Curriculum**   **Organisation**

boarding school, day school, qualification, school leaving certificate, co-educational, curricular activity, coursework, extracurricular activity, optional subject, public examination, private tutor, discipline, attendance, academic, achievement, vocational, rote-learning, corporal punishment, term/semester, interactive

4. You have been asked by your head teacher to write a friendly email to a new student who is about to join your school. The purpose of the email is to:
- welcome them to your city and school
- tell them what they need to buy before they join the school
- inform them of all the key terminology at your school. This could include abbreviations and short forms that are vital to getting around your school, such as: Upper School Area = USA, LS = Life Skills; cafeteria = tuckshop/refectory/lunchroom.

Developing the skills

When you encounter a new word, look up its meaning and then 'place' it in relation to words you already know on that topic. Having a wide vocabulary that you really understand will help you write precisely to inform and explain.

Glossary

hieroglyphics – word pictures

5. Read about Ancient Egyptian schools. Then answer the questions below.

Ancient Egyptian Schools

In Ancient Egypt, wealthy families sent their sons to school by the age of 4. Young girls, however, were not educated unless they were princesses or members of nobility, close to the Pharoah, the highest power in Egypt. A young boy's career was decided for him by his father, before he started school and he was only educated in what would be useful to his future career. For example, if he was to become a potter, he would only learn how to make pots and pans. If he was to become a blacksmith, he would learn about metals and metal work. Being a scribe or a tax collector, which required reading and writing **hieroglyphics**, was highly valued. These professions paid well but the skills they required took several years to master. Young scribes had to spend long hours at their teacher's house copying out hieroglyphics on papyrus with a reed brush and ink. Mistakes on the papyrus, or even talking, could be punished by a rod on their backs.

a) Which group of Egyptian girls was allowed to have an education?
b) What was the name given to Egyptian script?
c) What was considered bad behaviour? How was a young scribe punished?

6 Now read about ancient Indian schools and answer the questions that follow.

Ancient Indian Schools

In ancient India, schools were in **hermitages**, deep within the forests, run by formidably strict *Rishis* or *Gurus* who were their teachers. These schools were given to the teachers by the King or the temples and everyone could go to school. Young men and women were sent to live with their teacher's family until they finished their education anywhere between the ages of 15 and 25. They slept on the floor and cooked their own food. Students began studying at dawn. They were taught to read, write, chant and memorise in **Sanskrit**. They studied the scriptures, mathematics, grammar, yoga and the natural world. They were given homework and could ask questions but most often the teacher wanted them to find their own answers to difficult questions. Lessons consisted of lectures sitting at the teacher's feet followed by practical exploration and meditation in the forest. Service to the teacher had to be unquestioning at all times. Punishment for students could include **fasting**, **banishment** from lessons and unpleasant chores.

a) What were ancient Indian teachers called?

b) Where were schools in ancient India located?

c) What was included in the curriculum? What language was it taught in?

d) Name two of the punishments students might be given.

Glossary

hermitage – a quiet place where people live away from others
Sanskrit – an ancient Indian language
fasting – not eating food
banishment – being sent away

7 Write a school magazine article describing and explaining what you have found out about schooling in ancient times and how it compares with the present day. Comment on what has changed and what has not. Include information on:

● what was studied
● learning styles
● teachers
● discipline.

Make sure you use the correct vocabulary precisely.

Language booster

Your article might include some of the following 'compare and contrast' phrases to help comment on the different kinds of schooling:

similar to, different from, although, better, worse, however, not unlike, in contrast.

Asking 'Did you know…?' questions is another way of engaging the reader.

Going further

Repeating the same words can sound boring. Using a range of synonyms correctly will help you to keep the reader's interest.

8 Complete the table below, adding the **synonyms** in the list to the correct row.

school		
student		
teacher		
vacation		
busy		

learner, college, hard at work, holiday, tutor, campus, professor, occupied, break, pupil

> **Language booster**
>
> A **synonym** is a word that means the same, or almost the same, as another word. For example, synonyms of 'big' include 'large' and 'enormous'.

9 Now read the extract below. In pairs, discuss which aspects of the 'school of the future' are already common in schools today.

What does the school of the future look like?

Some well-funded corporations are working to help design the schools of the future. This is their vision for the 21st-century, high-tech school.

'Smart card' IDs will provide instant registration with one swipe. These smart cards will also be used in the cafeteria, recording students' preferences and tracking purchases and their nutritional value. So, no more French-fries for lunch and double doses of fizzy drinks!

Students will move effortlessly through the elegant chrome and glass building carrying nothing but their laptops or tablets. No more heavy school bags! The building will automatically control lights and air-conditioning or heating based on the light levels and temperature, thus conserving energy. There will be solar panels on the roof to provide an alternative source of energy.

Students may visit the 'interactive learning centre', basically a library with only e-books and journals. So, if you are one of those people who likes the smell of books, you're out of luck! The school aims to be largely paperless, with a few printers 'just in case'. It will have high-speed access to the internet and the world's best educational websites and databases.

10 In your pairs, imagine that 50 million US dollars were going to be spent to transform your school. What kind of school would you like to have?

11 Write a short report to your school governors describing your plans. Suggest changes to the following areas:
- school buildings and classrooms
- the library
- the cafeteria.

Use a variety of synonyms and accurate technical terminology. You must give a reason for each of your suggestions.

> **Top tip**
>
> Use headings and subheadings to make your report easier to read.

4.3 How do we learn?

In this section you will learn to:
- speak clearly using the most effective words to explain and describe
- choose the correct vocabulary and level of formality for the listener.

Getting started

1. Note down everything that comes to mind when you think back to your favourite primary school teacher.

   What was his/her name? What can you recall about their classroom? What was your first day at school like? What are your earliest memories of school? Think about your five senses. What smells, sounds or sights do you remember most?

2. In pairs, share the information about your teacher and ask some questions about your partner's primary school experience.

Exploring the skills

When you were talking together about your experiences, you will have noticed that the wider your vocabulary, the more able you were to describe a person or a situation accurately and vividly. Just as when you are writing, the most accurate choice of noun, verb, adjective or adverb will make your speaking more effective.

Language booster

The main parts of speech are nouns, verbs, adjectives and adverbs. As you widen your vocabulary, you should be aware of what part of speech a word is:

noun – a word that refers to a person, thing or idea, for example, *teacher*, *student*

verb – a word that expresses and action or a state, for example, *to study*, *to be*

adjective – a word that describes a noun, for example, *short*, *clever*

adverb – a word that adds information about an action, for example, to study *hard*, to walk *slowly*

3. Now read the text about Mrs D'Souza. Some key words have been underlined. Identify what type of word each one is and add it to the correct column in the table on page 79. We have done a few for you.

> Mrs D'Souza was a <u>fabulous</u> <u>teacher</u>. She was <u>tall</u> and <u>dark-skinned</u> with <u>thick</u>, <u>curly</u> black <u>hair</u> that <u>was</u> <u>securely</u> <u>fastened</u> by a <u>net</u>. She <u>wore</u> <u>beautiful</u> <u>print</u> <u>dresses</u> and <u>high-heeled</u> <u>shoes</u> that <u>clicked</u> on the <u>tiled</u> <u>floors</u> of the classroom. She <u>smelt</u> of <u>roses</u> and <u>talcum</u> <u>powder</u>. She was <u>always</u> <u>ready</u> to <u>comfort</u> little first years who <u>were</u> <u>crying</u> as they said goodbye to their parents.

Noun	Adjective	Verb	Adverb
teacher	fabulous	was … fastened	securely

4 Now make a few notes about one of your first teachers. Then tell your partner about the teacher, trying to use the best adjectives and verbs that you can to 'capture' what the person was like.

Developing the skills

Remember that in order to communicate well your vocabulary must be as descriptive and precise as possible.

5 You will now hear from a young woman about how the brain learns. Listen to the extract twice.

a) The first time, note down only key vocabulary.

b) The next time you listen, take notes. Think about:
- how emotions affect our learning
- what food and water the brain needs
- physical conditions that affect the brain
- the best conditions for learning.

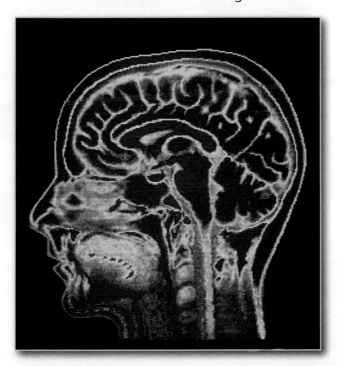

6 In groups, share your notes. Add any information you missed and highlight any key words that were new to you all.

7 Now, using your notes, discuss the questions below with a partner.
- How have emotions recently affected your learning? Have you been happy, sad or anxious?
- Talk about a time when you were happy and relaxed while you were learning something. How well did you learn? What did you learn?
- Do you have a balanced and healthy diet that supports your brain in its learning? What could you do to improve this?
- Do you take 'brain breaks', where you do some physical exercise or move around?

8 In your group, gather together the information you know about the best conditions for learning. Make a note of the key words you would use if you were giving a talk to a class of younger students. What do you think would be essential for younger students to know?

9 Use the key words to help you deliver a two-minute talk to your partner

> **Top tip**
>
> Remember to use a combination of information using key words and advice like: *The brain needs a lot of water. Make sure you drink water regularly while you are working or studying.*

Going further

Just as when you are writing, when you speak about a topic, it is important to use vocabulary that is appropriate to the listener. For example, you need to think about how formal you need to be. When you are chatting to your friends your language will be very informal. When you prepared your talk for younger students, you probably made an effort to use language that you thought they would understand. Perhaps you explained some technical or scientific points.

However, a talk for teachers would sound very different from a talk designed for students. Think about the level of formality and vocabulary used in the following:

Talk to teachers: *Emotions can impact greatly on the way we learn. Stress and anxiety can inhibit learning.*

Talk to students: *Feelings can affect the way we learn. Worry and stress can prevent us from learning so well.*

The student version is less technical and more informal than the teacher version.

10 You are now going to listen to two audio clips about mind maps. **Mind maps** are similar to concept maps but include much more detail.

As you listen, group the **key words** in this talk into 'teacher-speak' words and phrases and 'student-speak' words and phrases. After the talk, see whether you can convert the teacher-speak words into student-speak and vice versa.

Teacher speak	Student speak
key words	important words
images	
	.

11 Using what you have heard, work with a partner to prepare two separate talks: one for teachers and another for younger students. Both talks must include:

- basic information on mind mapping
- how mind mapping improves memory and creativity
- the benefits of mind mapping to teaching or learning in the classroom
- a demonstration of how to create a mind map.

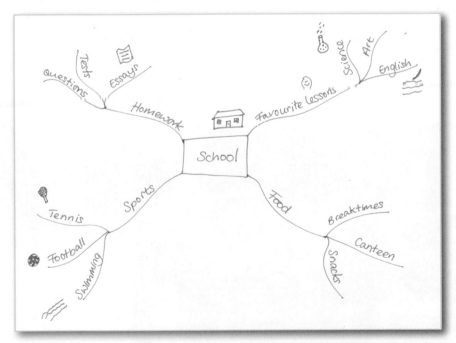

12 Give your talks to the class – did you all manage to show the difference between a talk aimed at teachers and one aimed at younger students? What were these differences?

Listening skills in focus (L1, L2 and L4)

In this section you will learn to:
- select details from different kinds of spoken texts
- use clues before you start listening to help you understand a text
- understand what is implied but not actually stated in a formal talk.

Getting started

1 Think about which aspects of the school curriculum are going to be necessary once you leave school. Do one of the following and make notes.

a) Ask your parents or another adult what they do in their jobs on a daily basis. Which of these skills did they learn at school?

b) Pick a job or a career that you would like to pursue. What skills and knowledge will you need to do that job?

2 Make a table like the one below to list **skills** and **knowledge** that you are acquiring at school and investigate their real-world uses. Fill in the last gap and then add some more rows with your own ideas.

Skill/knowledge from school	Use in real world	Career that requires this
Organisation: handing in work on time, keeping a diary	Meetings, deadlines, projects	All careers!
Understanding chemical symbols	Reading labels, buying vitamins	Biologist, teacher of biology, medical professional
Reading maps	Getting directions	

Exploring the skills

It will help you to understand spoken text if you can get some idea of the context – that is, where the people are, or the reason why they are there. You may be given some information before you listen to an extract. This will help you start to focus on the sort of things the speakers will be talking about. If you are not given much information, try listening out carefully for clues. For example:

Who – who is speaking? There could be several speakers. Listen for different voices.

Role – what do the participants in the extract do? What is their job or profession?

Context – where or when is the conversation happening? What do you think has just happened or is going to happen?

Point of view or **opinion** – this is harder to listen for. It tells you what the speaker(s) feels or think about the issue being talked about.

Keep these pre-listening tips in mind during the following task.

3 You are going to hear about a child **prodigy** called Adora Svitak. She is a young woman who has published books and spoken at conferences and who runs her own blog and teacher-training series.

Listen carefully to the information and then answer the questions below.

1: At what age did Adora begin teaching?

2: What is Adora's view of technology in the classroom?

3: What does Adora think adults can learn from children?

4: What was Adora's first book called?

5: What is Adora's favourite subject at school?

6: Which social networking site does Adora use?

School and the real world

Developing the skills

Here is another chance for you to practise your pre-listening skills.
Re-read the tips on page 83 and remember to use the clues. Read the
questions first and look out for the key question words before you listen.

4 Listen to three senior school students talking about the ideas of Alvin
Toffler, author of a book called *Future Shock*. One of the students,
Zara, has just watched an online clip of Toffler speaking about his
concerns regarding public education in the USA. Zara shares her
thoughts on the talk with two of her friends, Jeremy and Anna.

Alvin Toffler

Glossary

radical – very important
obsolete – no longer in
use, out of date

a) Why is Jeremy feeling overwhelmed?

b) Which parts of her schooling does Anna enjoy? Does she think
schools should be scrapped?

c) How old is Alvin Toffler? Why does his age surprise the other students?

d) What was the purpose of public education in the 18th and 19th
centuries in the USA or UK?

e) What are the similarities between the old factory and the current
school?

f) What does Jeremy want to do in the future? Who would he like to
learn from?

g) Name two roles that teachers could have in the new education
system.

h) Why does Jeremy want to stay up late?

i) Why is Anna unsure about working with younger students in
Art classes?

j) Explain two features of the 24-hour school.

5 With a partner, discuss the answers you gave to question 4. Talk about the following from your own viewpoint:

a) Which aspect of your current schooling resembles a factory or an industry?

b) Which aspects of current schooling are actually useful and practical?

c) Which aspects of your schooling do you think are not that useful to your generation and should be changed?

Your discussion could include topics such as:

the school, timetable, curriculum, organisation, rules, classrooms, use of computers, teaching methods

Going further

You sometimes have to listen 'between the lines' to understand what someone implies but does not actually say. Notice how a speaker might make a comment or ask a simple question when they want to guide your thoughts in a particular direction, without being obvious.

As you answer the next set of questions, you will find that sometimes you have to use clues to answer the questions, and not just select details from what the person says.

6 Listen again to Jeremy, Anna and Zara talking about present and future schooling. Can you read between the lines?

1: What is Jeremy's current attitude to school? Has it always been this way?

2: What kind of a relationship do you think Anna has with her grandmother?

3: Which phrase tells you that Anna is quite fond of school? Does she want to shut down schools?

4: What does Jeremy mean by the word 'system' when he talks about education? What does he think is inadequate about it?

5: Why do Anna and Jeremy disagree slightly on the idea of a 24-hour school?

6: Name two things that you learn about Jeremy from this conversation.

7: From the conversation, what can you work out about Zara?

8: Which three aspects of future schooling appeal most to the 3 teenagers?

The big task

In groups of three or four, you are going to research, plan and give a presentation on your ideal school. Imagine that this is a school of the future, the kind of school you would want your children to go to or would like to go to yourself. Make sure you think about accurate vocabulary to describe the school and its technological wonders.

1 You must research and include the following in your presentation:

- the name of the school and its aims/philosophy – logo or badge optional
- the school building, where it is located and how it works – classrooms, hall, cafeteria, toilets, library
- the curriculum – what is taught, how, when and why
- the teachers – how they teach, their attitude to teaching and learning
- the rules and culture of the school – uniforms, assemblies, timings, organisation, punishments
- links to the world outside school – how these will be achieved.

2 Think about how you will present this school to your classmates and teacher. You could use one or more of the following:

- a role-play or drama with music
- a short film/audio recording
- a photo story
- a day-in-the-life of your school
- a PowerPoint presentation with a voiceover.

3 Once you have done your presentation, write it up as a newspaper article that outlines the importance of funding and creating this school for your local community.

Check your progress

Here are the Reading, Writing, Speaking and Listening skills you learnt about in Chapter 4.

Use this table to decide how good you are at the different skills, and make a note of what you need to be able to do in order to move up a level.

READING	
I can ...	
Higher	usually understand and pick out all the details I need from texts, including diagrams and charts
Middle ↑	often understand and then pick out many of the details I need from texts, including diagrams and charts
Lower ↑	sometimes pick out a few of the details I need from texts, including diagrams and charts

WRITING	
I can ...	
Higher	use a good range of vocabulary correctly and confidently when writing to inform or explain and can express quite complex ideas
Middle ↑	use some variety of vocabulary when writing to inform or explain and can express straightforward ideas clearly
Lower ↑	use a limited range of basic vocabulary correctly when writing to inform or explain and can express simple ideas so that they can be understood

SPEAKING	
I can ...	
Higher	usually find the most effective words to explain or describe something usually choose exactly the right level of formality
Middle ↑	sometimes find the right words to explain or describe something sometimes find the right level of formality
Lower ↑	use a limited range of vocabulary, and may hesitate or search for the right words to explain or describe something understand the need to find the right level of formality, but find it hard to adapt

LISTENING	
I can ...	
Higher	pick out exactly the details I need when listening to texts, including complex ones, using the clues in the questions to help usually understand what is implied but not actually stated in a formal talk
Middle ↑	pick out many of the details I need when listening to texts, using the clues in the questions to help understand some of what is implied but not actually stated in a formal talk
Lower ↑	sometimes understand and pick out some of the details I need when listening to straightforward texts sometimes use the clues in the questions to help me answer straightforward questions understand straightforward formal talks

The big picture

In this chapter you will:

- think about competition both in the environment and in the human world

- read and talk about competition in nature where animals fight for resources

- think and write about what drives us to compete against each other and to want to win in competitions ranging from sports to scholarships.

Thinking big

1 On your own, look at the pictures and think about any competitions you have entered or would like to enter.

2 In pairs, rank the following statements from 'most true' to 'least true' in your opinion. People enter competitions:
- to prove they are the best
- to gain the admiration of others
- to get the prize/reward
- to increase their self-esteem
- to make money
- to show they are superior
- because they enjoy the game/business/ sport/subject
- to push themselves to their limits
- to perform better.

3 When do you think competition is unhealthy?

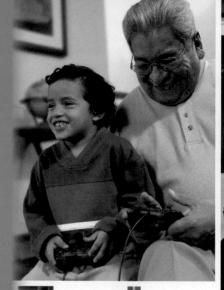

Chapter 5

Competition

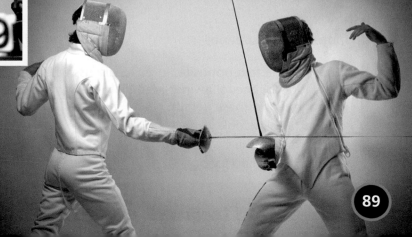

Competition in nature

Reading skills in focus (R2 and R3)

In this section you will learn to:
- use text features to pick out key points, facts and details
- find related details in a text in preparation for summarising.

Getting started

1 Look at the following photos. Think about what the animals or plants are competing for in each photo.

2 In pairs, make a list of resources (things they need) that animals compete for in nature.

3 Now write down five questions or topics you would like to know more about to do with competition in nature.

Exploring the skills

When you are reading any text, you should use all its features to help you understand it. The following can help you to find the information or detail you need quickly:

- headings
- photos and illustrations
- fact boxes
- diagrams.

4 Skim read the text opposite. In pairs, discuss where in the text you would look for the following. Identify the features in the text that helped you find these details:

- what a shark looks like
- where sharks live
- how sharks find food
- shark attacks on people
- how big a shark is.

5 Now read the text carefully and answer the following questions.

a) Where do sharks live?

b) What happens when a shark's tooth falls out?

c) How do sharks hunt? Give **two** details.

d) Why can sharks swim fast? Why might this be an advantage?

e) Do you think another animal would attack the shark? Give **one** reason why.

f) Write two sentences to describe what a shark looks like. Use at least three adjectives.

g) You are on a beach in South Africa and your friend refuses to go into the water because he/she is afraid of a shark attack. What would you tell them?

h) Give one fact that you found surprising about great white sharks.

Top tip

Non-fiction texts often use fact boxes to help you find the information quickly.

THE GREAT WHITE SHARK

The great white shark is an eating machine. All it does is swim, eat and breed.

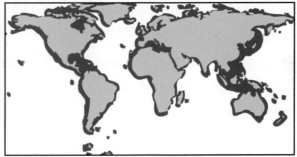

Blue shading = areas where great white sharks are found

Habitat
The great white shark is the largest predatory fish on the planet. It lives in temperate coastal waters all over the world but can swim very long distances across oceans and is capable of swimming 12 000 miles in nine months.

Skeletons
Because sharks have skeletons made of cartilage, which is more flexible and lighter than bone, this ruthless predator can swim at up to 15 mph.

Hunting
The great white shark does not compete for food, is at the top of the food chain and is therefore an apex predator. It hunts alone and usually eats dolphins, seals and sea lions

Fact box
Length Up to 6m
Weight 2250kg
Speed   Up to 43mph

which it typically attacks from below. However great white sharks will eat whatever they find.

Teeth and jaws
The great white has long rows of teeth which are continually replaced when old ones fall out. It can grow up to 20 000 teeth in a lifetime. Both its upper and lower jaws move and this makes them more powerful than any other creature in the world.

Great white's reputation
Great whites, and sharks in general, have a bad reputation. But the statistics do not match with the man-eater fame of sharks. In fact, fewer than 60 people are attacked annually by great whites and of these only 10% of the attacks result in fatalities.

Competition in nature

Developing the skills

Different texts use different features for different reasons. In addition to the list on page 90, non-fiction texts often use:

- captions
- bold/capital letters
- bulleted lists
- tables/diagrams

- maps
- quotations
- navigation bars.

6. Read the text opposite about the killer whale and answer the questions.
   a) Which text features listed above does the text use?
   b) What type of text is it?
   c) Where would you expect to read it?
   d) Compared with the text about sharks on page 91, which is easier to read? Give one reason for your choice.
   e) Which text is the more informative? Give one reason for your choice.
   f) Which text includes quotations? Why do you think they are used?

7. Reread the text on whale watching and answer the questions.

   Where would you look or click on the page, if:
   a) you only spoke French
   b) you wanted to join an expedition
   c) you wanted to give money to the foundation
   d) you wanted to watch a video of an expedition?

8. Summarise in one sentence what you do as a volunteer on the expedition.

9. Do you agree that the expedition is the *Experience of a lifetime!* Give one reason for your answer.

Going further

In the exam you may be asked to write a summary. It is useful to find and organise related details in a text before writing a summary, according to the task.

10. You have been asked to write a short summary of either why the great white shark or the killer whale is such a good hunter. Look back at the text about your chosen animal. Then copy and complete the table below with the relevant details.

Skeleton/size	Hunting	Teeth/jaws

BIOSPHERE EXPEDITIONS.ORG

| Home | About | Photo gallery | Video | Events | Results | Donate | Contact |

EXPERIENCE OF A LIFETIME!

Fascinating creatures of the deep: studying whales in the Atlantic Ocean

Price/dates

'Best Ten Wildlife Holidays' *Travel* Magazine.
'Best in Outdoor Pursuits' Travel awards 2013

This conservation work expedition will take you off the coast of Iceland to study orcas, or killer whales. You will photograph whales and record them as part of a long-term scientific survey. You will listen to and make recordings of whale **clicks and whistles** to tag the whales. All this in an effort to find out a whale's life history and its **pod's migration** patterns across the oceans.

PRICE = Expedition contribution $2000

Dates
2–11 April, 14–23 April and 26 April–5 May

Check availability & sign up

Fact box

Orcas typically measure 6-8m but can be up to 10m in length and usually weigh between 6 and 10 tonnes (6–10 000kg). Killer whales usually have 40–50 teeth. The orca is an apex predator because it has no predators other than humans. However, whales are still hunted and now have **protected status**.

Killer whales often live and hunt in pods: a group of whales work together to encircle and herd **prey** into a small area before attacking.

Glossary

outdoor pursuits – activities you do outside, for example diving, biking, canoeing
clicks and whistles – sounds whales make to communicate
pod – a group of whales
migration – moving from one place to another to find food
protected status – classified as an endangered animal
prey – animal hunted for food

Adapted from
www.biosphere-expeditions.org/azores

In this section you will learn to:
- use paragraphs correctly
- link ideas to write a smooth-flowing paragraph
- use a variety of connectives to write a summary.

Getting started

Humans also seem to enjoy competing against each other. It may not be competing for food or light like animals or plants, but for many other reasons. Sport is one area where people enjoy seeing who will win.

1 In pairs:
- Talk about any sports, games and activities that you play. At what level do you play?
- Brainstorm all the sports you know. Then classify them into two lists with headings. Discuss your classifications.
- Note down any interesting words or ideas from your conversation.

2 As a class, list five of the biggest sporting events in the world. Now rank them. Which event is the most important?

3 On your own:
- Look at the photos and at the list of words in the table below. Add three words or phrases of your own that you use often when talking about competition in sport.

cross the finishing line	
score points	
win the cup	

- Next, choose four of the words or phrases. Write a sentence using each word.

Exploring the skills

A **paragraph** is a group of sentences which discuss one main idea.

- Paragraphs break up the text and make it easier to read.
- They organise information into meaningful chunks.
- A new paragraph usually introduces a new idea.
- Often there are one or two supporting details in a paragraph which give more information about the main idea.

A **topic sentence** captures the entire meaning of a paragraph or a group of paragraphs. It often appears at the start of a paragraph.

Haile Gebrselassie is known as one of the greatest long-distance runners. In his career he has broken 15 world records, won gold medals and set new standards in long-distance running. Haile Gebrselassie, an Ethiopian, had to run 10 kilometres daily to go school and this laid the foundation for his running career.

— topic sentence
— supporting facts

4 Silently read the newspaper article below.

5 In pairs, identify the following:
- the topic sentence
- where each new paragraph starts
- the main idea in each paragraph
- the supporting facts or details in each paragraph.

WORLD CUP 2022

THE BID FOR the 2022 competition was awarded by Fifa to the desert state of Qatar. This will be the first time the World Cup is staged in the Middle East.

Qatar's bid included a commitment to provide air-conditioned stadiums and pitches. To do this, the super-rich nation will use a solar-powered cooling system to keep temperatures at a constant 27C, in contrast to the summer average of 41C. A group of Fifa officials visited the facilities and went to see a prototype of one of the air-conditioned stadiums.

Qatar, which is one of the world's wealthiest countries, showed Fifa officials plans for stadiums shaped as boats and sea shells. It also proposed to transport fans to some matches on boats and provide sea views from seats at matches.

Fifa president Sepp Blatter gave Qatar's bid a boost when he said that the Arab world deserved to stage a World Cup. The fact that Qatar had successfully hosted the 2006 Asian Games showed that it was able to organise big international events.

At first, Qatar had been considered by experts as an outsider among the bidders for the 2022 World Cup. Other countries in the running were the USA, Australia, South Korea and Japan. Qatar was the smallest country bidding to host the event, but was also one of the richest. As a result, the country promised it would spend £2.6bn on stadiums and £26bn on infrastructure.

Developing the skills

To write well you need to join different ideas together smoothly.
Connectives join sentences together. Some examples are 'and', 'but',
'so', 'although', 'because,' 'in spite of' and 'besides'.

6 Combine the sentences below to make one paragraph using
connectives from the box. You may need to use some connectives
more than once.

as	but	in spite of	which	also	and	because	although

Most people agree that the 2010 World Cup was a resounding
success. It was held in South Africa. The winners of the
tournament were Spain.

Many commentators agree that South Africa was also the winner.

South Africa showed that Africa can host a tournament as big as
the World Cup. The weather was cold. The welcome from South
Africans was warm. The welcome was friendly. South Africa has a
reputation for violent gun crime. The tournament turned out to
be peaceful.

Connectives not only link ideas within a paragraph. They also link one
paragraph to the next.

7 In pairs:

● Identify the connectives in the reading passage 'World Cup 2022'
on page 95.

● Make a list of all the connectives you found and any others you
know and complete the table, inserting the connectives into the
correct box.

Sequence order	Time order	Cause and effect	Contrast
At first	In the morning	As a result	in contrast

Going further

Summarising is a skill we all use every day. A good **summary**:
● includes the main points/ideas
● uses your own words
● is ordered logically
● does not include your opinions.

8 First, reread your ideas from task 5 for the main points of each paragraph in the 'World Cup 2022' article. Then read the summary below of the Qatar bid.

  a) Which of the features listed on page 96 does it use?

  b) Identify the connectives.

  c) What ideas or sentences from the original article does it include?

  d) Find two details from the original article that are not in the summary.

  e) Do you think it summarises the main points? Give your opinion.

> Qatar has been chosen as the surprise host for the 2022 World Cup. Although many people did not think Qatar had a serious chance of winning the bid, this small but rich country persuaded Fifa officials it was time to let the Middle East stage the World Cup. Besides showcasing air-conditioned stadiums, Qatar also showed plans promising to invest $26 billion in infrastructure and $2.6bn on stadiums.

Top tip

Reread your summary and check you have:
• Included a topic sentence
• used connectives.

9 Write a summary of a recent sports competition at your school/college or in your local area. Start with a topic sentence.
For example:

> The Inter-regional School Football Championships were the most exciting event in this year's school sports calendar.

5.3 Competition and the arts

In this section you will learn to:
- build a conversation by asking and answering questions
- be an active listener and add new ideas.

Getting started

1 In pairs, discuss the following:
- What do you know about the *Got Talent* show?
- What type of performances are allowed?
- Would you like to audition for the *Got Talent* show? If yes, why? If no, why not?
- Why do you think people want to appear on such TV shows?

Exploring the skills

Asking questions is a very useful way of building a conversation. You can use questions to:
- open a conversation
- ask a question back
- change the direction of a conversation
- request information or opinions
- develop an idea
- ask someone to repeat something.

When replying to questions, try to avoid short answers. Build the conversation using examples. The best way of giving examples is to provide answers to questions without them being asked, especially if you are given a 'closed' questions, such as, 'Did you watch *Vietnam's Got Talent*?' For example:

Answer: 'Oh yes. I watch every week.	**answers question: 'When'**
I saw the violinist yesterday while I was visiting my grandmother.	**answers questions: 'What', 'When' and 'Where'**
I didn't think she was very good.	
What did you think?'	**asks question back**

2 Two friends are discussing *China's Got Talent*. Read the dialogue below and identify the questions.

Ju: Did you see *China's Got Talent* yesterday?

Bao: Oh yes. I'm **hooked**. I watch it every week.

Ju: Oh, I missed it last night. What happened?

Bao: The 20 girls on a bicycle **act** got **knocked out**, but, well, I didn't think they should win anyway. So, who do you think is going to win?

Ju: Well, I quite like the young girl pianist. I particularly liked it when she mixed in a jazz section with a classical piece. Mind you, the panel of judges don't seem to like her performances very much. They always complain that she doesn't have much **charisma**. Although I didn't approve of the way the judges talked to her the other day. Did you see that?

Bao: Yes, that was shocking: they were so harsh that they almost **reduced her to tears**. But I'm not sure a pianist should win anyway. You know everybody plays the piano now. For instance, I heard the other day on the radio that between 25 and 40 million children are learning the piano now in China. And I'm not sure she's that special, although I did hear she practised over 12 hours a day.

Ju: Wow – that's a lot! So what do you think about the violinist?

Bao: Hmm. Not sure. Don't you think he's a bit **pushy** and self-important? Obviously, it's never easy to play at that level and it's a bit unfair to judge him on the strength of his attitude rather than his performance, but he is so **intent on** his own success.

3 Reread 'Exploring the skills'. In pairs, discuss the purpose of each question in the dialogue above. Then copy the table below and complete the first two columns to show how each question is used.

4 Next, reread the answers given to each question. Then complete the third column of the table with **one** example or way that the partner gives more information.

Question	Type of question and how it is used	Examples given in answer
1 Did you see *China's Got Talent* yesterday?	To open the conversation. The question assumes that the friend also watches the TV show.	I watch it every week.
2		

5 In pairs, practise reading the dialogue aloud, taking turns to read the different parts. Discuss who you think is guiding or controlling the conversation.

Developing the skills

Did you know you can build a conversation using different types of questions?

> Type 1 is the **What** question, asking for information:
>
> What did you see/hear?

> Type 2 asks for **the opinion or response** to what you saw or heard:
>
> What did you like/not like (most)? How did it make you feel?

> Type 3 question is the **Why** question and asks for reasons for the opinions expressed:
>
> Why do you think this?

Often when we want to build a conversation, we need to give an example. You can use these phrases to introduce the example.

> *For example*   *For instance*
>
> *To give you an example*   *Let me illustrate*

To develop a conversation from your example/opinion, it is useful to support it by adding the reason why. This broadens the discussion to more general matters.

For example:

> *The* Got Talent *contest is a waste of time.*
>
> *For instance, we all sit down on a Saturday evening to watch when we could be using that time to practise an instrument! I think all of us get more fulfilment actively playing an instrument than passively watching someone else play.*

6 In pairs, identify the phrase(s) that introduce an example in the conversation in task 2. What happens to the conversation afterwards? Discuss how the example works in the conversation.

7 Give an example to support each of the following statements. Don't forget to give reasons why, to back up your example.

- The *Got Talent* contest encourages us all to sing or dance or play an instrument.
- The *Got Talent* contest has made young people obsessed with fame and money.

8 In pairs, have your own conversation about the *Got Talent* contest in your country. If you have not seen the programme, then use one that is popular in your country. Start the conversation like this:

> *Have you been watching the* Got Talent *contest?*

Going further

The aim of a conversation is often to appreciate what your partner says by actively listening and taking turns. You can help develop the conversation even more by adding new ideas. You can do this, first by listening carefully and then by:

- showing that you have listened to their point (even if you have a different opinion) by rephrasing what your partner has said
- then giving your opinion
- then asking a question back.

For example:

> I didn't approve of the way the judges talked to the pianist the other day. — **rephrasing what your partner has said**
>
> Yes – I agree that was shocking. — **agreeing** The judges were so harsh that the girl was almost crying. But I'm not sure a pianist should win anyway. You know everybody plays the piano now. — **giving your opinion** What do you think? — **asking a question back**

9 Choose one of the topics listed in the box on the right. Tell your partner about the topic, giving examples and reasons for your opinion.

Your partner should listen very carefully because they must repeat back to you what you have said.

10 Now your partner chooses a second topic listed in the box. Listen carefully to what they say about it. Then follow again the three steps in 'Going further'.

11 In pairs, you are going to have a conversation of no more than 10 minutes. The aim is to keep the conversation going. Each choose one of the following themes. Write a list of five questions you want to ask your partner about their chosen topic.

- Buying music
- Painting
- Playing an instrument
- Films
- Video games

Topics

- The latest film on the market
- The last competition you entered
- The latest video game on the market

Top tip

Don't forget to listen actively to what your partner says.

Competition in business

In this section you will learn to:

- understand and pick out facts in short informal dialogues
- recognise and understand opinions in short informal dialogues
- recognise and understand facts and opinion in longer, more formal dialogues.

Getting started

Businesses usually want to sell you things or ideas. They are competing for your money and your time in order to become the market leader.

1 In pairs, discuss and decide who the market leader in your country is for:

- footwear
- cars
- computers
- fast food.

2 Discuss and give a definition of 'market leader'.

3 Now discuss which of the following competes better for your time and your money.

- Buying a book from the local bookshop or buying the same book on the internet.
- Buying a CD of your favourite band or going to the cinema to see the latest movie.
- Saving some money to buy a computer or going to a festival.
- Working overtime on Friday evening to earn double wages or staying in and watching TV.

4 Discuss and agree on a definition of 'competition' in business. Write it down. Compare your definition with another pair.

Exploring the skills

An **opinion** is a belief or judgement which is not based on fact or knowledge and which cannot be proved. For example:

Everyone needs a mobile phone nowadays.

You can often tell the difference between a fact and an opinion by looking out for adjectives. For instance:

This is a phone. —————————— fact

This is a wonderful phone. ————— opinion – we cannot prove the phone is wonderful.

This is the best phone. ————————— opinion – we cannot prove the phone is the best.

5 Skim the advertisement opposite for a mobile phone package.

6 In pairs:

  a) Identify the opinions in the advertisement.

  b) Decide if you think the phone is free. Give reasons for your answer.

  c) Discuss if you think it is the 'best offer yet'. Give reasons for your answer.

  d) Note down ideas about why companies advertise their products.

Great savings on the latest mobile phone deals

Free HTC Wildfire

✪ **Only $12 monthly subscription***

✪ **200 mins talk time**

✪ **200 texts**

✪ **and a massive 1GB of data usage**

It's the best offer yet!

* 24-month tie in

Developing the skills

When speaking, people rarely introduce their opinions with 'I believe …' or 'I think …' but will often try to convince you of their opinions by

- mixing facts with opinions
- telling you why they think something is useful/beautiful/good etc.

7 Now listen to a conversation between two people about a mobile phone. Then, in pairs, discuss:

5.1

- Why was the original MOB phone popular?
- What have the makers done?
- Copy and complete the following table which lists the features of the phone. What do Sami and Yara say about how those features might be useful.

Feature	Why it is useful
Sense interface	Lets you flick from one screen to another by touching the image
3.2" touchscreen	
Friendstream app	
5-megapixel camera	

- Do you think we have to agree it's a stylish little package?
- Do you think Sami does a good job of showing Yara his new phone?

8 Listen again to some phrases and statements from the listening passage. Write the letters a) to j) in your notebook and identify the facts and opinions by writing F next to facts and O next to opinions, as listed below.

  a) The first phone was so cool.

  b) I really liked the Sense interface.

  c) The Sense interface lets you flick from one screen to another by touching the image on the screen.

  d) The makers have updated it.

  e) Now it's even better than awesome.

  f) It's got a 3.2-inch touchscreen.

  g) It's perfect for me because I love looking at media and video clips.

  h) Social networking is looked after by a Friendstream app.

  i) It also has a 5-megapixel camera with autofocus and flash.

  j) It's a stylish little package.

Going further

Numbers and percentages often indicate that something is a fact.

9 Later, you are going to listen to an interview about the history of mobile phones. First, in pairs, prior to listening discuss:

  a) What do you know about the history of mobile phones?

  b) Look at the photo of one of the first mobile phones. What has changed about mobile phones since then?

  c) Do you think you will get more facts or more opinions in this interview? Why do you think that?

10 These are all words you will hear in the listening passage. Match each word on the left to its definition.

  a) antenna

  b) estimation

  c) forecast

  d) grow like wildfire

  e) handset

  f) predictive texting

  g) vibrate function

  h) wildly incorrect

  A when mobile phone guesses the word you want to write from the first few letters

  B mobile phone

  C setting so that the phone shakes slightly instead of ringing to warn you someone is calling/texting

  D very wrong

  E spread very quickly

  F guess

  G predict

  H long thin metal part that sends and receives radio signals

11 Listen to the passage a first time and answer the following question.

What has happened to the popularity of mobile phones?

12 Listen again and copy and complete the following table to chart the history of mobile phones.

Date	What happened
1985	First mobile phone appeared that did not have a battery the size of a briefcase
1996	
2000	
2001	
2003	
2007	

13 Listen again to the last paragraph and complete this table which lists the percentage of people who own a mobile phone in different countries.

Percentage	Country	Percentage	Country
40%	USA		Singapore
	India		Saudi Arabia
	Nigeria		Hong Kong
	China		

14 Read the following text (it starts from Dr Suhuyini's second speech in the listening passage). Identify two opinions.

> **DR SUHUYINI:** Mobile phones have got smaller and lighter and because of this the popularity of mobile phones has grown like wildfire.
>
> **INTERVIEWER:** What numbers are you talking about?
>
> **DR SUHUYINI:** Well, in the 1980s one mobile phone company forecast a world market of 900 000 phones by the year 2000. But they got it really wrong – their estimation was wildly incorrect. By 1998 more mobile phones were sold worldwide than cars and PCs combined. Today, 900 000 mobile phones are sold every three days.

15 On your own write notes on the three most important features for you in a mobile phone. When and why do you use them? Why are they important?

16 In pairs, discuss what is important to you in a mobile phone and why.

17 As a whole class, discuss:
- Why do you think mobile phones spread 'like wildfire'?
- Why do you think the features of a mobile phone keep changing?
- Do you think a new feature on a phone is always a benefit?
- What does this say about your society?

The big task

You are the reporter for your school magazine and have been asked to write a review of the annual school talent show which was also recorded for a local TV channel.

1 On your own, brainstorm what type of acts you think will appear in your school's talent show. Think about:

- dance
- solo singing
- groups/bands
- music/instruments
- circus/novelty acts.

2 Now decide:

- which acts performed
- what happened on the night
- who you/the audience liked best/least/how the contest made you feel
- what the winner's reactions were
- what this means for the school.

3 Write a first draft of your review.

4 Now go back and check your review. Add a title (make sure the title is less than five words). Check:

- spelling
- that you have at least one fact
- that you have at least one opinion.

5 Write a final copy of your review.

6 Hold a class competition and vote for the best review of the talent show. Before you decide, think about how you will mark the reviews. For example, will you give more marks for:

- an interesting review
- accurate English
- good presentation skills?

Here are the Reading, Writing, Speaking and Listening skills you learnt about in Chapter 5.

Use this table to decide how good you are at the different skills, and make a note of what you need to be able to do in order to move up a level.

READING I can ...		WRITING I can ...	
Higher	confidently use text features to understand and then pick out most of the key points usually pick out all the related details I need from a text I have to summarise	**Higher**	use paragraphs correctly and confidently when writing link quite complex ideas together, using a variety of connectives, to form smooth-flowing paragraphs in a summary regularly use a variety of connectives to help me write an effective summary
Middle	use text features to understand and then pick out key points pick out many of the related details I need from a text I have to summarise	**Middle**	sometimes use paragraphs when writing sometimes link my ideas, using connectives, to form a smooth-flowing paragraph in a summary
Lower	sometimes use text features to understand and then pick out key points pick out the basic related details I need from a text I have to summarise	**Lower**	make limited use of paragraphs when writing sometimes join a few ideas together, using some basic connectives, to form paragraphs in a summary

SPEAKING I can ...		LISTENING I can ...	
Higher	build a conversation with confidence, by taking my turn at asking and answering questions be an effective listener and often add my own new ideas	**Higher**	understand and then pick out exactly the facts I need when listening to short informal dialogues usually recognise and understand opinions expressed in informal and formal speech
Middle	help build a conversation, by responding well to questions be a competent listener and sometimes add a few of my own ideas	**Middle**	understand and then pick out many of the facts I need when listening to short informal dialogues sometimes recognise and understand opinions expressed in informal and formal speech
Lower	join in a conversation by giving short answers to questions be a fair listener and try to respond to other people's ideas	**Lower**	sometimes understand and pick out some of the facts I need when listening to short informal dialogues understand straightforward informal and formal speech

The big picture

In this chapter you will:

- think about work – the different kinds of work people do

- consider the kind of work you would like to do

- research, talk and write about ways to find work and to succeed at work.

Thinking big

1   Look at the photographs. On your own, note down ideas about the following:

- What different kinds of work are shown in the photos?

- Which of these jobs do you think is the most interesting?

- What would be the rewards and drawbacks of each job?

- Which of these jobs would you like to do? Which ones wouldn't you like to do?

2   In pairs, look at the photos. Talk together about what you know about each of these jobs and the different types and places of work pictured. Ask your partner questions about what they would like and dislike about the work shown in the photos.

3   Discuss your choice with another pair.

- What is the most important thing about work for you – to make money, to do something you enjoy, to help others?

- What do you think would be the advantages and disadvantages of travelling a lot for your work? Would you prefer to work locally? Why?

- Do you prefer to work in a group of people, or on your own? Explain your reasons.

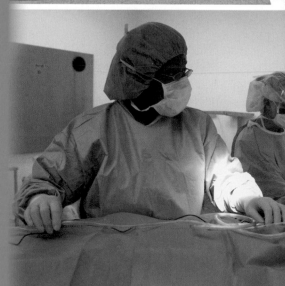

Reading skills in focus (R3)

In this section you will learn to:
- select facts from a range of texts which also contain personal opinions
- recognise the language used to introduce facts and straightforward personal opinions.

Getting started

1 Before you can decide what kind of work you would like to do, you have to develop some awareness of what kind of person you are. Read the questions below and discuss your ideas with a partner.
- What skills do you have – what kind of things you are good at doing? Are you good at working with computers or at communicating with other people?
- What do you enjoy doing? Do you enjoy working indoors or outdoors? Do you like working on your own or with other people?
- Make a note of your answers.

Exploring the skills

As you already know from earlier chapters, it is useful to be able to pick out descriptive information, opinions and facts when you are reading texts. A **fact** is something that you can prove is true. For example, in the extracts on page 111, the facts about Leila are:
- She's 21.
- She works for herself.
- She set up her business a year ago.

The **opinions** are:
- Leila works too hard. (This is the writer's opinion.)
- Leila is happy. (This is Leila's own opinion.)

2 Read the descriptions of four different types of work personalities below. Then read the descriptions on the next page. In pairs, match each person to the correct type, and identify the facts that reveal this.

Creative: has lots of ideas and is always thinking of new products.

Technical: enjoys seeing how things work and being involved in the technical details.

Managerial: is good at organising people and processes.

Independent: can see what needs to be done and will take risks to make it happen.

Leila, 21, works for herself. She set up her own business a year ago and it is very successful. It is sometimes difficult, but she enjoys making decisions. I think she works too hard, but she says she's happy!

Rashid, 19, is great at working with people, and he seems to really understand what people are good at. He often has to organise meetings and projects. Some people think he talks a lot though!

Kaya, 22, is a web designer. She often comes up with new ways to present information when no one else can think of any ideas. At school, her teachers thought she didn't work hard, but now everyone can see how talented she is.

Imran, 20, prefers to work alone. He enjoys making things work and repairing them when they do not work. He knows a lot about the machinery he works on. I find him a bit quiet though.

3 Read the personality types again and decide which type of worker you would be. Explain your choice. Think about your answers to the questions in task 1 and use facts about yourself to support your answer.

Developing the skills

In a text there are often signs in the language that show whether something is a fact or a personal opinion. Opinions are often given in personalised language, with phrases such as 'for me' and 'I find'. Facts may be given as numbers, showing an exact amount of something that can be counted and proved.

4 Look at the extract below from a survey about work. This combines facts and opinions. It tells us that 750 boys and 600 girls want to run their own business. This is a fact shown by the statistics in the graph. What opinions can you find?

1.   Do you want to run your own business?

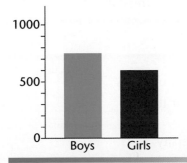

Number of people who want to run their own business

2.   What is important for you about work?

" For me, it is the chance to make a difference. I want to work as a doctor, because I believe that the most important thing is to be able to help people who are ill or injured. " Marco, Rome

" I'd like to be a journalist, and write stories and interview interesting people. I think travelling to new places is really exciting, and I also feel that sharing information is essential. " Yoshi, Tokyo

Here is more information from the survey you looked at on page 111.

Young people and work

We interviewed lots of different young people for our survey on 'Young people and work'. Some of the people were still at school and others had just started work. This report shows the information we collected.

3. Would you prefer to work inside or outside?

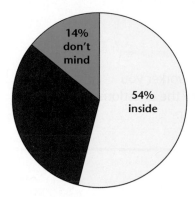

14% don't mind

54% inside

4. Do you want to go straight to work or go to college or university first?

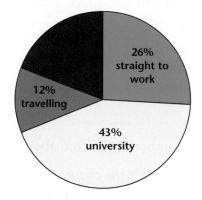

26% straight to work

12% travelling

43% university

5. Where would you like to work?

❝ *Definitely in an office – I like to be indoors with my own desk and computer.* ❞ Emilia, Brazil

❝ *I think I'd like to work outdoors – I enjoy being outside and I think it would be more relaxing and interesting than being inside all day.* ❞ Domingo, Mexico

❝ *I'd like to travel with work – I wouldn't like to be in the same place all the time – that could get boring.* ❞ Eric, Nigeria

6. Where would you like to be in 20 years' time?

I'd like to be running my own company. I know exactly what I want to do and I'm really keen to work for myself.

Ruben, Switzerland

I'd rather not be working at that point – I want to be looking after my family.

Ana, Guatemala

I hope to have a good job in a big company – I'd like to be in charge of a small team of people but I don't think I'd like to be the Managing Director – it would be very stressful!

Theo, London

5 Read the survey again and find the relevant facts to answer these questions.

a) What percentage of people in the survey do not mind whether they work inside or outside?

b) What percentage of people in the survey want to go to university immediately after school?

c) What do 12% of the people in the survey want to do before they go to work?

6 Now answer the questions below. Are the answers facts or opinions?

    a) Why does Emilia want to work indoors?

    b) What two words does Domingo use to describe an outdoor job?

    c) What does Ana want to be doing in 20 years' time?

    d) What does Theo think it would be like to be in charge of a large company?

7 With a partner, discuss how you would answer questions 3 to 6 of the survey. Share your ideas first and then make notes.

Going further

If a text contains both facts and opinions, you will have to study it very carefully to interpret the information it contains. Look out for language clues and think about whether what it says can be proved, or whether it is the opinion of the writer.

8 Read the following text, then copy and complete the flowchart below.

> Many young people are nervous about leaving school and starting work. If you are lucky, there will be several options. The three main options open to young people are further education, training for a specific job, or starting work straight away.
>
> If you go into further education, you can specialise in a particular area. You might have to spend money on the course, but at the end you might get a better job because of it. However, many people feel that it is better to start earning money as soon as possible, rather than continuing studying.
>
> Training on the job is a useful alternative. You are taught a lot of useful skills while you earn some money. I believe this is an excellent way to achieve your goals.
>
> Finally, you could get a job straight away. There is often a lot of competition for jobs, so you will have to be prepared to try hard. Some people who try this option think that you often can't get the job you really want unless you have extra training or qualifications.

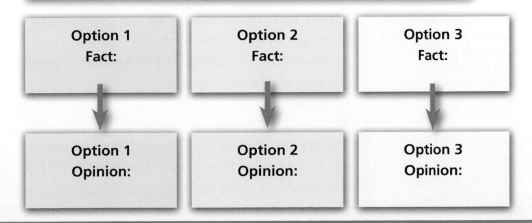

Option 1 Fact:	**Option 2** Fact:	**Option 3** Fact:

Option 1 Opinion:	**Option 2** Opinion:	**Option 3** Opinion:

Job applications

In this section you will learn to:

● use the appropriate tone and style when you are writing a letter or a magazine article.

Getting started

1 Match each situation to the best type of communication.

a) You want to tell all your friends about what you did at the weekend.

b) You want to contact one friend quickly to arrange a meeting time.

c) You want to apply for a job.

d) You want to contact someone you haven't met to ask for information.

| **A** text message | **B** formal letter | **C** informal email | **D** formal email |

Exploring the skills

Just like your speech, your writing style also needs to suit different situations and different people. You will use different styles of writing and language when you write to a friend and when you write to someone you don't know. You might use different vocabulary, as well as different sentence structures and punctuation.

2 Read this letter from Murad to Samir. Is it written in a formal or an informal style? Discuss your ideas in pairs and find phrases to support your opinion.

Hi Samir,

How's things? I hope you had a great holiday. Did you go to the beach a lot? I've been working this summer in a restaurant. It was really hard work, because it's very busy. I was rushed off my feet!

At first I didn't like it, but since the first week I haven't looked back. It gave me the chance to save some money and make some new friends.

What have you been up to? Write soon and tell me what you've been up to!

Murad

P.S. My sister hasn't had a good summer break – she broke her leg three weeks ago! She fell off her bike and she's really fed up!

Here the writer uses informal language for writing to a friend. Murad starts:

Hi Samir,
How's things?

But to a teacher, you might start with:

Dear Mrs Rodia
I hope you are well.

This is an example of how you can adjust your tone to suit your audience.

3 You may come across **idioms** in informal writing. Beware, as they may not mean what they seem to mean! Find out the meaning of any idioms in Murad's letter that you do not know. What do you think the two below mean?

I've had a ball!
This has turned everything on its head.

Developing the skills

When you are writing, consider whether it is for a formal or an informal audience, and adjust your **tone** and **style** accordingly.

Many ideas can be expressed using either formal or informal vocabulary:

- *job*   *position, role*
- *loads of*   *many/much*
- *I love …*   *I am very keen on*

Each pair of phrases has the same meaning, but when they are used depends on whether their context is formal or informal.

4 Read the following letter. Is this a good letter of application?

Dear Mr Santorum

Hi – I hope you're ok. I saw your advert, and I'd like to apply for the job. I'd love to work in a music shop and I think I'd be great at it. I love listening to music and watching videos – I could do it all day! I've got loads of young friends, too, so they'd all come in and buy things.

Can't wait to hear from you!

Lissa Carlos

5 Discuss with a partner how Lissa's letter on page 115 could be improved. You could group your answers under the headings 'Vocabulary', 'Content' and 'Tone'.

6 Read the following letter. Discuss in pairs how it is different from the previous letter.

Dear Mr Santorum,

I recently saw your advertisement in the newspaper, for the position of part-time sales assistant in your music shop, and I would like to apply for this position. I am seventeen years old and I am a student at Newton College.

I feel I would be a good candidate for the job. I have experience of working in a shop, as I worked in a clothes shop last summer. I am also very keen on music, so I could bring a great deal of relevant knowledge to the role.

I would be very happy to come for an interview to discuss this. I am available to start work immediately.

Yours sincerely,
Mia Henley

Notice the clear paragraph structure. Paragraph 1 introduces the writer, explaining why she is writing and where she saw the advert.

Paragraph 2 gives more detail about why she would be suitable for the job.

Paragraph 3 gives her availability and offers to come in for an interview.

7 Now read the job advert below and write a letter of application.

> **Vacancy**: part-time waiter or waitress required for pizza restaurant.
> Minimum age 16 years.
> Must have relevant experience and be able to work on Saturdays.
> Write to Giuseppe Blanco, Napoli Pizzeria

> **Top tip**
>
> To start a formal letter, you use 'Dear', with the person's name. If you don't know the name of the person to whom you are writing, use Sir/Madam.
>
> To end a formal letter, if you have addressed the person by their name, use 'Yours sincerely'. If you used 'Dear Sir/Madam,' use 'Yours faithfully'.

Going further

When you are writing, consider who will be reading it and adjust your tone to fit. This means using appropriate language and structures.

8 Read the descriptions a) to d) and match them to the writing A to D:

a) a letter thanking your grandma for a present

b) a letter thanking your supervisor for their help on your work placement

c) a letter asking for information about a job

d) an email to a friend about your new job.

A
Hi Nina!
You'll never guess what –
I've got a job in that great
clothes shop!

C
Dear Sir/Madam
I was interested to read about
the position of assistant on
the news desk, and I would be
grateful for more information.

B
Dear Mr Khan,
I would like to take this
opportunity to thank you for
your advice last week.

D
Dear Grandma,
Thank you so much for the
present you sent to me – I love it.

9 Imagine are writing an account of your work experiences for the school magazine. Your readers are parents and other students. Decide which of the introductions below would be the most suitable.

A *I've just spent three weeks doing work experience at the hospital in town. It was great – I was rushed off my feet though!*

B *I have recently spent three weeks on a work placement at the local hospital. It was an interesting and very enjoyable experience.*

C *Have you ever considered the work placement scheme? I've just come to the end of a three-week placement at our local hospital, and I'd recommend it to anyone.*

10 On your own, write a magazine article about a work placement experience you have had, or you can invent one. Remember to adjust your language to suit your audience.

Top tip

Think about:
• how full forms and contracted forms are used
• the tone of the vocabulary:
  – which is most sophisticated
  – which engages the reader best
  – which describes the experience in the most detailed and informative way.

Job interviews

Speaking skills in focus (S6)

In this section you will learn to:
- pronounce words and speak clearly to be understood in a conversation
- speak up confidently and clearly.

Getting started

Remember that speech is an essential way to convey information. If speech isn't clear, information will be passed on incorrectly or not at all.

1 Look at this picture.
- How do you think the person being interviewed feels?
- How would you feel in this situation? Why?

Note down your ideas.

Exploring the skills

In order to be understood in a conversation it is important to pronounce words correctly and speak as clearly as possible.

2 Listen to the following extracts of speech. Are they easy or difficult to understand?

6.1

3 Listen again. What is the problem in each situation?

4 What problems could be caused in each situation by misunderstanding?

5 Have you ever had a similar experience, in English or in your own language, where it was difficult to hear what a person was saying? What problems did it cause you?

6 You are going to practise talking clearly in different situations. Make notes about the following, but don't write down every word you are going to say:

   a) information about your date of birth, your age and your address

   b) times of a train or bus journey, and where stops are made – you can make this up using information from where you live

   c) food you like to eat in a restaurant or café.

7 Now work in pairs. Sit with your back to your partner so that you cannot see each other. You could move your chairs apart if there is room.

Take turns to give each other the information you made notes about above. Your partner writes down what they hear.

8 Compare the information your partner wrote down with what you said. Discuss what you found easy and difficult about each other's speech.

> I could understand your numbers very clearly.

> I couldn't hear the name of the place where the bus would stop.

Developing the skills

In formal situations, you may find that you don't pronounce words as clearly as you would like. If you are slightly nervous, you may speak more quickly than usual.

9 Read the questions below and discuss them, in pairs.

   a) Have you ever had a job interview? If you have, what was it like? If you haven't, what do you think it would be like?

   b) If you feel nervous in a situation such as a job interview, what do you do?

10 Listen to the openings of two job interviews. Then, in pairs, choose words from the box, or any others you think are suitable, to describe how the candidates are feeling.

> nervous confident embarrassed happy shy calm

11 Listen again to a short extract from each of the interviews.

In pairs, role-play a similar interview. In one version, the candidate should be nervous. In the other version, the candidate should be confident. Record your conversations, and then listen back to them. Did you succeed in sounding nervous or confident?

12 Read the following questions and decide whether they would be asked by the interviewer or the job candidate.

a) Could you tell me about your experience?

b) Could you tell me more about the position?

c) Will I be able to do any training for the position?

d) Why do you think you would be suitable for the job?

In pairs, discuss your ideas, speaking clearly and thinking about your pronunciation.

13 With your partner, read aloud the following answers to two of the interview questions. Again, think about your pronunciation and speak clearly. Which one do you think is the best answer to each question?

Question a) answers

I haven't got much experience, but I learn quickly.

I've never done anything like this before.

I've got a lot of relevant experience – I've worked in an office for six months and I've completed a course at college.

Question d) answers

I don't know really, but it sounds fun.

I believe I have useful skills and I am very keen to learn.

I get on with people, and I'm good at most things.

14 In pairs, make notes about all of the answers in task 13. Discuss why each one is suitable or not. Think about the language used and the ideas expressed.

15 You will now listen to a job interview. As you listen, think about whether the person will get the job.

16 Listen to the interview again. What does the candidate say about:

a) his grades from college

b) his skills

c) what he enjoys at work?

Going further

Recording yourself speaking is good practice for exam situations. Listening to yourself will show you where and how you can improve your pronunciation and clarity of speech.

17 You are now going to work in pairs to prepare role-plays for a job interview, taking turns to be in the interviewer and the candidate.

Record your work, both as you prepare your ideas and after you have practised. Listen to how clearly you speak, and see if you can improve this each time you do the role-play.

Individually:

a) Choose a job from the box below, or think of a different one.

> **waitress   shop assistant   assistant in sports centre**

b) Make a note of the skills that would be useful for the job you have chosen.

In pairs:

c) Think of questions that you might be asked in an interview for each job you have chosen.

d) Consider how you would answer these questions. Share ideas about how you could give examples to support what you say.

18 Now prepare each role-play together. Think of how you will start and end the interview. Decide on at least three questions and answers for each job. Remember to think about using the appropriate tone and language for a job interview.

19 Record yourselves as you carry out each role-play. Then listen to it. Are you surprised by what you hear? Can you think of ways to improve it?

6.4 Unusual jobs

In this section you will learn to:
- predict to help you understand and select details
- select details to make notes or fill in forms when listening to a range of texts.

Getting started

1 Discuss the following points with a partner.
- Can you think of any unusual jobs? Compare ideas and make notes.
- What are the advantages and disadvantages of unusual jobs over jobs that you consider to be 'normal'?

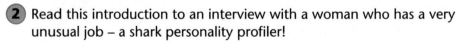

Exploring the skills

When you are listening to longer texts, you may have to pick out specific details. It is helpful to predict the kind of information you might hear. If you are making notes, be clear which headings you will use; if you are going to fill in a form, read through it to see what information it asks for. This will help you to listen out for the information you need.

2 Read this introduction to an interview with a woman who has a very unusual job – a shark personality profiler!

Interviewer: Hi Mandy – well, this is a job I've never heard of before! Can you tell me about it?

Mandy: Hello. Yes, well I work in Australia with sharks. My job is to put tags on them to see how they behave, how often they feed, and where they go – that sort of thing.

3 In pairs, discuss what else you might hear in the rest of the interview. What other questions might the interviewer ask? For example, the interviewer might ask how long Mandy has done this job. In this case, you might hear her reply with a number of months or years.

4 Listen to the rest of the interview. Were any of your predictions in task 3 correct?

5 Listen again and note down the information you hear about the following:

   a) what Mandy likes about the job

   b) what you need to be able to do for this job

   c) why an animal might attack you.

Developing the skills

If you are given a form to fill in, you can work out what to listen for. Read through it and consider the information you will need to fill in the gaps, such as names, ages and places. Make sure you listen carefully for these. The information you put in the form must make sense. Unless you are asked for full sentences, just write a word or short phrase.

6 You are going to hear more interviews about unusual jobs.

   Look at the pictures. Listen and match each one to a speaker.

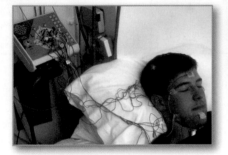

7 Read the following cards and think about the kind of detail you will need to pick out to fill in the gaps.

1.

Name of person: Kamila

Name of job:

How long person has done the job:

Where do they work?

Overall feeling about the job:

2.

Name of person: Max

Name of job:

How long person has done the job:

Where do they work?

Overall feeling about the job:

---

8 Listen again and copy and complete the cards.

9 Discuss the questions in pairs.

   a) What do you think are the advantages and drawbacks of each job?

   b) Which ones do you think are the most and least interesting? Why?

   c) Which one of these jobs, if any, would you like to do?

3.

Name of person: Jannah

Name of job:

How long person has done the job:

Where do they work?

Overall feeling about the job:

10 Read the article. Which city is being discussed?

Work in the digital era

EVERY FRIDAY EVENING, in a modernised warehouse in east London, there is a meeting for business start-ups, software developers, and investors – people who can offer money to help new businesses turn their ideas into reality. Shoreditch, as this area is called, is one of the world's fastest-growing digital 'hubs' – drawing in entrepreneurs and investors from all around the world. While the rest of the city struggles with financial problems, this area thrives. It has already produced some astonishing successes:

TweetDeck is a social-media application that was bought by Twitter for £25m. The music website, Last.fm, was bought by the American television network CBS for £140m!

From *Sunday Times Magazine*,
6 November 2011

Language booster

Match the words to the definitions.

1	modernised	A	an 'app' – a simple computer program that performs a specific task
2	reality	B	a person who can think of ideas for new businesses
3	warehouse	C	someone with the technical skills to program computers
4	financial problems	D	the central or most important part of a particular place or activity
5	start-up	E	improved and made more up-to-date
6	investor	F	something which actually happens
7	application	G	difficulties caused by not having enough money
8	software developer	H	an old industrial building
9	hub	I	a person who makes money by investing in new businesses
10	entrepreneur	J	a new business: literally, one that is 'starting up'

---

11 Listen to this report about one of the start-up businesses in Shoreditch. Which industry does this new business work in?

6.7

12 Read the form on page 125 and think about what information you have heard. Listen again and copy and complete the form with notes about the new business.

Name of business: _____

Where Julia is from: _____

Julia's age: _____

Ages of people involved: _____

The industry Julia works in: _____

Her software searches the internet for:

1: information about _____

2: what _____ are saying

3: product _____

13 Listen once more. Discuss the following questions with a partner.

    a) In what way does this business rely on the internet?

    b) Do you think this kind of business would have been possible 20 years ago? Explain your reasons.

Going further

Reading through questions before completing a task is one way to help you succeed in exams. You can use prediction techniques to help you with longer and more complex texts.

14 Read the questions below and think about what information you can expect to hear.

    a) Where does Edith work now?

    b) What did she do first?

    c) What did she decide to do?

    d) Where did she move to after this?

    e) Why was she able to do voluntary work?

    f) Did she enjoy the conservation project?

    g) What does she need to do her job?

15 In pairs, discuss the questions and compare your predictions.

16 Now listen to a journalist talking about how her career has changed as the internet has developed.

17 Now listen again and answer the questions in task 14.

Language booster

Match the words for types of work with the correct definition.

a) Voluntary   **1** work that you do all week, at regular hours

b) Part-time   **2** work that you do without getting paid for it

c) Full-time   **3** working for part of the week or for a shorter day than most people do

d) Flexible work   **4** work that can be done at different times during the week

e) Self-employed   **5** running your own business

The big task

In this chapter you have looked at different kinds of work. Now you are going to think about what would be your ideal job and how you would go about getting it.

1 In pairs, discuss your future – what would be an ideal job?
Note down some ideas about the work you would like to do.

- Why does it appeal to you?
- What skills and qualities does this job need that you have?
- Where can you do this job?

2 Do some research to find out more about your ideal job. Record your findings individually. Prepare a short fact sheet with information about the job, for example:

My ideal job: architect

An architect is a person who designs houses and other buildings. To be an architect you have to study at university for three years. You also have to complete training courses.

You need to be good at design and technology, and have good mathematical skills. It is important to be creative, but you also have to get on well with the people you are working with.

Architects often work in big companies, but you can be self-employed.

3 How do you think the job described below would be advertised? Write an advert for this job of the kind you might see in a newspaper or magazine. Include as much detail as you can about what the job involves and what kind of person should apply. Also remember to include details of who the applicant should write to.

Wanted: young architect to join busy city-centre company. Must have relevant degree and training. Good design, technology and mathematical skills essential. Applicants should be creative and have good people skills. Write to Serena Matayo, Block 6B, High Street.

4 Present your advert to the class.

5 Now imagine that you are writing a letter of application for this job. Think about how you can respond to each of the points in the advert. Make notes about your relevant skills and experience. Remember to use the correct level of formality for the job application letter.

6 Prepare your letter. Remember to use the correct style and register for a formal letter, and use the letter-writing conventions from this unit.

7 In pairs, act out an interview for the jobs you have both chosen. Swap letters. The interviewer should think of five questions to ask the candidate based on their letter.

Remember to speak clearly and confidently in an interview situation. Record yourselves to see how you sound.

Check your progress

Here are the Reading, Writing, Speaking and Listening skills you learnt about in Chapter 6.

Use this table to decide how good you are at the different skills, and make a note of what you need to be able to do in order to move up a level.

READING	
I can ...	
Higher	confidently distinguish between facts and opinions in complex texts consistently recognise and understand the language used to introduce facts and opinions
Middle	distinguish between facts and opinions in straightforward texts often recognise and understand the language used to introduce facts and opinions
Lower	distinguish between facts and opinions in simple texts sometimes recognise the language used to introduce facts and straightforward opinions

WRITING	
I can ...	
Higher	consistently and confidently use the appropriate tone and style when writing a letter or magazine article
Middle	sometimes use the appropriate tone and style when writing a letter or magazine article
Lower	write a simple letter or magazine article, but tend to use the same tone and style without adapting it to reader and purpose

SPEAKING	
I can ...	
Higher	express quite complex ideas effectively consistently speak with confidence and clarity
Middle	express most of my ideas so that they are understood speak clearly and with some confidence, so that I am generally understood
Lower	express simple ideas, though may need support from my listener attempt to speak clearly, but may hesitate or search for words

LISTENING	
I can ...	
Higher	pick out exactly the details I need to make notes or complete forms consistently use prediction to help me understand and successfully find the right information
Middle	pick out many of the details I need to make notes or complete forms sometimes use prediction to help me understand and find the right information
Lower	pick out a few of the details I need to make notes or complete forms try to use prediction to help me understand and find the right information, but have limited success

The big picture

In this chapter you are going to think about just how fragile our planet is. Think about this quote by Carl Sagan, a famous astronomer:

The Earth is the only world known so far to harbour life. There is nowhere else, at least in the near future, to which our species could migrate. Visit, yes. Settle, not yet. Like it or not, for the moment the Earth is where we make our stand.

Thinking big

1 On your own:

- Look at the photographs opposite. Which show environmental issues and what issues might they represent? Which issue is most important to your part of the world?

- Now look at each photo more carefully. Write down the issue(s) represented by each one. Are some of them linked to each other? Are there other ways you could group these images?

- Number the photos, in order of their importance as global issues, where 1 is the most important/urgent.

2 In pairs:

- Compare your order with your partner's. Are there some surprising differences? Are there some similarities?

- Explain why you think some global issues are more urgent and important than others.

3 In your group:

- See if you can agree on the three global issues we need to tackle most urgently.

- Brainstorm some of the things we could do as individuals about these issues.

Chapter **7**

Environment and wildlife

Our carbon footprint

In this section you will learn to:
- find and select facts and details from graphs
- understand texts containing pie charts and bar graphs
- understand what is implied but not actually written in a piece of text.

Getting started

1 There is a lot of debate about what is actually happening to our planet. What have you heard? Consider the following topics and make notes.

  a) Wildlife species are disappearing rapidly.

  b) We are running out of freshwater sources.

  c) Pollution is a serious issue.

  d) Global warming is taking place.

Exploring the skills

To understand reports and newspaper or magazine articles properly, you often need to be able to read and understand graphics such as charts and graphs.

Let's look at pie charts. They are called pie charts because they are circular and resemble a pie or a pizza. Each wedge or section stands for a percentage (out of 100%).

Pie charts help us to break down information into categories and see how each contributes to a bigger picture.

Here is a simple pie chart that shows the main activities that make up the total of a typical person's **carbon footprint** in some countries of the more economically developed countries (**MEDCs**).

The blue wedges represent direct contributions to CO_2 **emissions**, while the yellow wedges represent indirect contributions to CO_2 emissions. Which ones do you think we might have more control over?

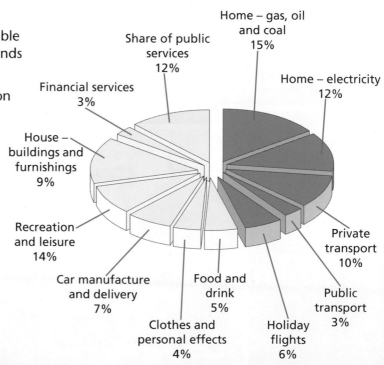

Share of public services 12%

Home – gas, oil and coal 15%

Financial services 3%

Home – electricity 12%

House – buildings and furnishings 9%

Recreation and leisure 14%

Private transport 10%

Car manufacture and delivery 7%

Food and drink 5%

Public transport 3%

Clothes and personal effects 4%

Holiday flights 6%

2 Read about global warming and greenhouse gases. Then answer the questions that follow.

The Greenhouse Effect

The Earth gets energy from the Sun in the form of sunlight. The Earth's surface absorbs some of this energy and heats up. [...] The Earth cools down by giving off this energy in a different form, called infrared radiation. But before all this radiation can escape to outer space, greenhouse gases in the atmosphere, like carbon dioxide (CO_2), absorb some of it, which makes the atmosphere warmer. As the atmosphere gets warmer, it makes the Earth's surface warmer, too. This is called the greenhouse effect.

Greenhouse gases

Greenhouse gases trap heat in the atmosphere, which makes the Earth warmer. This can have disastrous effects on the Earth's weather and change the environment with harmful effects on wildlife, plants and humans. People are adding several types of greenhouse gases to the atmosphere which can make matters even worse.

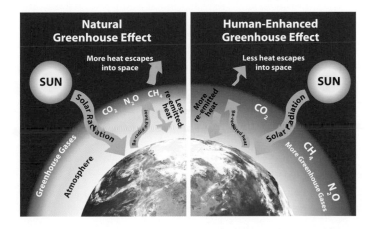

From *A Student's Guide to Global Climate Change*, EPA

a) What is the name of the energy that the Earth reflects off its surface?

b) Look closely at the diagrams above. State one major difference between the natural greenhouse effect and the one caused by human activity.

c) Why is there more radiated heat in the right-hand part of the diagram?

Developing the skills

Let's look at simple bar charts. What do they tell us? Bar charts are usually used to:

- compare groups or categories of data
- make generalisations quickly or observe a trend or pattern easily
- ask questions about what the data shows and why.

Now look at the bar chart of carbon emissions by country in 1990 and 2008. The labels tell you what the different parts of the chart show.

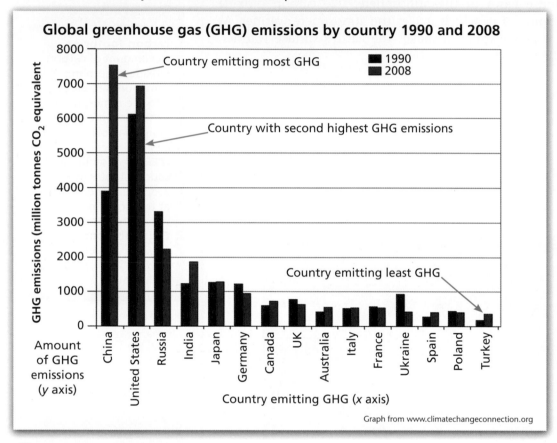

Global greenhouse gas (GHG) emissions by country 1990 and 2008

Graph from www.climatechangeconnection.org

3. Answer the following questions about the bar chart above.

a) What does GHG stand for?

b) What is the unit used to measure GHGs?

c) Using the correct units, say which country had the highest emissions of GHGs in 1990.

d) Name the three countries that had the lowest GHG emissions in 2008. How high were these emissions?

e) Which country had the highest greenhouse gas emissions in 2008?

f) Name a country in which greenhouse gas emissions remained exactly the same in both 1990 and 2008. How much was this?

g) What was the amount of Russia's GHG emissions in 2008? What was the amount for the United States in 2008?

Going further

Writers do not always say things directly. Often we have to **infer** or work out a writer's thoughts, feelings or attitudes.

4 Read the article below in which a journalist thinks about his use of paper and its impact on the environment.

A Waste of My Time?

Yesterday, I gathered up all my old newspapers. My wife is always reminding me to recycle, but the recycling bin was outside, it was raining … and I couldn't be bothered. I shrugged my shoulders as I picked up a paper which had just fallen on the floor. After all, what have my old newspapers got to do with global warming? Nothing, right?

Wrong. As I picked up the newspapers, I noticed a report about greenhouse gases in the USA. In fact, it was this chart that caught my eye. It shows the different causes of greenhouse gases. It was 'Deforestation' that stood out. That meant forests being cut down for farming, housing, and, yes, paper.

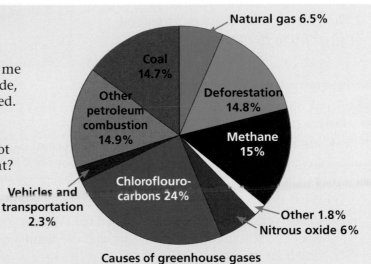

Causes of greenhouse gases

I sighed. I was responsible for that blue sector. I stepped out into the pouring rain, and walked over to the recycling bin. I knew I was doing the right thing.

Which of these statements best describes the writer's attitude at the start of the article?

● He always recycles and has to remind his wife, who forgets.

● He usually recycles things but does so out of habit, not because he really understands why.

● He's really committed to recycling, even when it's raining.

5 What does *I shrugged my shoulders* suggest about the writer's attitude to recycling? What single word in the text signals his change of attitude when he sees the chart?

Writing skills in focus (W1)

In this section you will learn to:
- use details to develop ideas when writing descriptions
- make descriptive writing convincing using the five senses.

Getting started

Read this short poem on your own:

> *Fresh water is liquid silver,*
> *More precious than a king's palaces,*
> *More dazzling than a sultan's jewels.*
> *Thousands tread dust for days to seek it,*
> *Yet others waste and lose it.*
> *'Our planet's full of water!' they say.*
> *I say, 'Try to drink it then.'*
>
> **Mike Gould**

1 Think about these questions, make notes and then share your ideas with a partner.

a) Are there any words or phrases you don't understand? Have a guess at their meaning. If your partner does not know either, use a dictionary to help.

b) What do you think the **message** or the point of the poem is?

c) In line one, what is water compared to? Why do you think the poet chose this comparison? This kind of 'picture in words' is called an **image**.

d) Find two more examples of where the writer creates vivid pictures to make his point. Explain why he makes these comparisons.

e) Be really honest and describe *your own* attitude to water and how much you use/waste?

f) With a partner, discuss which of the five senses the poet uses in his poem.

> **Top tip**
>
> When you describe a personal experience, use the five senses of *sight*, *touch*, *sound*, *smell*, and *taste* to help the reader enter your world.

Exploring the skills

To describe experiences or issues well, you need to use details to develop your descriptions. Adding **examples**, **facts** and **images** can really make your writing come to life and engage the reader. For example:

> *We have a problem with water.* ***We have plenty of it, but it's the wrong sort.*** — develops and builds on opening sentence

Did you know that __about 70% of our planet is covered in water,__ but only __about 3% is fresh water?__ Just consider that as you let **sparkling, clear water escape** *from your tap as you clean your teeth.*

—facts add detail and make comparisons

well-chosen verb makes us sound careless

vivid picture in words (an 'image') that brings facts to life

2 Now look at this sentence about water usage.

We need huge amounts of water for all our everyday needs.

You are going to take this **topic sentence** and develop it into a full paragraph.

a) First, add an example or explanation that develops what is said here. It could be about what our everyday needs are.

We need huge amounts of water for all our everyday needs. Just think about...

b) Now build the paragraph by adding new sentences, using the facts below. You may need to use **connectives** (*and, or, but, in addition, because*) to turn these facts into sentences and join ideas together.

- Recommended daily requirement for sanitation, bathing, cooking, consumption = approx. 50 litres per person.
- 1 billion+ people have to use less than 6 litres per day.

c) Finally, make your writing come to life. For example, add a vivid image (a 'picture in words') which gives an idea of what it is like searching for water each day. You could start:

For many, the best sight in the world is...

Developing the skills

Adding more detail also means thinking how you can add content or ideas.

A student is writing an article about his childhood memories. He is describing his first swimming lesson.

I remember going to the pool. I stood by it with all the other kids, until the teacher told us to go in. I sat down on the edge. Suddenly, someone splashed me. It was horrible.

There is much more information the student could have added here. For example:

- more detail on how he behaved (did he sit down 'quickly', 'happily'?) and what he did
- what the pool was like (indoor, outdoor, modern, old)
- descriptions of the other students/teacher.

3 With a partner, think about the five senses. Write down what you think the child above could see, touch, smell, hear and even taste.

See	
Hear	children laughing, water slapping the sides of the pool
Smell	
Touch	
Taste	

4 Now rewrite the text, adding further detail.

- You can change or alter the text but it must still be about a boy's first swim.
- Write a minimum of 75 words.

5 A student was given a task in which she had to imagine life in the future in a world which is short of water. Beforehand, she was given some basic information on:

- the effects of lack of fresh water on health
- our overuse and waste of water
- the contamination of fresh water supplies, such as industrial waste in rivers.

As you read, identify where in the text she has used:

- facts and examples but also added her own original details or extra content
- vivid imagery or powerful verbs to reveal her feelings or views about the situation.

> Today, in 2065, I live in a world without water. I am 15 years old, but I look 50, my skin is starting to crack and look parched like a desert road. My muscles are weak and I lack energy. My family's life revolves around water: finding or buying it, conserving it or storing it, dreaming and thinking about it. My father's job? He is lucky – he works in a desalination plant, converting salt water to fresh, but he doesn't get any extra favours or water rations.
>
> I **interrogate** my father about the past – a time when everyone had water. He tells me about lush trees in the city parks, swollen with emerald leaves, and how he could enjoy **soothing**, **warm** baths, or cool, refreshing showers, whenever he wanted them. Back then, he was told that drinking about 8–10 glasses of water a day was ideal for a healthy lifestyle. Now, we're lucky if we get one glass, which I treat as if it were the finest meal on Earth. But he also tells me how companies and countries allowed poisonous chemicals to pollute rivers and lakes. When he was a boy, **2 million tons** of sewage and human waste was dumped into water.
>
> I often plead with him to tell me why he and his friends didn't do more if they knew this? Why they left us with this dreadful legacy? He has no answer.
>
> From www.openworldthailand.com

verb suggests strong questioning

adjectives suggest comfort

factual info backs up statement about companies

Going further

One of the techniques the writer above used was to 'zoom in' from the general to the specific or a 'close-up'. For example:

> *lush trees* (general) – *swollen with emerald leaves* (specific/close up)

6 Which is the general description in the line below, and which the close-up detail?

> *I describe the beauty of the forests, the winding rivers, the scent of evening rain on blossom.*

Language booster

Adding vivid adjectives to well-chosen nouns to make **noun phrases** is a great way to add detail. For example, we can tell more about the writer's views when she adds the adjectives, 'soothing' and 'warm' to 'bath' to make *soothing, warm bath*.

7 Imagine the writer steps outside and describes her village or town, and how shortage of fresh water has affected it. Complete this paragraph by adding 'close-ups' to the general description. Remember to make use of the five senses to help you think of the details to include.

> *As I step outside my door, I see the wide field in front of me, with …*

8 Now, write a newspaper article of 150–200 words about the importance of water. Describe:

- how precious fresh water is
- any water problems in your part of the world
- what steps you are taking to save water.

You can use any of the factual information in this unit, but you must add your own ideas, and make your readers think of water as a fantastic, life-giving resource.

Checklist for success

Use the information in the unit, but add your own ideas and examples.

✔ Include vivid descriptions of fresh water; how it feels.

✔ Use imagery of the five senses to let the reader 'into your world'.

7.3 Pollution – slow poison?

In this section you will learn to:
- express your ideas clearly using the correct verb tenses
- respond clearly, accurately and appropriately to others in conversation
- communicate your ideas clearly and confidently in a more formal talk.

Getting started

1 Think about the following questions in pairs. Make notes on any interesting ideas.
- What are the sources of air, sea, water and land pollution around you?
- What issues or problems does pollution cause in your daily life?
- Who or what is responsible for this pollution?
- Who can do something about it? What should be done about it?
- What can you do about it? What are your rights against pollution?

2 Now quickly note your thoughts on pollution in your city or region. Don't worry about whether all the details are correct or not. If you have questions, note those down as well.

Exploring the skills

The sentences below are in the simple present tense (e.g. *leads, creates*) or the present continuous tense (e.g. *is shrinking, are becoming*). This is because they are referring to facts that are considered current or true over a long period of time.

a) The burning of fossil fuels *leads to* serious air pollution and also creates more greenhouse gases in our environment. (simple present tense)

b) The water table is *shrinking* in many parts of the world. (present continuous tense)

c) Our freshwater sources *are becoming* too polluted for fish and other organisms to survive. (present continuous tense)

Language booster

The first verb in every sentence *must* agree with the subject (the person or thing doing the action) of the sentence.

The **simple present tense** is used to describe routines, facts, likes and dislikes or attitudes and opinions.

The verb 'to play'		
Subject	**Verb that agrees**	**Example**
I/you/we/they	Verb with no 's' ending	I play, they play
he/she/it	Verb with 's' ending	he plays, she plays, it plays
The verb 'to be'		
Subject	**Verb that agrees**	**Example**
I	An exception: 'am' is a special form of the verb 'to be' which only agrees with 'I'	I am
you/we/they	are	you are, we are, they are
he/she/it	is	he is, she is, it is

The **present continuous tense** is used to describe events as they are happening or that are still happening. It is usually constructed using the verb 'to be' and another verb with an '-ing' ending.

Subject	**Part of 'to be' that agrees**	**Example**
I	am	I am playing
you/we/they	are	you are playing, we are playing, they are playing
he/she/it	is	he is playing, she is playing

3 In your pairs, tell each other three facts that you have recently learnt in science or geography. Write down each other's facts. What tenses are you using?

4 Tell each other three facts about what is happening in the room where you are at this moment. Write down each other's facts. What tenses are you using?

5 With your partner, play this explanation word game:
- Taking turns, use the verbs in the box and the labels on the diagram below to describe what is going on.
- Think about when you will use the simple present tense and when you use the present continuous tense.
- Give a point to your partner for each tense that they use correctly.

contain	cause
spew	rain
pollute	mix
rise	be

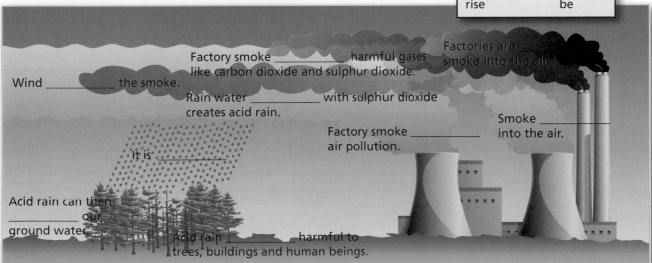

Factory smoke _____ harmful gases like carbon dioxide and sulphur dioxide.

Factories are _____ smoke into the air.

Wind _____ the smoke.

Rain water _____ with sulphur dioxide creates acid rain.

Smoke _____ into the air.

Factory smoke _____ air pollution.

It is _____

Acid rain can then _____ our ground water.

Acid rain _____ harmful to trees, buildings and human beings.

Developing the skills

When you are discussing a topic with a partner or in a group, you need to listen and then respond clearly, accurately and appropriately, even if the situation is quite informal.

6 Read these extracts about air pollution. If there are any words you do not know, discuss them with your partner and see if you can work them out from the rest of the sentence. Only use a dictionary as a last resort. Make a note of any new words.

The air we breathe

Air pollution is a severe problem – one that we ignore at the risk of our health and our economy.

Lung cancer is now the most common cancer in the industrialised world, and heart disease is the second-biggest cause of death in some places. Smog hangs heavy over cities like Beijing, Shanghai and Hong Kong, where children grow up with asthma and other respiratory illnesses. Every year, cities lose billions of dollars due to health costs and lost productivity.

These problems all go back to air pollution, whose consequences are long-term, sometimes fatal and almost always borne by the public.

Much of the time, air pollution is invisible, but its effects are not. Millions of people in Asia are breathing dirty air – with terrible health consequences, from respiratory disease to strokes, lung cancer, and heart disease.

Economies in Asia have grown rapidly, but often at the price of its people's health and wellbeing.

From www.greenpeace.org

A silent killer

Air pollution is a world-wide problem. Carbon monoxide is a colourless, odourless, poisonous gas produced by the incomplete burning of carbon in fuels, mainly by cars and trucks and also by forest fires and the burning of agricultural waste. In the USA, about 77% of the pollutant comes from transportation sources. In cities, as much as 95% of all CO_2 emissions may come from automobile exhaust. Carbon monoxide is a deadly poison which binds to haemoglobin molecules in blood, reducing the amount of oxygen carried to body tissues.

From 'Carbon Monoxide' from *Environmental Science in the 21st Century* – an online textbook by Robert Stewart

(7) In groups of two or three, talk together about air pollution in your part of the world. You can talk about your home countries, or the country where you live now if it is not the same.

- What causes the pollution?
- What is being done about it?
- Are there health consequences for people in your city or region?

Going further

Now you will work together to give a talk in a more formal situation. You can feel confident that you have plenty of ideas and will know which tenses to use. You have gained a clear understanding of various types of pollution and the problems that air pollution in particular can cause.

(8) In your group, prepare a six-minute talk about air pollution:
- the dangers it poses to our health and wellbeing
- and what could be done about it.

Your audience will be your classmates and teacher. Make sure each of you speaks for about 2 minutes.

- Try to ensure that your talk flows naturally and that each person's speech connects to the others'.
- You could use connective clauses like:

As Sarah pointed out when she introduced air pollution, the health hazards are often hidden…

or

If we know that carbon dioxide is a released by burning fossil fuels, then we need to consider what this means for our lungs…

> **Top tip**
>
> In order to give a speech that flows well and naturally, you need to spend some time planning together and making sure that your sections link well to each other. Also, be clear about your facts and key words, and decide together what they mean.

Where has all our wildlife gone?

Listening skills in focus (L1, L2 and L4)

In this section you will learn to:
- use key words to help you pick out important details
- use key words to understand and answer multiple-choice questions
- understand what is implied but not actually said during an interview.

Getting started

1 You have already seen the effect human activities may have on our habitats and on pollution levels. What does this mean for wildlife and the many animal and plant species that share the planet with us?

2 In pairs, discuss:
- Which animal or plant species have recently been considered 'endangered' in your region?
- Which wild animals, birds or plants were you used to having around you when you were a child? Are they still around? Will they be around for your children?

Exploring the skills

In Chapter 4 you learnt about using what you read before you start listening to a spoken text in order to answer questions about it. You can develop this skill even further.

- Read the questions provided before you hear the extract so that you know what you are listening for.
- Identify any **key words** in the question, apart from the question words like 'where' or 'how many'. Take this question as an example:

  'Who is responsible for the death of so many tigers?'

The word *who* tells you that your answer is likely to be the name of a person or a group of people. You know that you will need to listen out for the words *death* and *tigers*, because you can guess that you are likely to hear the answer close to these words. To help focus your mind, underline the key words in the question before you start listening to the text.

- Sometimes, you will have to be extra alert and listen out for words or phrases which mean the same, or something close to the same, as the key word in the question.

Suppose you have been asked the question:

Give two ways in which mankind has been responsible for the drop in numbers of wildlife.

You might decide to underline '<u>mankind</u>', '<u>responsible</u>' and '<u>drop in numbers</u>'.

Then you hear the speaker say:

The numbers of birds, animals, marine and freshwater creatures have declined by almost one third, according to the charity called the World Wildlife Fund. They say that most of the blame for this terrible situation lies with human beings. Mankind has been responsible for this drop in numbers – through habitat destruction and pollution.

When you hear the key words you will know that the answer is likely to be given soon, and indeed it is: 'habitat destruction and pollution'.

Here is another, more tricky question:

Who, according to the World Wildlife Fund, has caused a decline in the numbers of wild animals?

You might decide to underline the key words '<u>caused</u>', '<u>decline in numbers</u>' and '<u>animals</u>'.

The answer is more difficult to find, because you have to understand that 'has been responsible for' means the same as 'caused by'; and also that 'this drop in numbers' means the same as 'decline in numbers'. Only then can you understand that the answer is 'mankind'.

3 Here are some more questions Remember to read them carefully and underline key words before the recording is played to you.

7.1

a) What is the problem the organisation the World Wildlife Fund is concerned about?

b) In what year did countries in Europe make a promise to prevent the extinction of certain animals?

c) What is the reason wildlife organisations fear that the situation might get even worse in years to come?

4 Next, a journalist tells us some facts and figures about conservation. Listen to what he has to say about this and answer the questions below.

7.2

a) What kind of animals are named in the so-called Red List?

b) How many species are on the Red List?

c) What proportion of the world's birds are in danger of disappearing forever?

d) What percentage of the world's assessed plants are endangered?

e) Over the last five centuries, how many species of animal have been made extinct because of humans?

Where has all our wildlife gone?

Developing the skills

Often, after you have identified the key words in the question, you will have to listen out for words or phrases which mean the same thing. To help you do this confidently, you will need to have as wide a vocabulary as possible.

You are now going to explore your understanding of key words associated with wildlife and conservation. You might hear some of these words in the interview you will listen to in the next exercise.

5 Copy the table and place a tick or a cross in the first two columns. Next, highlight any words that you might need to look up.

Then, in pairs, see if you can teach each other some of these words.

Key word	Seen/heard it before	Can spell it	Meaning/definition
conservationist			
activist			
legal			
dedicated			
remote			
carnivores			
predators			
poachers			
habitats			
encroachment			
destruction			

6 You are about to hear an interview with Prerna Bindra, a journalist and wildlife conservationist. She won the Sanctuary Wildlife Service Award in 2007 for her legal and practical work towards the conservation of wildlife in India, particularly the tiger.

Listen to the first part of the interview and answer the questions below.

You will listen to the recording twice. After the first listening, check your answers and prepare to fill any gaps.

7.3

a) What kind of house did Prerna live in as a child in India?

b) What kind of bird laid its eggs just outside Prerna's home?

c) What kind of animal can be found only in Gir National Park?

d) What were Prerna's two great loves as a child?

e) What career did Prerna take up as a result of these two great interests?

With your partner, compare your answers and discuss whether you identified the best key words.

> ### Top tip
>
> Remember to underline the key words first. You can discuss with a partner which words you have identified and compare your ideas.

Prerna Bindra

Going further

Sometimes you have to understand what people mean from what is implied but not actually said. You have to pick up on the clues.

7 Choose the answer which best completes the sentence – A, B or C – as you listen to the second part of the interview with Prerna.

i) India is:

- **A** the most popular country in the world to visit
- **B** the country with the biggest population in the world
- **C** the world's second most densely populated country

ii) Village people might kill tigers because:

- **A** the tigers have killed the villagers' cattle
- **B** the tigers' furs make good coats for the villagers
- **C** killing tigers is popular with tourists

iii) In the past, people:

- **A** thought that tigers were signs of good luck and fertility
- **B** did not respect the tigers which lived near their homes
- **C** thought that tigers would trample down the crops in the fields

iv) Many years ago, elephants:

- **A** were given poison by the local people
- **B** were never given huge spaces to live their lives freely
- **C** were loved by people and even worshipped as a god

v) The speaker, Prerna, believes that people and wild animals like tigers:

- **A** can live happily together in the same area
- **B** can live together happily so long as people are educated
- **C** can live happily side-by-side but not in the same space

vi) The speaker, Prerna, thinks young people:

- **A** should never take up a career in wildlife conservation because it is too hard
- **B** should think about a career in wildlife conservation because it is always a good laugh
- **C** could take up a career in wildlife conservation if they enjoy a challenge

vii) The speaker, Prerna, is:

- **A** enthusiastic
- **B** easily depressed
- **C** desperate

viii) Prerna's message to young people is:

- **A** there are many ways you can work for conservation
- **B** study hard at college and look after yourself first
- **C** they are too young to help with nature conservation

The big task

In groups of three or four, you are going to organise a presentation of the most pressing environmental or wildlife concerns for your local city or region. In order to do this, you might want to consider one of the big issues you have been studying and how this relates to your local city, town or environment.

1 Using the information in this chapter as prompts, do your own research and identify local sources of information. The issue you choose could be one of the following:

- Global warming and our carbon footprint
- The water crisis
- Pollution – air, water or land
- Disappearing wildlife.

2 Invite junior students at your school or your partner school to view your presentation. Your presentation should:

- describe the problem and explain why or how it came to be this way
- explain what some of the solutions might be
- suggest how listeners could get involved.

3 Think about how you will organise your presentation. Make sure you explain any real objects or exhibits. In order to grab their attention, here are a few suggestions.

- Include a multimedia presentation – a mixture of reading, viewing, listening and presentations. You could even include a skit or short play as part of your presentation.
- Use visuals or big pictures to grab attention, but be prepared to explain the science and the geography behind these big pictures.
- Think about bringing in real evidence from your city or region to prove your points – this could include photographs and facts and statistics about land, water, sea or air pollution in your city, waste dumping, the plight of wildlife or disappearing green areas.
- Arrange, if possible, to interview local experts or teachers at your school to find out their thoughts on your chosen issue.
- Suggest actions you can take as individuals, students and a school to help tackle the issue locally.
- Invite suggestions from your audience to 'act local and think global.'

Here are the Reading, Writing, Speaking and Listening skills you learnt about in Chapter 7.

Use this table to decide how good you are at the different skills, and make a note of what you need to be able to do in order to move up a level.

READING	I can ...
Higher	confidently understand and pick out the details I need in texts which contain graphs and charts usually understand what is implied but not written
Middle ⬆	sometimes understand and pick out the details I need in texts which contain graphs and charts understand some of what is implied but not written
Lower ⬆	pick out a few details I need from straightforward texts which contain graphs and charts attempt to understand what is implied but not written, but with limited success

WRITING	I can ...
Higher	consistently and confidently use details to develop ideas when writing descriptions make descriptions convincing by referring to the five senses appropriately
Middle ⬆	use details to develop ideas a little when writing descriptions sometimes make descriptions convincing by referring to the five senses
Lower ⬆	include one or two details when writing descriptions attempt to make descriptions convincing by referring to one or more of the five senses

SPEAKING	I can ...
Higher	express quite complex ideas effectively, using correct verb tenses consistently respond with confidence and clarity to others in conversations
Middle ⬆	express most of my ideas so that they are understood, using mostly correct verb tenses often respond clearly to others in conversations
Lower ⬆	express simple ideas, but will make errors in verb tenses attempt to respond in conversations, but do not appear confident and I may not always be completely understood

LISTENING	I can ...
Higher	pick out exactly the details I need by using key words consistently understand and answer multiple-choice questions by using key words usually understand what is implied but not actually stated
Middle ⬆	pick out many of the details I need by using key words often understand and answer multiple-choice questions by using key words understand some of what is implied but not actually stated
Lower ⬆	pick out a few of the details I need by looking for key words sometimes understand and answer straightforward multiple-choice questions by looking for key words attempt to understand what is implied but not actually stated, but with limited success

The big picture

In this chapter you will:

- write and talk about what you understand by 'culture'

- read about ways of life in different countries, how celebrations are an expression of culture and how cultural objects and art influence the societies in which we live

- discuss which cultures are being squeezed by the modern world.

Thinking big

1 In pairs, look at the photographs.
- Make notes on what is shown in each photo.
- Guess which society or nation each one is linked to.
- Write one question you would like to ask about each of the photos.

2 In groups, make a list of things that make your culture (where you live now) special. Think about the following areas:
- arts
- celebrations
- different ethnic groups
- food
- lifestyle
- religions
- sports.

3 In pairs, compare your lists. Discuss any differences as a class.

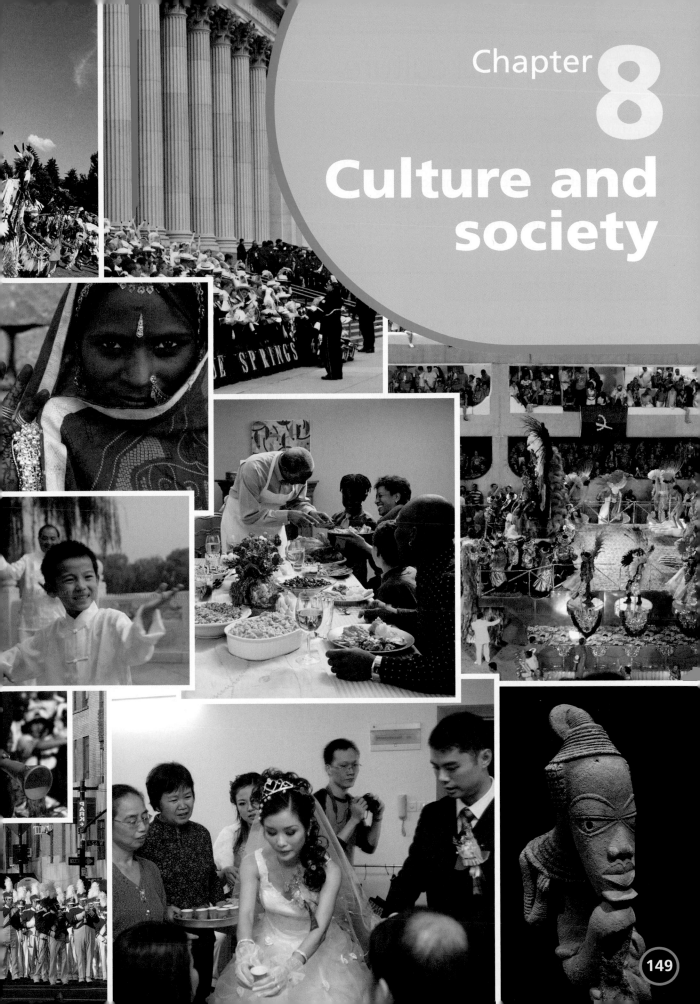

Chapter 8

Culture and society

8.1 Art and culture

Reading skills in focus (R2 and R3)

In this section you will learn to:
- understand and select information
- identify the overall viewpoint and understand the main points in a text
- see connections between ideas and make notes to summarise a text.

Getting started

People usually think of 'the arts' as an expression of the **culture** of a particular place. But what really counts as art?

1 Which of the following do you think count as art?

a) carpet weaving   c) photography   e) hip hop

b) calligraphy   d) ballet   f) pottery

> **Glossary**
>
> **culture** – the common beliefs, way of life and artistic expressions of a community

2 Add three more examples of important forms of art in your culture.

3 In pairs:
- Discuss and agree on a full list of all forms of artistic expression.
- Decide which of the arts you have listed are practised in your country.
- Discuss if there are any differences between art forms practised by young people and traditional art forms.

Exploring the skills

We can all have different views about the same situation. The main **point of view** in a text (both written and spoken) is the standpoint from which an author talks about a topic. It is often:
- for/in favour/positive/approving of an idea OR
- against/negative/disapproving of an idea.

4 In pairs, discuss and make notes on this statement: *Hip hop is art.* Give reasons for your opinion.

5 Speeches often have a strong viewpoint. Read the speeches of two people (opposite) about hip hop, then copy and complete the table.

	Positive points about hip hop	Negative points about hip hop	Overall point of view
Speech 1			
Speech 2			

Good afternoon. My name is Sarah. I would like to talk to you about a national dance competition that I recently attended. Now usually I love dance competitions but at this one I was dismayed to find that over half of the entries were hip hop or street dance.

Hip hop or street dance is a new form of dance where dancers usually dance to rap music. Of course, I understand that hip hop can be enjoyed by all and I can see that it might be popular at the local club. But this is not a good enough reason to welcome it as an art dance form at a national dance competition.

What happened to tap? And ballet? And salsa and African dance? These forms of dance have a long and creditable history and require hours and hours of practice to achieve high level of technique and mastery. Hip hop does not require this level of practice and cannot be compared to these other higher dance forms. Not surprisingly, dancers now think that they can get away with less practice and this decreases agility and coordination.

In my opinion, hip hop's widespread obsession with tricks like balancing on your head reduces dance to mere show and not art.

Making hip hop an art form also gives status to something which started as a form of aggression when dance should be about grace, beauty and culture.

I am not alone in thinking this. Several dance teachers have also noticed a similar trend and complained that the current popularity of hip hop takes attention and money away from the more classical forms of dance.

There has been too much encouragement of hip hop and I urge dance schools around the country to encourage young people to learn the basics of dance through concentrating on classical dance.

Hi. I'm Chu and two years ago I met a lot of hip hop dancers who all belonged to an underground street culture – all with super human strength and abilities. They could fly in the air. They could bend their elbows all the way back. They could spin on their heads for 80 times in a row. I'd never seen anything like that.

Seeing these dancers changed the meaning of dance for me. When I was growing up, my dance heroes were people like Michael Jackson. And it seemed like those dance heroes were disappearing – only in the background of music videos. But after seeing hip hop, the truth is, good dancers have not disappeared at all. They're here, getting better and better every day and our new dancers come from hip hop and street culture. Dance is changing and evolving. Dance is now using technology. Online videos and social networking between dancers have created a global laboratory online for dance, where kids in Japan are taking moves from a YouTube video created in Detroit, copying and then changing it within days and releasing a new video. And this is happening every day. And from the bedrooms and living rooms and garages, with cheap webcams, come the world's great dancers of tomorrow. And because these dancers can now talk across different continents, hip hop can now start to transform dance and change the world.

Developing the skills

You have read Sarah's and Chu's opinions about hip hop. However, you may have a different point of view.

(6) Now answer these questions about the speeches, giving your opinion.

a) What solution does Sarah offer to the 'problem' of hip hop?

b) What is your view of Sarah's solution?

c) Which of Sarah's points do you agree with and which do you disagree with?

d) What is your view of Chu's idea that hip hop can *transform dance and change the world*?

e) Do any of Sarah or Chu's ideas seem unreasonable? Why do you think that?

f) Which speech has a formal style? And which an informal style? What effect does this have on how persuasive you find each speech?

g) Which speech is the most persuasive? Give reasons for your answer.

h) Which speech is the most inspirational? Give reasons for your answer.

Going further

If you have to write a summary, it is usually a good idea to make some notes first. Remember, notes are not written in sentences. They are usually single words or phrases to just give you the basic meaning.

This set of notes summarises the last paragraph of Chu's speech on hip hop dancing:

- dance is changing
- technology helping the change
- people all over the world can see one another dancing
- hip hop is changing all over the world

(7) Look at the photo on page 153. Calligraphy, or the art of writing, is an important part of traditional Chinese culture. Read the transcript (page 153) of a dialogue between a Chinese girl and her father living in the US. Then make some notes ready to write a summary of:

a) the girl's point of view

b) the father's point of view.

> **Top tip**
>
> Notes are not sentences. They are usually single words or phrases to help you remember an idea.

Girl: Hi Dad. Look at this. We just got the list of subjects we can choose for higher secondary school. And I was thinking about taking Fine Arts.

Dad: Wonderful. I approve, but any reason why?

Girl: Well, I'm really good at drawing and I love painting – all that colour. A lot of people have admired the paintings that I have done.

Dad: Why don't you specialise in calligraphy instead? You are also really good with your brush and ink. You know that universities in China prize calligraphy above other art forms. Calligraphy was **revered** as a fine art long before painting.

Girl: But Daaaad. You know that I will never get into a Chinese university. And I want to work in colour. Calligraphy only uses black ink and paper and concentrates on learning characters by heart. I reject the old-fashioned idea that colour is distracting.

Dad: But it's also a way of staying Chinese. That's important.

Girl: But calligraphy isn't creative – it is just copying what ancient scholars wrote years ago.

Dad: Okay, but don't just dismiss the idea. What about studying calligraphy after school and then doing Art as your school option?

> **Glossary**
>
> **revere** – admire and respect something greatly

8) In pairs, share your notes with each other and give comments. Check that the notes:
- are short
- use own words
- give information about each point of view.

Language booster

Read the list of words below. Sort them into two lists: words that mean 'have a good opinion of' and those that mean 'have a bad opinion of'. Find the words in the dialogue.

> revere   reject   prize   approve   admire   dismiss

Complete the following phrases about your own culture.

One thing my culture prizes is …

One thing my culture rejects is …

8.2 Celebrations and culture

In this section you will learn to:
- use examples to support your point of view when writing
- use powerful language to make your opinions persuasive
- include opposite points of view to develop your own.

Getting started

1 In pairs, look at the photos and discuss three different celebrations in your own communities using these headings to help you:
- Name of celebration
- When it is celebrated
- Where it is celebrated
- Why it is celebrated
- How people celebrate.

Durbar festival

2 On your own, choose one celebration and make notes for a short one-minute talk. Don't forget to use the headings above to structure your talk.

3 In groups, give your talk to the rest of the class.

Exploring the skills

When you write or speak, you can support your opinion and be more convincing and persuasive by giving reasons and examples.

An example can be from your own experience or what you have seen or heard. Examples back up your opinion because:
- they give proof that something exists
- they show how/when/where something takes place.

4 Every year in Katsina, northern Nigeria, there is a Sallah Durbar (a big traditional celebration). Look at the photo of the Durbar above and, in pairs, write five questions you would like to ask about Katsina and the Durbar.

> **Glossary**
>
> **emir** – a ruler or chief (in the Islamic world)
> **retinue** – group of advisers for chief, ruler or other important person

5 Now quickly read the extract from a travel brochure about Katsina and the Sallah Durbar. Does it answer any of your questions?

Katsina

With its renowned hospitality and unspoiled countryside, Katsina has something for everyone.

The environment
Looking for an active holiday? Katsina is the perfect base to explore the rugged desert. For example, take a full-day hike with one of our experienced guides from the Nigerian Field Society.

The town
Looking for something more relaxing? Take pleasure in wandering the streets, soaking up the atmosphere of a traditional fascinating Hausa city. Afterwards, you can unwind sitting by the side of fountains sipping your favourite iced drink in the shade of a peaceful courtyard.

Food
More of a foodie? What about savouring both local and international cuisine from the buffet of the resident-acclaimed chef at the Hotel al Kabir?

History
Like sightseeing? Take a tour and visit historic monuments such as the **Emir's** Palace which is considered one of the oldest palaces in Hausaland. The compound is built in typical round style out of sun-dried clay bricks, and the interiors of the rooms have beautiful artistic designs.

The Sallah Durbar
Looking for more excitement? If you possibly can, visit Katsina during one of the most spectacular festivities in Nigeria to celebrate the end of the great Muslim festival, Eid al-Fitr. After prayers, follow the parade of ornately dressed horsemen and the emir himself in ceremonial robes with his splendid **retinue** through the town to the square. Here, groups of horsemen race across the square at full gallop, with swords drawn, until a few feet before the emir. After all the action, there is drumming, dancing and singing which continue into the night. The Durbar expresses the joy and happiness for the Muslim festival and allows all to celebrate their cultural heritage.

6 Read the travel brochure extract again. It gives five reasons and examples for visiting Katsina. Copy and complete the table about why you should visit Katsina.

Position statement	Reason given	Example
You should visit Katsina because ...	If you like active holidays ...	You can go on a hike with a guide from the Nigerian Field Society.
	If you ...	

Developing the skills

You can persuade people by describing things in a strong, positive way. For example:

The fireworks were good.	**less persuasive**
The fireworks were spectacular.	**more persuasive**

7 Reread the passage on Katsina. Find strong, positive words in the passage that mean the following:

- eat
- enjoy
- walk slowly
- drink
- well known
- praised
- old
- in nice clothes

8 Now complete the table with all the strong and positive phrases that are used to describe Katsina.

What	Descriptive phrase
Katsina	*renowned hospitality* *unspoiled countryside*
the environment	
the town	
the food	
the monuments	
the Durbar	
the emir	
the salute for the emir	

9 Write five sentences about your community and region using strong positive descriptive phrases. Use the following prompts to help you:

- the countryside
- the town
- the food
- the history/monuments
- the things to do.

10 You are going to write a letter to a friend, persuading them to come and stay in your home town during a festival or celebration. Use the diagram below to plan your letter.

- Give examples of what you can do together during the festival.
- Make your town and the celebration sound appealing and be persuasive by using lots of positive language.

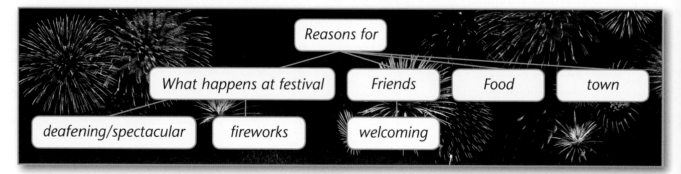

11 Next, write the first draft of your letter.

Checklist for success

✔ Have I written about the festival?

✔ Have I given good reasons and examples?

✔ Have I used strong positive words and phrases?

✔ Have I checked my spelling and punctuation?

Going further

You can often be more persuasive by acknowledging another viewpoint and then trying to overcome this with your own arguments.

12 The Lord Mayor's Show is a traditional parade in London. Read the following text, which argues that we should cancel the celebrations. What phrases are used to acknowledge another viewpoint?

I think that the amount spent on the Lord Mayor's celebrations is too much, and for this reason we should cancel it or severely reduce the amount spent on the festivities.

While I fully understand that we need to celebrate and, in truth, I take great pride and joy in celebrating how wonderful London can be, I believe there is good evidence to show that we spend too much on the celebrations. Last year we spent over $50 million on fireworks, displays, pageants and floats. Meanwhile, London's hospitals and schools are in a very bad state. Our hospitals badly need this $50 million to invest in new equipment.

13 Match each viewpoint with its opposing argument.

Acknowledge other point of view	Oppose the argument
a) While it is true that some people suffer injuries during the celebrations,	1. however, the numbers of children that are involved every year in preparing for and celebrating the march-past is enormous.
b) In the eyes of some, Independence Day is just a celebration of the military;	2. we could make sure there are extra trained first aid helpers on hand during the festivities.
c) To some extent it is true that fewer adults take part in the celebrations;	3. in fact, the entire nation wakes up on this special day to celebrate life and freedom.

14 Write sentences to overcome or oppose the following arguments with an argument of your own.
- While it is true that the celebrations are expensive, …
- To some extent it is true that the festival is just entertainment …

15 Write a 200-word blog arguing in favour of holding a traditional or Independence Day celebration in your country.
- Plan your argument: think of three main reasons for holding a traditional or Independence Day celebration in your country or another country in your region.
- Write your blog: don't forget to acknowledge another viewpoint and overcome this with your own arguments.

Modern culture

Speaking skills in focus (S2)

In this section you will learn to:

- use examples to support your opinions while speaking
- include facts and expert opinions to support your point of view
- use rhetorical questions to make your speaking effective.

Getting started

1 In pairs, discuss the following questions.

- Do you play computer games? If you don't, why not?
- What types of games do you or others play?
- How much time do you or others spend playing per day/week?
- Who do you think is the 'average' gamer?
- Why do you think people play computer games?

2 Now, in groups of four, feed back to your group what your partner told you.

Exploring the skills

You can be more persuasive when speaking if you use facts or examples to support your opinion. Facts or examples often give reasons or answer the question: 'Why do you think that?'

For example:

> *Gaming is an important part of young people's culture.*
> (Why do you think that? Because ...)

Reason/example:

> *Many young people prefer computer games to traditional board games such as chess.*

3 Organise the following examples (a to d) to support Opinion 1 or Opinion 2.

Opinion 1: We should limit the number of hours young people spend on gaming.

Opinion 2: Gaming can solve the problems of the world.

a) Some online games like *World Without Oil* encourage you to adopt real-life habits, like thinking of ways to reduce the amount of oil you use.

b) The majority of fee-paying online users are under the age of 20, and 10% are under the age of 16 in China.

c) Thirteen per cent of under-18s who use the web are addicted to online gaming, according to a recent report.

d) Games encourage you to persevere and work hard to achieve a mission.

4 In pairs, research and think of two examples to support both points of view for the following opinion.

Computer games are (not) an important part of modern life.

Now each choose one of the opinions. Interview your partner about why they hold their opinion. Start like this:

So, could you explain a bit more why you think computer games are (not) an important part of...

Developing the skills

Facts are a powerful means of supporting your opinion. Facts that are 'expert opinions' will make your argument even stronger. Why is this?

Facts and expert opinions:

- show you have done some research
- give your audience a better idea of exactly when, where and how something takes place.

For example:

Many young people play computer games.	weak fact
Five million people under the age of 20 play computer games more than three hours a day in the Middle East.	strong fact
Evidence shows that playing computer games more than three hours a day means you are more likely to become addicted to gaming.	stronger/strongest fact

Top tip

You need to do research on the internet or in the library to gather powerful facts or evidence.

5 Read this speech about gaming. Add the labels using the words in the box below.

Hi. My name is Soo Kyung and I'm an online game designer. I've been making games for about 10 years now. And during that time, as I am sure you are all aware, we are sold the story that online games are violent. Not only that they also encourage violent behaviour.

So I'm going to investigate these ideas and put them to the test. I am going to argue that these ideas are just a myth. I am going to show you that these negative ideas about gaming are, in fact, incorrect.

Let us look at the games. Are they actually violent? In fact many games do not feature any violence. For instance hundreds of millions play games like 'Farmville' where you spend time constructing a house, a family and electronic city. Other games are brain teacher games such as 'Dr Kwashimana's Brain Training.' Then there are the active sports games by Wii which encourage us all to get up and move – to play tennis, play golf, dance, ski and even do yoga. None of these games is violent.

Next let us look at whether games encourage violence. Critics say that video games where you become an active participant in the killing, mean you will resort to violence in the real world too.

An easy way to test this is to look at whether violent crimes have increased together with the boom in video games sales. Is this the case? In fact, the evidence shows that violent crime in America, Japan and China, the three biggest video-game markets, has dropped over the past decade at the same time as sales of video games have soared.

example	personal introduction	use of 'you' or 'we' to involve the audience
repetition	numbers/facts to support opinion	use of expert opinion
speaker's point of view	acknowledge other point of view	

Going further

Good presentations often use rhetorical questions. Rhetorical questions are asked only for effect and they do not expect an answer. Instead, they ask the audience to think further. For example:

Obviously computers are useful to us in many ways that go beyond a book. But is usefulness the best way to measure the value of something?

6 Now insert one or two rhetorical questions into the following introduction to a speech on the benefits of spending your free time away from the screen.

Obviously I use the computer to do my homework. My free time is precious. Free time I save for doing things off screen. Free time is for chatting to friends, playing basketball and reading.

7 You are going to give a presentation on an aspect of computer games. Choose one of the following titles.
- Computer games are addictive.
- Computer games are a waste of time.
- Reading is better for you than gaming.

Example:

Chosen presentation	Computer games are a waste of time
My viewpoint	I disagree that video games are a waste of time
Supporting point 1:	Other games, for example, chess are thought to be strategic
Expert evidence	
Supporting point 2:	
Supporting point 3:	

Instructions for giving a presentation
- First choose your presentation title.
- Next, decide your point of view. Do you agree with the title?
- Then do your research. Use the internet or the library to find out three pieces of information or examples which support your point of view.
- Make notes for your presentation.
- Now practise giving your presentation. Make sure you know exactly what you are going to say – practise it to yourself several times.
- Use the hints in the 'Checklist for success' to make your presentation clear and persuasive.
- Give your presentation to your group.

Checklist for success

✔ Clearly state the reason for the speech early in the speech.

✔ Use 'we' to include the audience.

✔ Use examples to support the points made.

✔ Include expert opinions to support the points made.

✔ Use repetition, often in groups of three.

✔ Ask rhetorical questions to make listeners think further.

Listening skills in focus (L2 and L3)

In this section you will learn to:
- understand and select relevant details in spoken texts
- recognise and understand opinions in a range of spoken texts
- recognise and understand conflicting opinions in an informal spoken text.

Getting started

Many traditional cultures from the countryside are disappearing. It is not just people's lifestyles that are disappearing, it is also the knowledge they hold of their cultures that is being lost.

1 Look at these photos. They both show houses in the Middle East.

In pairs, discuss the following questions.

a) Which photo shows a town (urban) life and which a country (rural) life?

b) Where would you prefer to live? Give one reason why.

c) Do you think the photos are a good reflection of urban and rural life where you live now?

2 In pairs, brainstorm and then copy and complete the table with things that you associate or link with country life and town life in your country.

Think hard – maybe some activities are associated with both country and town life.

Town life	Country life
Commuting to work	Commuting to work
Going to the cinema	Using mobile phones
Using mobile phones	

Exploring the skills

There are many situations when you might hear a lot of information in a short space of time. You need to be able to find out quickly whether someone is giving you facts or their opinions. If they give you facts it is often easier to trust them. Luckily you can spot opinions from particular phrases people use to introduce them. For example:

> *The majority of people live in cities.*

Fact – you can prove this fact by finding out how many people live in cities.

> *It's normal that most people live in cities.*

Opinion – you cannot prove 'it is normal'.

Checklist for success

Phrases and words that introduce opinions:

- ✔ 'It's normal that …'
- ✔ 'It's a shame that …'
- ✔ 'It's wonderful that …'
- ✔ 'It's terrible that …'

- ✔ 'Obviously …'
- ✔ 'never'
- ✔ 'always'
- ✔ 'better/best'

3 In pairs, listen to some statements about living in the country and in the town. Sort the statements into fact and opinion. Be careful, some of them are a mix of fact and opinion. Explain how the statement can be proved if it is a fact.

Opinion	Fact	How fact can be proven
The overcrowding in our cities is terrible.	The majority of people live in cities.	Find out the numbers and percentage of the national population that lives in the major cities.

4 Two young people from different countries talk about their home life. Listen a first time and answer the question.

Who has a rural life and who has an urban life?

5 Listen again. Are the answers the speaker gives to these questions facts or opinions? For example:

Where does she live?

She says she lives in an enormous and luxurious house. This is opinion because you cannot prove it is luxurious – what is luxurious to one person may not be to another.

Person 1

a) Where does she live?

b) Is there a school in her village?

c) How does she feel about going to school?

d) What does she think about Abuja?

e) How does she keep in touch with her parents?

Person 2

a) Where does he live?

b) What happened to his parents?

c) How does he feel about where he lives now?

d) What is the house like where he lives?

e) What are his grandparents like?

6 Listen again to the first few sentences from person 2. Find two facts and two opinions.

Disappearing ways of life

Developing the skills

In the next exercise you will be asked to listen very carefully to what your fellow students say. The more carefully you listen, the better you will be able to do the writing task.

7 Write a 200-word article for your school magazine about the advantages you find of living in either an urban or a rural environment. Prepare for the article using the instructions below:

First, listen to others
- On your own, list or make notes of the advantages of the places where you live or have lived – and whether they were rural or urban.
- In groups, take turns to give a short talk about the advantages and disadvantages of where you live or have lived.
- All other members in the group should listen carefully and make notes.
- One person should serve as scribe and collect all the facts and opinions about living in town or country environments.

Next, plan the article
On your own, use the collected group notes about living in an urban or rural environment to plan your article. You can use a concept map to help you plan.

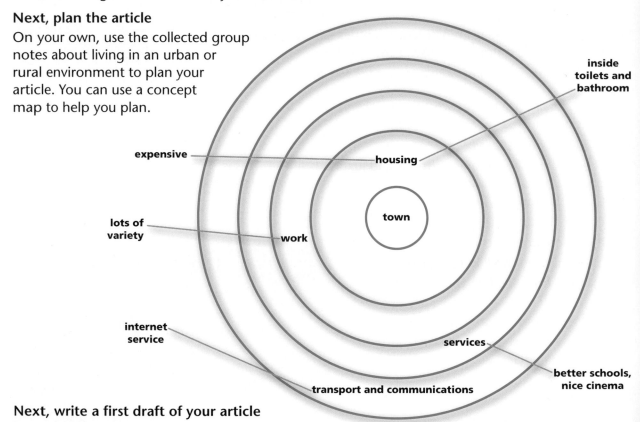

Next, write a first draft of your article
Then check your article and rewrite it. Check that you have:
- written about 200 words
- acknowledged other ideas and argued against them with facts and examples
- mixed facts with opinions
- used strong, positive words.

Going further

A dialogue, or conversation between two or more people, is often more difficult to understand because different people are likely to hold different opinions about the same thing. When listening, you have to work out who holds which opinion. For example:

Person 1: It's normal for people to move to towns and cities for work.

Person 2: You should encourage people to stay in the villages to protect rural lifestyles to make sure the languages and knowledge don't die out.

8 You are going to listen to a short dialogue between a girl and a boy from Indonesia who talk about disappearing cultures.

Before you listen, as a class, brainstorm everything you know about Indonesia.

Look at the photos and think about the types of traditional lifestyles the people have.

Now listen to the dialogue and answer the questions.

8.4

a) What special skill and knowledge did the grandmother have?

b) Why doesn't the girl have this knowledge today?

c) What does the girl say has been lost?

d) What is the girl's opinion about the death of a language?

e) What is the boy's opinion about the death of a language?

9 Listen again. Write down the two methods the girl gives for protecting a language.

10 In pairs, discuss what languages you know of in your own culture that are in danger of dying.

Discuss whether you think it's normal for village lifestyles to disappear. (This is an opinion.)

11 Write two sentences about why it is important to protect different languages.

12 Write two sentences about how you can make sure minority languages stay alive.

The big task

Nomadic communities are groups that move from place to place as part of their lifestyle, often to reach new sources of food and water. Did you know that many nomadic communities are disappearing? For example, many people from a European travelling community, the Roma, have abandoned the traditional way of life, including travelling, and now live within mainstream society.

Write a 250-word article for your school magazine about a community whose culture and way of life is disappearing. The last paragraph should give your opinion about whether and how we should preserve the community.

1 First, brainstorm your topic.

- In groups of four, choose a culture that is in danger of disappearing. If you cannot think of one near or in your country, then your teacher can help you.
- Copy and complete the first two columns of the table below.
- Each person in the group researches one of the questions from the 'What I want to know' column.
- Take it in turns to feed back to your group. Your group must listen carefully to what each person has to say.
- On your own, complete the last column of the table.

What I know	What I want to know	What I learnt
Roma have abandoned travelling as a way of life.	What …? Where …? How …? Why …?	

2 Now plan your article.

- In the first part of the article, write engagingly about what you know about your disappearing culture.
- In the second part of the article, write your opinion. Think of three reasons why and how we should preserve your disappearing culture.

3 Now write your article. Use as many as possible of the following features.

- Use expert opinions (e.g. laws/conventions/evidence/important people).
- Use facts to support the points made.
- Use examples to support the points made.
- Acknowledge other viewpoints.
- Use repetition.
- Ask rhetorical questions.
- Clearly state your opinion in the last paragraph.

Here are the Reading, Writing, Speaking and Listening skills you learnt about in Chapter 8.

Use this table to decide how good you are at the different skills, and make a note of what you need to be able to do in order to move up a level.

READING
I can ...

Higher	confidently understand and select details from complex texts, and produce concise notes for a summary
	consistently identify the overall viewpoint and main points, recognising connections between related ideas
Middle	understand and select details from texts, and produce adequate notes for a summary
	sometimes identify the overall viewpoint and main points, recognising some connections between related ideas
Lower	select a few details from straightforward texts, and produce notes for a summary
	identify the overall viewpoint and a few more obvious points, recognising a few connections between related ideas

WRITING
I can ...

Higher	consistently and confidently use examples to support a point of view
	make my arguments persuasive by deliberately choosing powerful language and by utilising opposite points of view to develop my own effectively
Middle	sometimes use examples to support a point of view
	make some of my arguments persuasive by using powerful language and by including opposite points of view to try to develop my own
Lower	use one or two examples to support a simple point of view
	try to make my arguments persuasive by using powerful language, and by trying to refer to opposite points of view to develop my own, but find this difficult to do

SPEAKING
I can ...

Higher	consistently make effective use of examples and expert opinions to support my point of view
	use rhetorical questions effectively to make my speaking persuasive
Middle	sometimes make use of examples and expert opinions to support my point of view
	use rhetorical questions to try to make my speaking persuasive
Lower	try to include examples, including expert opinions, to support my point of view
	recognise the effect of rhetorical questions but do not use them

LISTENING
I can ...

Higher	understand and pick out exactly the details I need when listening
	confidently distinguish and understand opposite opinions in a range of spoken texts, including more complex, formal ones
Middle	understand and pick out many of the details I need when listening
	often recognise and understand differing opinions in a range of spoken texts
Lower	pick out a few of the details I need when listening
	identify straightforward opinions in simple spoken texts
	recognise conflicting opinions in simple spoken texts

The big picture

In this chapter you will:

● think about transport – how people all over the world travel from one place to another

● read, write, talk and think about how transport has changed in the last hundred years, and how it continues to change.

Thinking big

1 Choose two photographs that you find interesting.

● Make notes about the types of transport illustrated in the photos. Note down some ideas covering what you know about them, and why you find them interesting.

● Why are different kinds of transport popular in different places around the world?

2 In pairs:

● Discuss the photos with your partner and share what you know about them. Talk about the countries shown and think about when these different kinds of transport are or were used. Ask your partner questions to look up any information that you don't know.

3 On your own, note down ideas about the following:

● How and why do methods of transport change over time?

● What advantages and disadvantages can you think of for some of our main forms of transport today?

● What is your favourite mode of transport? Explain why.

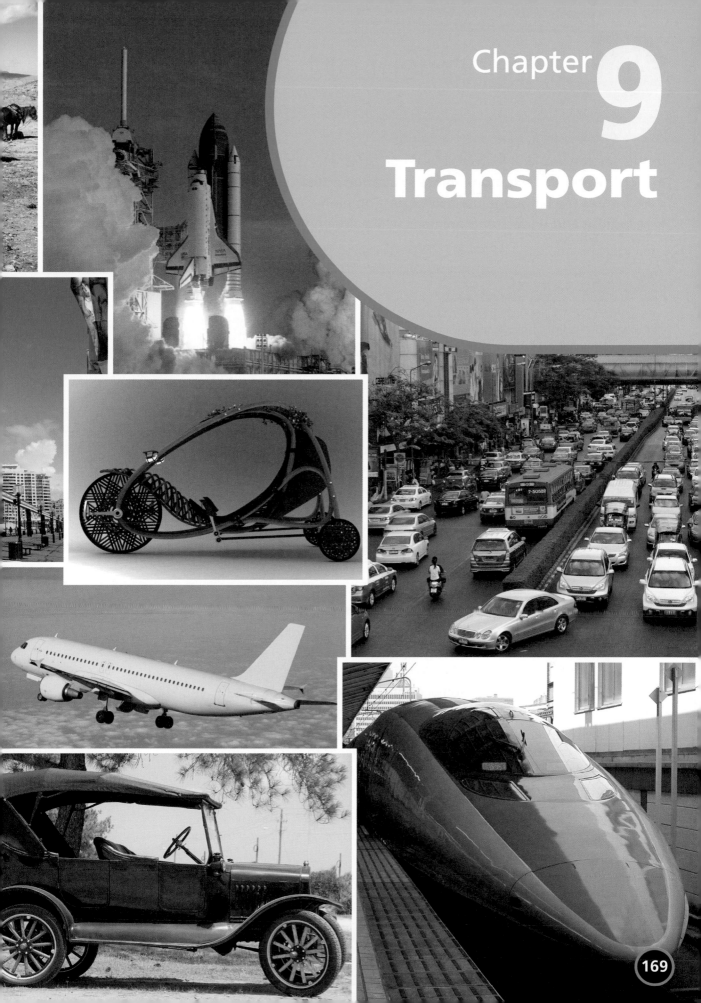

Chapter 9
Transport

9.1 Development of transport

In this section you will learn to:
- identify and understand opinions in a range of texts
- recognise the language used to express opinion
- recognise and understand opinions which are implied but not actually stated.

Getting started

1 Read the points below and discuss your ideas about them with a partner.

- Think about a journey you have been on recently. What transport did you use and what did you like or dislike about it?
- What are the advantages of cars? Are there any disadvantages?
- How do you think transport influences our lives today?

Exploring the skills

When you read a text, it is important to be able to tell the difference between facts and the writer's opinion. Remember:

- A **fact** is something that can be proved, such as a date.
- An **opinion** is what one person or group of people thinks or feels. It cannot be proved beyond doubt.

A writer may use phrases such as *in my opinion* and *I think* to express their point of view. However, if not, a reader still needs to recognise that a comment may just be personal opinion.

Opinions that are presented well are often supported by facts:

> *The development of new forms of transport is the main reason why we have so many opportunities today … we can send items around the world at speeds that were unheard of 100 years ago.*

In this example, *The development of new forms of transport is the main reason* is an opinion, a personal point of view. The fact that follows may be true, but it would be possible for someone to argue that there is another reason of equal or greater importance.

2 Read the text and answer the questions below.

Europe today has many different forms of transport – cars, buses, trains and planes. I think that the development of these forms of transport is the main reason why we have so many opportunities today – we can travel to work, so we can choose from a wider range of jobs. We can send items around the world at speeds that were unheard of 100 years ago. We can go on holiday and visit friends and family.

But this has only been possible in recent years. What did we do before motorways, air travel and the railways? In my opinion, life must have been more difficult and less interesting.

a) Give four types of transport named in the text.

b) Identify four things which transport allows us to do.

c) Identify two sentences where opinions are expressed.

d) Find two phrases the writer uses to say what he or she thinks.

e) Do you agree with the opinions being expressed?

Developing the skills

Remember that in order to distinguish between fact and opinion you need to:

- recognise how facts are presented in a text – look out for dates, numbers and other information that can be proved to be true
- look for phrases that signal the writer's own opinion, such as *In my opinion*, *I think that*
- consider whether something can be proved – if not, it is probably an opinion rather than a fact.

3 Read the text below and on page 172 about how transport has developed, then answer the questions.

Transport at speed, and travel for leisure, have always been possible – life was very different before transport created the opportunities we have today. This started to change in Britain in the 1800s, when railways became an important form of transport.

In 1803 the steam locomotive was invented by Richard Trevithick. In 1825, the first public steam railway was built in the north of England, from Stockton to Darlington. Many people watched the train set off on its first journey, but they were scared when it let off steam and lots of them ran away!

In 1829, the first intercity railway joined Liverpool and Manchester. The train that ran on this railway was designed by George and Robert Stephenson. It was faster and used less coal than earlier models: they called it 'Stephenson's Rocket'.

A lot of money was spent on developing the railways, and 'railway mania' began. Building the railways provided lots of jobs and the work was hard but well paid. By 1873, there were 275 000 people working for railway companies.

It appears that this development of the railways shaped modern Britain. They helped businesses grow, as things could be moved around the country more quickly. They allowed people to travel for pleasure – to the seaside, to football matches and other places of interest. People even became healthier, because food that was transported quickly was fresher when it arrived. For these reasons, many people believe that the railways are the most important development of the last 200 years.

4 Read the sentences below. Then read the text again and complete the facts.

Key facts about transport in Britain

Invention of steam locomotive in _____
by _____

First public railway built in _____

First intercity railway went from _____
to _____

Inventor of 'Stephenson's Rocket' _____

Number of people working for railway companies in
1873 _____

Top tip

When you read a text with lots of facts, it can be useful to make short notes to help you remember key information:

1803 – first steam locomotive

1825 – Stockton–Darlington railway

5 What does the writer think about the following topics:
- the transport system we have today
- the development of the railways?

6 What is your view of the writer's opinions? Do you agree that the railways are the most important transport development or do you think that other inventions have been more important?

Look at the photos to help give you some ideas, or use any of your own. Research some facts to support your argument.

Going further

Adjectives such as *great*, *vast* and *scenic* signal an opinion about what someone has seen or experienced. They add more information to a factual account and give you an idea of how the author feels without them having to say it directly.

7 Read the following extract from an account of a journey.

> Taking thirteen days, passing through nine countries and nine time zones, the main feature of this trip was a journey on the legendary Trans-Siberian Railway.

a) In this extract, the writer gives a number of facts: for example, the journey took 13 days. Identify two more facts.

b) The writer also introduces his opinion with the word *legendary*. What do you know about the Trans-Siberian Railway? Find out what might make it *legendary*.

8 Read the rest of the text. What is the writer's overall impression of the journey?

> Coming from a family that has always had strong connections with railways, I had always been interested in trains from being a small child.
>
> Therefore, I suppose it was only natural that I would always wonder about what it would be like to travel on the world's longest train journey, on the Trans-Siberian Railway.
>
> This 7650 mile journey by train across two continents was a great adventure which far exceeded my expectations and stirred the emotions. It took me nearly half way round the globe, providing the opportunity to see vast contrasts of scenic beauty, culture and climate in a short space of time. The thoughts and recollections from the journey will no doubt continue way into the future.
>
> For those who think the Trans-Siberian Railway is just another ride on a train – well, apart from it being the longest train journey in the world, it is much more than that: it's an adventure and one of the very few left on our planet that can be completed by absolutely anyone.
>
> From Clive Simpson www.trans-siberian-railway.co.uk]

9 Think of more adjectives the writer might have used to describe this journey. Then, in pairs, invent sentences about the journey using these adjectives.

Consider how the writer could express a different opinion about his journey, using negative adjectives. For example:

> *It was a boring / an unimpressive / an uncomfortable journey*

10 Read the whole text again and identify:

a) three facts about the journey (think about the distance travelled, where the writer went and why he went)

b) some of the writer's opinions about how he travelled and what he saw on his journey.

The impact of transport

In this section you will learn to:
- use relative pronouns to join sentences
- use a variety of structures when writing descriptions
- join your ideas and sentences using connectives (connecting words and phrases).

Getting started

1 Read the questions below and discuss your ideas with a partner.
- In what ways can transport provide people with more opportunities?
- Would you prefer to travel abroad to work, or would you rather go abroad on holiday or for sightseeing?
- Do you think it is good that more people are able to travel wherever they want, or are there disadvantages in this?

Exploring the skills

When you write, you can use a variety of sentence structures to join your ideas together and extend them. In Chapter 3, you learnt about ways to combine simple sentences to make compound and complex sentences. Here you will look at more ways to join or extend sentences using relative pronouns.

Relative pronouns

Where introduces information about places, for example:

> *This is the park <u>where</u> we like to play.*

Who introduces information about people, for example:

> *Mr Moss was the teacher <u>who</u> encouraged me most at school.*

That or *which* introduce information about things, for example:

> *These are the trainers <u>that</u> everyone wants at the moment.*

2 Nisha has moved to a new country to start a job. She is emailing her friends and family at home to tell them about her first few days in a new country. Read the text. How did Nisha travel to the island, and where did she spend the first night?

Look at this photo. That's the boat I arrived on. I flew to the main airport then took a **ferry** to the island. The ferry, which was quite small, was good fun because I met some friendly people and I also saw dolphins on the journey!

This is the helpful lady who showed me where to catch the ferry. It was really busy at the **port**, and my guidebook, which was quite old, didn't have the right information in it!

I was really glad she helped me because I was lost!

And look – this is the hotel where I stayed on the first night. The place where I'm working is a long way from the ferry port, so I stayed here for the night and set off again the next morning by coach. The hotel, which was in the town centre, was really noisy but the breakfast was tasty!

Glossary

ferry – a boat for taking people on journeys, usually from one island or country to another
port – a place where lots of boats and ships arrive in a country

3 Read the text again and identify at least four relative pronouns.

4 In pairs, read the following sentences and discuss:
- the main idea of the sentence
- what information is given about the main subject.
a) This is our classroom where we study English.
b) This is my friend who lives next door to me.
c) I've got a bike which is quite old.
d) These are the tickets that we need for the plane.

Can you identify why each relative pronoun is used? Look back at page 174 to check your ideas.

5 In pairs, think of different endings for the following sentences. Remember to use the correct relative pronoun.
a) Here's the book …
b) There's the plane …
c) She's the girl …
d) Have you seen the hotel …
e) This is the airport …

The impact of transport

Developing the skills

When you are describing something, try to use a range of structures to add interest to your writing. Think about using sentences of different lengths, as well as of different types (simple, compound and complex sentences). Also try to use a variety of ways to add description – adjectives (describing words), noun phrases (see Chapter 3) or relative pronouns (see pages 174–175). For example:

> We reached the hotel early in the evening. It was breathtaking. The hotel, which was a small, white building, was set on the side of a hill overlooking the sea. In front of us we could see blue sea and a clear sky. The beach was spectacular. It had white sand and was surrounded by large palm trees. We could hear the waves gently crashing on the sand. The sky was full of beautiful colours because the sun was starting to go down.

- simple sentence
- relative pronoun
- compound sentence
- noun phrase
- complex sentence

6 Work in pairs. Discuss a holiday you have had or would like to have. You could draw a picture of a place you would like to visit.
- What do you like about the place?
- What can you do when you are there?
- How can you travel there?

7 Imagine you have been on a journey overseas for work, study or sightseeing. You are going to write an email to your friends or family to describe why you chose this place and how you travelled there.

a) First, make notes to help you structure your ideas. Look at the photos below and think about what each one shows. You can use these, or any of your own ideas.

> **Top tip**
>
> When you are writing, you can use adjectives to offer more information about your experiences. Using a variety of adjectives will also make your writing more interesting.

b) Read through your notes and think of ways you can expand them into simple and longer compound sentences.

8 Now write your email describing your journey.

You could start:

Look at these photos. This is the yellow taxi which I took to the city centre.

Top tip

When you are describing how you travelled, there are certain phrases to remember:
I travelled …
   by bike
   by car
   by bus / taxi / train
   on foot

Going further

Complex sentences can express more sophisticated ideas, for example to compare time and place or to add information. Sentences can be connected in different ways in order to make complex sentences. Connective phrases have different uses, as shown below.

Language booster

Connectives	Use
even though	to make a contrast – shows that something happened despite a problem or difficulty
because	to show cause and effect – gives a reason or reasons why something happened
although	to make a contrast – similar to 'even though' – introduces a statement which makes the main statement seem surprising
when	to add further information about an event

9 Read the following sentences. Referring to the table above, decide on the use or function of the underlined connective phrases.
  a) The plane, <u>which was very big</u>, had comfy seats.
  b) <u>Even though</u> I like driving, I take the bus to work.
  c) <u>When it is raining</u>, the bus is always busy.
  d) <u>Although I got up at 5 a.m.</u>, I missed the train.
  e) We walked to the cinema <u>because the underground was closed</u>.

10 Make notes on the following questions.
  a) What opportunities do you have because of transport in your area?
  b) What improvements could be made to the local transport system?
  c) How could an improved transport system improve young people's lives?

11 Now imagine you have to write an article for a school magazine to explain the importance of a good transport system to young people. Use your notes from above to help you structure your ideas.

Top tip

Try to give reasons for your ideas, using a range of sentence forms (simple, compound and complex) and connective phrases.

Problems with transport

In this section you will learn to:
- use a variety of grammatical structures when you speak
- vary the tense of verbs you use according to the situation.

Getting started

66 *Restore human legs as a means of travel. Pedestrians rely on food for fuel and need no special parking facilities.* 99 *Lewis Mumford*

1 Read the quote above and discuss in pairs what you think it means. Use a dictionary to look up any words you don't know.

Then consider the following problems that can be caused by transport:
- Pollution – what effects do different forms of transport have on the environment?
- Congestion – what is it like to be on a very busy road?
- Cost – how expensive are different forms of transport?

Exploring the skills

When you are speaking it is important to be able to express yourself clearly and fluently. This includes using the correct verb tense in the correct situation, depending on whether you want to talk about the past, the present or the future. For example:

I ride my bike to college. (present tense)

I walked to school when I was younger. (past tense)

When I'm older, I will drive to work. (future tense)

2 Read the speech bubbles below and identify the past, present and future tenses. One of them uses complex verb forms which are not any of these, called 'conditionals'. Can you spot it?

When my parents were young, they didn't have a car and they used to travel by bicycle a lot. It was better for the environment, and it was probably fun too. —————— **past tense**

Transport causes pollution, and I think cars, which often only have one person in them, are the worst for the environment.

In my opinion, aeroplane travel is the worst in terms of pollution. Each journey releases a lot of dangerous gases. It's also cheaper to fly today than it used to be, which means that people are flying more often and further.

People say that transport is progress, but in my opinion, digging up the countryside to make roads and railways isn't progress – it damages our environment. Soon there will be too many roads and not enough open spaces.

I think that in the future, people won't use cars in city centres at all. There will be new kinds of public transport which will be more environmentally friendly, and cheaper to use.

If we didn't have a good transport system, we wouldn't have all the things we take for granted these days. Businesses wouldn't be as successful, and life wouldn't be as interesting.

3 Identify which speakers think that transport was better in the past, and which think it was worse. Then read again, and identify the speakers who think transport will be better in the future, and those who think it will be worse.

4 Which of the comments above do you agree with? In pairs, discuss your ideas and give reasons for your opinions.

5 Listen to two people talking about their views on transport.

9.1

a) Why is Maria asking Luca these questions?

b) What does Luca think about the bus service?

6 Listen again and match the following incomplete sentences to make sentences you hear. Then decide which full sentence is a simple sentence, which is a compound sentence and which is a complex sentence.

a) It used to be quite quick,

b) I usually

c) Although it might make a difference now,

A) I don't think it will help in the future.

B) but now it's really slow.

C) cycle everywhere.

Developing the skills

Used to … is one way of talking about what things were like in the past and comparing them with the present. Read this example from the recording:

> *It used to be quite quick, but now it's really slow.*

It describes what the bus service was like in the past (quick) with what it is like now (slow).

> *It used to be quiet in my town, but now it's very busy.*

> *We used to walk to school, but now we get the bus.*

7 In pairs, think up more sentences to describe a situation that you knew in the past and how it is different now, using *used to*.

8 Read the following extract. Do you agree or disagree with the point of view? How does it compare with the transport situation where you live?

> I think there are lots of problems with transport today. For example, lots of people in my town drive to work every day. There is a good train service here, which goes straight to the city centre. However, the trains are lot more expensive than they used to be. They are too expensive for most people to use every day. But petrol is also very expensive – and I think it will get more expensive in the future.
>
> In my opinion, there should be a better bus service. Buses are cheap, practical and they don't cause as much pollution as lots of cars.

9 In pairs, think of similar sentences about transport that join ideas together in a variety of ways. Try to think of at least one example for each use. Look back at the 'Language booster' on page 177.

10 Which form of transport do you think causes the biggest problems?

a) Note down ideas about:
- how often it is used
- how many people use it
- how expensive it is to use and to run
- how much pollution it causes
- how it has changed over time, and how it might change in the future.

b) Can you think of any alternatives to this method of transport? In what ways are your alternatives better?

11 In pairs, discuss the notes you made in task 10. If possible, record your conversation. Then listen to it again and see if you can think of ways to improve the way you join your sentences and ideas. Have you used verb tenses correctly?

12 Act out your dialogue again, this time using more ways to join sentences and express your ideas. Make sure that you use the right tenses for your verbs.

Going further

You can use **modals** to express your arguments and opinions in a more sophisticated way. These are small words that can be added to a verb to show subtle shades of meaning, such as possibility, intention, obligation or necessity. For example: I <u>can</u> walk/I <u>ought</u> to walk/I <u>could</u> walk/I <u>should</u> walk.

Start with simple modals (e.g. can, must, should) before changing to the past (e.g. should have walked) and using more complex forms.

Read the following conversation.

    A   I should walk to college more often as it is good exercise.
    B   That is a good idea. I could walk with you.

Speaker A feels an obligation to walk to college. Speaker B suggests the possibility of walking with her.

13 Match the following incomplete sentences to make the correct full sentences.

    a) I should have set my alarm clock to wake me up early,

    b) I think the government should have spent a lot of money on railways,

    c) I could have cycled to school today,

    A) because the service is awful at the moment.

    B) although it was raining a little bit.

    C) because I overslept and I missed the bus!

14 You are going to role-play a dialogue between two people who are discussing the transport in their home town. Before you start, note down ideas about:
- what is good about the current system where you live
- what is bad about it.

When you have finished, team up with a partner. One of you will present the positive points and the other will present the negative points. Decide on your roles and spend a few minutes preparing your ideas.

Remember that this is a conversation between friends, so the language can be quite informal. However, try to use a variety of sentences correctly in order to join your ideas more fluently.

Act out your role-play, without looking at your notes.

Top tip

If possible, record yourself and listen to the conversation afterwards. Can you think of ways to improve it?

Listening skills in focus (L3 and L4)

In this section you will learn to:

- understand connections and differences between related ideas to answer multiple-choice questions
- understand what is implied but not actually said in a formal spoken text.

Getting started

1 Read the points below and discuss your ideas with a partner.

- What do you think the most popular form of transport will be in the future? Will it be cars, trains, bikes, or something new that hasn't been designed yet?
- What reasons do we have for needing new kinds of transport?
- If we are developing new kinds of transport, what qualities should they have?

2 Because of the problems with many of our current forms of transport, lots of people around the world are trying to design new types of transport. Look at these photos and match each one to its description below.

The future of transport

a) Using the power of the wind, this idea is perfect for when the journey itself is more important than the destination.

b) Great for short, personal journeys, for people who have always wanted to fly!

c) A sporty, futuristic vehicle, great for travelling around town.

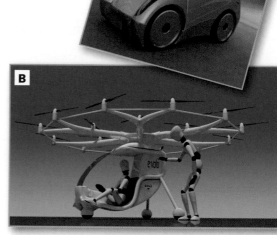

Top tip

Remember to study any images linked to a text as closely as you can. These will give you important information right away, and will help you to understand what you read or hear.

Exploring the skills

When you answer multiple-choice questions about listening texts, as with other listening tasks, first read the questions and underline any key words to help you listen out for the answers. If, on the first hearing, you are not absolutely sure which is the right answer, put pencil question marks by the possible answers and then wait for the second hearing before putting the right answer in the box.

3 Listen to a radio programme about future forms of transport. Which one of these forms of transport do you think is the most likely to be successful?

4 To prepare you to answer multiple-choice questions, let's first answer some True/False questions. Decide whether the statements below are true or false.

Remember:
- First, read the statements carefully to ensure that you understand them.
- Underline <u>key words</u> in the statements to help you focus.
- Then listen to the programme again.

The first one has been done for you as an example.

a) The speaker thinks that <u>big cars</u> are a <u>useful</u> way to travel around town.

> False – the speaker thinks that travelling around town in big cars causes pollution, is expensive and makes the roads too busy.

b) The Uno is designed to be used by one person.

c) The Uno uses expensive fuel.

d) The Multicopter can be used by more than one person.

e) The person controlling the Multicopter has to use a computer.

f) It can be used for long journeys.

g) The Passing Cloud idea is useful if you want to get somewhere quickly.

h) The design is of small, separate spherical shapes.

i) It uses an electric engine to move about.

Developing the skills

In exams you may be asked multiple-choice questions about listening texts. Again, you should read the questions first and underline any key words to help you listen out for the answers. Try to think of different ways in which the information could be presented, as you may not hear it in exactly the same form. For example, instead of 'it uses expensive fuel', you might hear 'it isn't cheap to use'.

5 Look at the picture and choose the best description. In pairs, give reasons for your choice.

a) Scientists develop new green form of transport.

b) Tourists travel into space for first time.

c) Astronauts carry out research into space travel.

Language booster

Match the words to the definitions.

a) bamboo
b) sustainable material
c) zero emissions
d) heat-resistant
e) synthetic material
f) waterway
g) infrastructure

1 a material which isn't damaged by high temperatures
2 water which can be used for transport
3 a tall plant, a bit like a strong kind of grass
4 not producing any pollution
5 a system which is needed for transport to work
6 material which can be used without damaging the environment
7 material which is made artificially; not a natural product

6 Listen to the descriptions of each design for new kinds of transport, then answer the multiple-choice questions below. **9.3**

i) Who designed the Bamboo Ajiro bicycle?

- **A** a student from Austria
- **B** a student from America
- **C** a student from Australia

ii) What are the advantages of bamboo?

- **A** it is strong and needs light to grow quickly
- **B** it grows quickly and is light and strong
- **C** it grows quickly and does not use much energy

iii) Which is the best description of 'aramid', the fabric used to make the Adhoc canoe?

- **A** an artificial material which is waterproof and resistant to heat
- **B** a material which is naturally waterproof and heat resistant
- **C** an artificial material which is waterproof and easily damaged by heat

iv) What is the Adhoc canoe powered by?

- **A** a fuel with low emissions
- **B** water
- **C** human energy

v) What is the Aquatic water taxi made from?

- **A** metal which is sustainable
- **B** metal which is not very heavy
- **C** metal which is soft to the touch

vi) How does it travel?

- **A** on waterways that are already there
- **B** on new waterways
- **C** on a new infrastructure

7 Listen to a presentation about space travel. What is the main reason for space flight, according to the speaker?

9.4

8 Listen to the text again and answer these multiple-choice questions.

i) Why is it now possible to travel into space?

    A we can afford it

    B we have the right vehicles

    C because enough people want to go

ii) What does the speaker say about sending human beings into space?

    A spacecraft can't go into space without humans

    B spacecraft must not have human beings on board

    C spacecraft can go with or without humans

iii) What example does the speaker give of a spacecraft which does not carry any passengers?

    A the shuttle programme

    B communication satellites

    C the space station

iv) What equipment is needed to make a spacecraft take off?

    A a rocket and gravity

    B tools and a satellite

    C a rocket and a launch pad

v) What is the most important reason why scientists want to explore space right now?

    A so they can discover other planets with vital minerals and metals

    B so they can find out about other planets and other life forms

    C so they can develop space tourism

Going further

Just as when you read, sometimes you have to work out what a speaker means by using clues. When we talk to one another we do not always 'spell out' exactly what we mean. In the same way, when you listen to a speaker, you have to be ready to understand what is implied but not actually said.

9 Listen to the text about space travel again. Answer the questions below in sentences.

a) Is the speaker positive or negative about what humans have achieved as regards space travel so far?

b) Explain two ways in which the speaker seems very hopeful for the future possibilities of space exploration.

In pairs, discuss your answers and explain which clues led you to these answers. In other words, what did you hear that helped you understand what was being implied?

The big task

Imagine that there is a competition to design a new system of transport for your town or city. You are going to work in a group to design an entry. You have to produce a leaflet which presents your idea, lists its advantages, and explains why it is needed.

1. What factors do you think are important for the new transport system? Here are some ideas:

   cheap   *environmentally-friendly*   *made of sustainable materials*
   convenient safe   *quick*   *healthy*   *easy to make*   *easy to use*

   Think about these and other ideas and make some notes.

2. Working in groups, talk about ideas for a new form of transport. Try to agree on:
   - what features are the most important
   - what type of material it should be made from (e.g. metals, plastics, carbon-fibre, sustainable materials, recycled materials)
   - what form of energy it should use.

   You will need to draw up a list of possibilities and discuss which ones are the most suitable.

   You can use the internet and other resources to get ideas and conduct research. You could also design an image of your chosen form of transport.

3. As a group, produce a leaflet for your competition entry. This will need to tell people how good your idea is, and why. You will need to:
   - Say what is wrong with the existing forms.
   - Describe your proposal and say how it works. Use diagrams and plans if necessary.
   - Explain why it is a good idea by listing its advantages.

4. Present your ideas to the class. Be prepared to explain your design and answer questions about it.

Check your progress

Here are the Reading, Writing, Speaking and Listening skills you learnt about in Chapter 9.

Use this table to decide how good you are at the different skills, and make a note of what you need to be able to do in order to move up a level.

READING	I can ...
Higher	consistently understand the opinions expressed in texts, including the more complex ones securely recognise the language used to express opinions and understand what is implied but not written
⬆ Middle	understand the opinions expressed in a range of different kinds of texts recognise the language used to express opinions and understand some of what is implied but not written
⬆ Lower	understand some basic opinions expressed in straightforward texts identify the language used to express opinions and understand literal meanings

WRITING	I can ...
Higher	use a wide variety of structures effectively when writing descriptions use a variety of connectives, including relative pronouns, securely to good effect when writing
⬆ Middle	use some different structures when writing descriptions use some different connectives , including relative pronouns, to link ideas and sentences
⬆ Lower	use some basic structures when writing descriptions use some basic connectives and understand how relative pronouns link ideas and sentences

SPEAKING	I can ...
Higher	confidently use a variety of grammatical structures when speaking confidently and accurately vary the tenses of verbs I use, according to situations
⬆ Middle	use a variety of grammatical structures with reasonable accuracy when speaking use some different tenses when speaking, though may make errors when I try to be ambitious
⬆ Lower	use some straightforward grammatical structures when speaking use some basic tenses well enough to be understood

LISTENING	I can ...
Higher	understand connections and differences between related ideas in quite complex listening texts when answering multiple-choice questions accurately usually understand what is implied but not actually said
⬆ Middle	understand some connections and differences between related ideas in listening texts when answering multiple-choice questions understand some of what is implied but not actually said
⬆ Lower	understand a few connections and differences between related ideas in straightforward listening texts when answering multiple-choice questions with a little success answer some straightforward questions about literal meanings

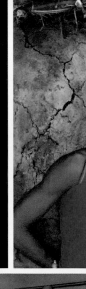

The big picture

Fashion is all around us: from the street to magazines to what everyone around us is wearing. In this chapter you will consider the importance of clothing, what is meant by 'fashion', how it expresses who we are and the rich, beautiful, cultural differences that make fashion what it is.

Thinking big

1 Look carefully at the photographs and pick the two that interest you most. What questions would you like to ask about each? Make notes on each one, using these questions as prompts.

a) Which time periods is the pictures from?

b) Can you identify the people in the picture?

c) Can you identify the country or culture represented in the picture?

d) Why does the picture interest you?

2 Consider the following and then write about:

● an item of clothing, shoes or jewellery that is special or lucky for you

● how your style of dress reflects your culture.

3 Now read the following quotes. Explain to your partner what you find interesting or thought-provoking about them. What do you learn about each speaker from their words?

❝I did not have three thousand pairs of shoes. I had one thousand and sixty.❞ *Imelda Marcos*

❝A fashion is merely a form of ugliness so unbearable that we are compelled to alter it every six months.❞ *Oscar Wilde*

❝I don't do fashion, I am fashion.❞ *Coco Chanel*

❝They think him the best-dressed man, whose dress is so fit for his use that you cannot notice or remember to describe it.❞ *Ralph Waldo Emerson*

❝I don't design clothes. I design dreams.❞ *Ralph Lauren*

❝Fashion is what you adopt when you don't know who you are.❞ *Quentin Crisp*

Chapter 10

Fashion

Reading skills in focus (R1 and R2)

In this section you will learn to:
- find facts and details from maps, diagrams and timelines
- understand and use maps, diagrams and timelines.

Getting started

1 Fashion can be a great outlet for creativity and artistic expression, but the desire to be 'in fashion' can also have negative effects. Think about the following points and note down your thoughts:
- How fashion moves across countries and cultures.
- Ways people use natural products such as silk, and where they come from.
- Puts pressure on people to spend money and change the way they look.

Exploring the skills

Reading information that is presented in different forms is a key skill for understanding complex texts. Processes may be described using diagrams, maps flow charts or timelines. To find detailed information in such a text:
- Read the questions first to ensure that you know what you are looking for.
- Read for detail. Look at the text and understand how it fits with the diagram.
- Look for labels, arrows, small print or shaded parts that explain the diagram.
- Notice dates and arrows in a timeline. See how they relate to one another.
- Look for the 'key' on a map. It might colour code countries, cities, seas, etc.

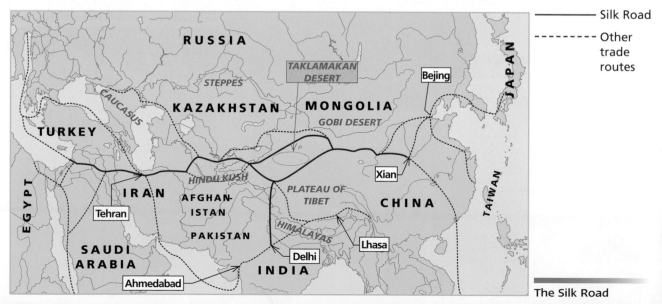

The Silk Road

2 The Silk Road was a major trading link across countries in Asia and the Middle East. Look at the map on page 190 and answer the questions using the tips above it.

a) In which Chinese city does the Silk Road begin?

b) Name two large deserts that the Silk Road touches.

c) Name two Indian cities along the trade route between Lhasa and Tehran.

d) Which countries would you cross if you passed through the cities of Lhasa and Tehran?

Language booster

3 Silk is one of the most valuable and luxurious fashion fabrics in the world. Match the following key words from the text 'How Silk is Made' to their correct meanings.

larvae	a fine, thread-like structure of a fabric or a metal.
cocoon	kept whole without breaking
chrysalis	the silky envelope spun by the worm while it is maturing.
emerge	the immature feeding stage of an insect in the process of its growth.
intact	the hard-shelled case of a moth or butterfly larvae
filament	to come out of a closed space

4 Read the text and diagram below to answer the questions on page 192.

How Silk is Made

The tiny silkworm is the caterpillar of the silk moth. Its life begins as an egg laid by the adult moth. Larvae (caterpillars) emerge from the eggs and are then known as silkworms. They survive by eating the leaves of the mulberry tree.

To become a moth, the silkworm spins a protective cocoon around itself so it can safely transform into a chrysalis. The chrysalis then breaks through the cocoon and emerges as a moth.

Once the silkworm has spun its cocoon, the chrysalis inside is destroyed by plunging it in hot water before it can break out of the cocoon. This is to ensure that the valuable silk filament remains intact. To make one yard of silk material, approximately 3000 cocoons are used.

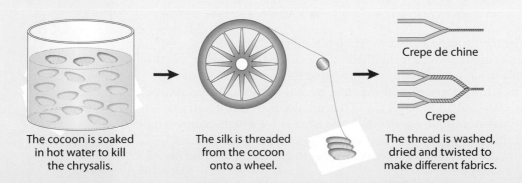

The cocoon is soaked in hot water to kill the chrysalis.

The silk is threaded from the cocoon onto a wheel.

Crepe de chine

Crepe

The thread is washed, dried and twisted to make different fabrics.

a) What does the caterpillar eat?

b) What comes out of the eggs laid by the moth?

c) Why does the silkworm weave a cocoon around itself?

d) What would naturally happen to the cocoon of the silkworm?

e) What is different about cocoons raised for silk?

f) Looking at the diagram, explain the purpose of the wheel in silk making.

g) Why are the cocoons soaked in hot water?

h) Summarise in 50 words the process of silk making from the diagram.
   Use your own words as far as possible.

Developing the skills

Sometimes writers find it useful to use timelines to clarify what they actually mean and you will need to be able to read and understand them.

5 Read the text below and answer the questions that follow.

The Story of Silk

According to Chinese legend, Lady Hsi-Ling-Shih is the Goddess of Silk. She was the wife of the mythical Yellow Emperor, who is said to have ruled China in about 3000 BC. She is credited with introducing silkworm **rearing** and inventing the **loom**. Another folk story says that a Chinese princess discovered silk when a silkworm in its cocoon accidentally fell into her hot cup of tea, loosening an amazing strand of silk.

Half a silkworm cocoon unearthed in 1927 near the Yellow River in Shanxi Province, northern China, has been dated to between 2600 and 2300 BC. More recent **archaeological** finds include a small ivory cup carved with a silkworm design. It is thought to be between 6000 and 7000 years old.

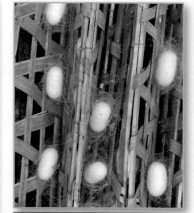

Silkworm cocoons

The stability of the Silk Road popularises the caravan trades

- 3000 BC Silk first produced in China
- 900 BC Spread of mounted nomadism – people moving from place to place.
- 753 BC Rome founded.
- 500s BC Chinese adopt nomadic style, wear trousers and ride horses.
- 1 AD Silk first seen in Rome

Although Chinese royalty prized silk making, its methods were kept highly secret for hundreds of years. Death by torture was the punishment for anyone who revealed the secret of silk-making. The Chinese made a fortune from trading silk for precious stones, sandalwood and metals along the Silk Route. It is believed that traders would pay up to 600 grams of gold for a high-quality length of silk. Eventually travellers and traders from other countries smuggled out silkworm eggs in order to create silk in other places.

Adapted from
www.silk-road.com/artl/silkhistory and www.madehow.com/Volume-2/Silk

a) How did the Chinese princess accidentally discover silk?

b) According to legend, what is the name of the person who invented the loom?

c) What evidence was unearthed in 1927?

d) What was the punishment for revealing the secret of silk?

e) Why do you think the Chinese wished to keep the secret of silk to themselves?

f) How much were traders willing to pay for a high-quality length of silk?

Going further

When you are faced with complex texts that include diagrams, maps and dates, it can be useful to simplify them, in your own words, to understand them better. This is will be a helpful study technique for all your subjects.

6) Look at the information you have gathered on silk and the Silk Road. As a class, create a colourful poster for younger students which:

- explains how silk is made
- answers frequently asked questions (FAQs) about silk
- uses the map on page 190 to trace and tell the story of one bale (large bundle) of silk along the Silk Road.

Do your own research to extend what you already know about silk. Present information in a variety of ways, including diagrams and maps, and use your own words.

Top tip

Note that you will be using the **present tense** when you are talking about the process of silk making. However, you will be using the **past tense** to talk about historical events in the past, such as the silk trade in ancient times.

In this section you will learn to:
- use a range of appropriate vocabulary in your writing
- use comparatives and superlatives correctly
- use formal and informal vocabulary appropriately.

Getting started

1 Look at photos of fashion in the past or in different parts of the world. Match the vocabulary below with the relevant photo.

a) bell-bottom trousers   e) salwar kameez

b) crinoline skirt   f) sari

c) drain-pipe trousers   g) leotard

d) bandana   h) cowboy boots

Exploring the skills

Building a wide and varied vocabulary is the key to sounding like an expert. Specialists show their understanding of their particular field by using the key vocabulary for that area. In Chapter 4 you studied vocabulary linked to education. In the same way, fashion writers use a range of verbs, adverbs and adjectives to describe clothing in great detail.

When you come across new vocabulary, try the following:
- Guess what the word means from its **context** – the words around it.
- Identify the form of the word – is it a noun, verb, adjective or adverb?
- Look for picture clues that might tell you what the word means.

- See if you can make sense of what the word might mean from its description. For example, *cut-off jeans* and *hipster trousers* both have clues that might help you guess their meaning.

- Look out for **metaphors** or **similes** used to describe fashion. For example: *The* **cup-cake** *bridesmaid dress is strictly out of fashion. The skirt tends to stick out* **like an upside-down plastic flower**.

(2) Quickly gather some useful vocabulary for today's fashion – clothes, hairstyles, shoes.

(3) Now let's look at a fashion blog, by Xiaohan Shen, at www.xssatstreetfashion.com.

As you read, note down specific nouns and verbs related to fashion and style.

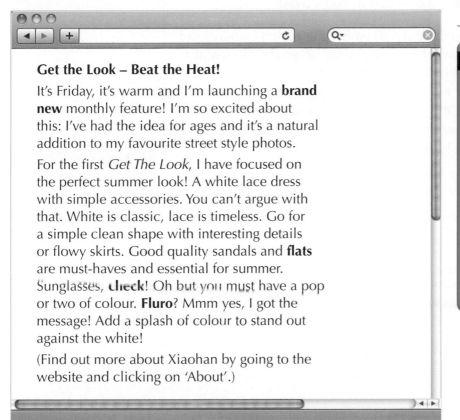
From www.xssatstreetfashion.com/category/get-the-look

(4) The blogger uses key adjectives, too, such as *perfect*. What do *simple*, *timeless*, and *classic* mean in the context of fashion? Write a brief explanation for each.

Language booster

Now, consider these other aspects of the blogger's **style**.
- Written in the present tense: *I have the perfect summer look*, to express the immediate, 'here and now' feel of the blog, which contains current views and news.
- Uses **imperative verbs** to give advice: *Go for...*, *Add a ....*
- Has a light, casual tone and uses informal vocabulary: *Sunglasses, check!*

Language booster

A **metaphor** is an imaginative way of describing one thing as another, e.g. *Sheets of rain poured down the windowpanes. Armies of dark clouds gathered menacingly on the horizon, promising more rain.*
A **simile** is a comparison in which a person or thing is described as being similar to another. Similes normally use the words 'like' or 'as, e.g. *His teeth are as white as pearls. The two sisters fight like cat and dog.*

Glossary

brand new – a completely new idea or feature
flats – flat shoes without a raised heel
check – another word for a tick mark that says you have already got it
fluro – abbreviation of 'fluorescent': a particular set of colours that pick up and reflect light; for example, highlighter pens come in fluorescent colours

Developing the skills

You can compare ideas or thoughts within a text by using different types of adjectives.

The **comparative** is the form of an adjective that expresses *more* or *less*. This is often formed by adding '-er' to the adjective: *short – short<u>er</u>*. For example: *In the 1970s, jeans were much <u>wider</u> from knee to ankle.* However, there are some irregular exceptions to this: *good – better; bad – worse*.

The **superlative** is the form of the adjective that expresses *most*. This is often formed by adding '-est' to the adjective: *short – short<u>est</u>*, but there are some irregular exceptions: *good – best* or *bad – worst*.

5 Now write a short blog of about 150 words comparing clothing and fashion in the past with what is popular today in your region. Make sure you include at least two of the following:

- dates and preferably a photo to illustrate your points
- what was popular at the time in clothes and hairstyles
- reasons why these were popular and who led fashion at that time
- how all of the above have changed today.

Make sure your blog has the same friendly tone as the one on page 195 and uses vocabulary appropriate for fashion. You could begin:

   *'**Check out** this must-have outfit...'*

> ### Glossary
> **check out** (informal) – look at

Language booster

You will be using the **past tense** to describe clothing and fashion in the past. For example:

Bell-bottom trousers <u>were</u> popular between the late 1960s to the 1970s. These <u>were</u> trousers that <u>flared</u> out from the knee to the ankle.

And the present tense to describe the fashions of today.

For example:

Nowadays, people <u>prefer</u> a narrower trouser leg for jeans or trousers. Funkier gathered or loose trousers inspired by Asian and African cultures <u>are</u> also popular.

Going further

It is important to choose words that give your writing the right tone. This will depend on why you are writing and for whom. A formal piece of writing demands formal vocabulary. So, although you may want to say, *white socks are really uncool these days*, you would write: *white socks are no longer considered fashionable, except for sport.*

6 Below are some examples of informal language used in blogs or in spoken language. Copy the table and fill in the gaps for both formal and informal language.

Informal/spoken/blog language	Formal language for a serious context
Check out...	Look carefully at...
	Dresses will be less structured and shoulder pads are softer and less pronounced.
	Denim jackets are an extremely popular fashion item this year.
Get yourself some flats asap!	
Get the new look!	
	Accessorising a plain outfit is often the most economical way to make it new again.
Silk shirts to die for!	
An outfit that works for day and evening; office to club, just like that!	

7 Read the situation below and then write the letter.

Until now your school/workplace has had a flexible, casual dress code. However, the new principal/boss has decided that neither staff nor students are allowed to wear denim in any form, at any time. You think that this is unfair as well as inconvenient.

Write a polite letter to the principal/boss in which you:

- explain the benefits of wearing denim, for example: *jeans match with everything, wash easily and last a long time*
- give evidence of how denim is popular worldwide, for example: *Surely you have noticed that denim is now accepted as a sensible and smart option around the world. Even Barrack Obama has been photographed wearing denim*
- persuade your reader that more extreme denim fashions may be frowned on, for example: *ripped jeans will not be worn.*

> **Top tip**
> You are writing a formal letter to the management of your organisation. Keep your language formal and accurate.

In this section you will learn to:
● use exactly the right words when speaking about culture and clothing
● use more specialised vocabulary appropriately.

Getting started

1 Culture can be defined as the combination of language, art, food, literature, clothing, music and ideas that are special to a particular part of the world. Fashion is therefore one part of culture.

In pairs, think about the following questions about what people wear and note down ideas or information that is new to you.

● What styles of hair or clothing do people in your area follow?
● What fashion trends are followed in your part of the world?
● What is the historical origin of the fashions that are worn on the street today?
● What colours of clothing are significant to particular occasions? For example, black is worn to funerals in some parts of the world while white is worn in others. Some brides wear white to their wedding while others wear red or vibrant colours.

Exploring the skills

To talk knowledgeably about clothes and culture and to discuss them, it is important to learn the general vocabulary around fashion as well as the specific vocabulary you need to make your point.

2 In pairs, consider the following culture- or country-specific words to do with clothing and match them with the relevant photo:

a) sarong
b) jodhpurs
c) kimono
d) beret
e) kilt

(3) Vocabulary can also be categorised into groups of similar words. Look at the lists of words below related to culture and clothing.

Head-dress: turbans, crowns, tiaras, feathered hats, bowler hats, peaked hats, helmets, fur-lined hood, beret, bonnets, headscarves, veils

Styles of clothing: flared, tapered, gathered, baggy, fitted, high-waisted, low-slung, hipster, full-skirted, tight-fitting. loose-fitting

In groups of three, choose a set of words each to play Pictionary with. Take turns to make a sketch of a fashion item from the list above while others guess which one it might be. The time-limit for each sketch is 30 seconds. If you are unsure of meanings, check using a dictionary.

(4) Add your own words to the categories above and explain them to each other. Are some of these special to your own or another culture? Sketch the different styles of clothing, head-dress or decoration of clothing in your notebook.

Developing the skills

To talk effectively about cultural influences on clothing, you will need to develop your knowledge of some specific and detailed vocabulary.

(5) Read the text below which explains some reasons for wearing different types of clothing. Discuss it with your partner.

Clothing is so much more than just a covering for our bodies or protection from the environment. Clothing represents who we are, what we believe and even how we worship. Some cultures and civilisations define themselves through their clothing.

Of course, choices of clothing are also based on factors like gender, climate and geographical location. As we know from old paintings and photographs, clothing is constantly changing over time to reflect the needs of our lifestyles. Clothing is also worn for more complex reasons, for example, to show membership of a group like a basketball team. Some types of clothing are worn only at special ceremonies, like a graduation cap and gown or a wedding dress. Some clothing is worn to indicate emotions, such as joy or sorrow. Different cultures believe different colours are appropriate for mourning.

Some cultures have distinctive clothing that is associated with them. Silk kimonos are Japanese, saris are Indian and kilts are associated with the Scots. Fashion and traditional clothing can help us understand the people who wear them, as well as their cultural beliefs and values.

Different clothes for different folks

6 Work in groups to prepare notes for a short talk for your class on describing a specific type of clothing in your region or culture.

- Name and describe the item.
- How is this particular type of clothing different by gender: male/female?
- Explain the origin of this form of clothing: religious, cultural, climate, environment, group membership or ceremonial.

7 Now identify any gaps in this information and agree together on how you will gain information to fill these. For example, each of you could take responsibility for one type of clothing. Remember first-hand sources around you might be more reliable than internet searches. Think about teachers, parents, support staff, grandparents, family members that you could ask.

8 As a group, prepare to give the talk to the rest of your class, making sure you divide up the speaking equally. This will need planning and co-operation. You could bring in items of clothing or pictures to illustrate your presentation.

9 Bring a culturally rich piece of clothing along to your next lesson for a show-and-tell. For example, you could bring a robe, special piece of headwear, piece of jewellery, scarf or shoes. If it is too difficult to obtain this item of clothing, find a picture that would allow you to talk about it effectively. As you describe it, make sure you use accurate, authentic vocabulary. Be prepared to answer questions from the class and to ask questions about other people's items.

> ## Top tip
>
> The 'W' questions (What, When, Who, Where, Why) and 'How' are useful when framing questions. Remind yourself of the areas you have to cover and make sure you have a question organised for each one. Use ideas from the reading extract to help you with questions on page 199.

Going further

Using vocabulary accurately and sensitively to communicate your ideas effectively is a key skill. The wider your vocabulary, the better you will be able to explain exactly what you mean.

10 In pairs, find a magazine, newspaper or internet page which shows what people wear for sporting activities in your country or region. Use your now extensive fashion vocabulary to note down a brief description of the clothes that are used for these sporting activities. Consider some of the following:

- What traditions are being followed in certain sports? For example: white for tennis and cricket; coloured football shirts; patches; name labels.

- How do the physical requirements of the sport influence what is worn? For example: track pants; loose robes in martial arts.

- Are colours and categories meaningful in this sport? For example: black belt versus brown belt or yellow belt in karate.

- To what extent do people see these clothes as 'fashion'?

11 In pairs, use the material you have collected about sportswear to host a joint radio programme called 'Teen Talk' for teenagers in your part of the world. In your programme, aim to do the following:

- Describe the traditional clothing around certain sports, activities or martial arts.

- Explain why it has developed as it has.

- Discuss how sports fashions influence adult or teenage fashion today.

- Suggest ways in which teenagers could be fashionable and sporty at the same time.

Listening skills in focus (L1, L2 and L4)

In this section you will learn to:
- listen effectively to fellow students
- understand and select detailed information supplied by fellow students
- understand what is implied but not stated in a conversation.

Getting started

1 Although fashion is by and large a popular and rich aspect of our culture, the modern fashion industry can sometimes exploit both people and animals in its search for luxury and low-cost products.

In pairs or threes, discuss what you know and what you think about **one** of the following issues related to the fashion industry:

- the use of the furs/leathers of endangered species as a fashion accessory
- workers/tailors/embroiderers/craftsmen being paid an unfair wage relative to the profits made by big fashion companies.

Now make a note of some questions for a group to answer on the other topic. They will do the same for you. Try to answer their questions and highlight any points that you will need to research as a group.

Exploring the skills

In the last task you had to listen carefully to what your fellow students were saying. You used this information to help you learn more and see where there were gaps in your knowledge. Together, you had to write some notes.

To do this, you needed to:
- listen attentively
- ask questions – to make them explain things in more detail when you were unsure – and listen carefully to the questions they asked you
- make use of as wide a vocabulary as possible.

Did you have to use any other skills?

2 Now you will work together on a listening task. You are going to hear a news story about an animal-rights group, *Animal Friends*, speaking out against the fur trade.

Answer these multiple-choice questions. Choose the ending which best completes each sentence:

i) Animal Friends believes that fur traders only care about:

    A the low population numbers of the animals

    B the quality of the animal's fur

    C the health and welfare of the animals

ii) What does the spokesperson think Animal Friends activists should be doing?

    A stay inside their cages

    B come and help him sell fur coats

    C help the authorities to improve animal conditions

iii) Why does the spokesperson think the fur trade will continue?

    A because animals will not become extinct

    B because no-one wants to look after the animals

    C because so many people want to buy clothes made out of fur

iv) Which word best sums up the spokesperson's attitude to fur farms:

    A cruel

    B realistic

    C angry

3 Now listen to the news story and answer the questions below.

a) What did the activists do to attract attention?

b) What were they protesting against?

c) What does the first protester say he was shocked to see when he went into the fur farms? Give two details.

4 Before listening to the news story for a second time, check your answers to the multiple-choice questions i) to iv) and questions a) to c).

In pairs, discuss your answers.

Now listen again.

Developing the skills

You are now going to work together again. Divide into two groups.

Group A reads numbers 1 to 4 of the *Fast Facts About Fur*.

Group B reads 5 to 8.

Discuss the meaning of the words in bold and be ready to summarise your information in your own words.

Fast Facts About Fur

1. More than 50 million animals are killed and slaughtered each year so that their **pelts** can be used in fashion.

2. Methods used to kill animals for their fur include gassing and **electrocution**. In the wild, fur-bearing animals are also caught and killed in traps.

3. The fashion industry now has the technology to create **alternatives** to real fur. Nylon or other synthetic options can easily be produced.

4. Fur seriously endangers **fragile animal populations** like racoons, foxes and otters. Continuing with this killing will upset the environmental balance and **disrupt** the food chain.

— Group A

5. Fur 'farms' or '**ranches**' have been around for thousands of years. Humans have always needed fur to keep themselves warm. They ate the meat of these animals and used their fur to keep warm and survive.

6. The fur trade was a **key contributor to the North American Economy** and is still necessary for the survival of local communities, for example in Canada and Siberia.

— Group B

7. People eat meat and wear leather shoes and have leather bags. What is so different about fur?

8. In some countries animals like rabbits can be a **pest**. Killing them for meat or fur is a useful way of keeping the **environmental balance**.

5 Now work in pairs, one person from Group A and one person from Group B, and give a summary of your Fur Facts.

Good listeners understand what other people may imply but not actually say. This is probably most important when you are listening to people who have different points of view.

You need to pay attention to the tone they use, their body language and, above all, to their language and their choice of words.

6 You are going to listen to two students talking about sweatshops and what they can do to prevent companies taking advantage of people who are desperately in need of a job. 'Sweatshop' is a slang (very informal) word that has been made up to describe factories where workers (often women and children) experience difficult working conditions, unfair wages and have no medical care. They often do not have unions or ways of voicing their opinions.

Take a look at the questions before listening to the recording.

First read questions a) to d).

a) Why is Celine glad to stop and have a coffee?

b) Name two things that Celine has bought.

c) How does Celine feel about her shopping?

d) How does Celine feel about the amount of money she has spent?

Now listen to the recording.

Discuss your answers in pairs.

Listen to the recording again. Which questions made you use clues to understand what is implied (meant but not actually said)?

Now read the rest of the questions.

e) What is Barry annoyed by first of all?

f) What really shocks him even more?

g) How much might some sweatshop workers get paid per day?

h) What is the key phrase used to describe a certain group of customers, for example, a particular age group?

i) Why does Celine think they should be careful when writing to companies?

j) What is Celine's idea to get more public support against sweatshops?

k) How does Celine feel about the campaign that she and Barry will start?

Now listen to the whole conversation and answer questions e) to k).

Check your answers. Put a star by the ones where you had to understand what was implied but not actually said.

Listen to the whole conversation a second time.

Check your answers.

The big task

You are going to organise a unique fashion show. You will present clothes that represent your very own style and your opinions on fashion.

1 First, read this flyer and summarise the main points quickly for your classmates.

Welcome to:

'Be Yourself' – a fashion show with a difference!

'Be Yourself' is organised by a group of teenagers interested in culture, art and design. We are aspiring designers, graphic artists and fashion enthusiasts who would like to see a forum for their work and that of their peer group. We want to give young people the chance to show just who they are, how they feel and the things that express their creative talent in marvellous fusion of fashion, culture and teen couture.

Being a 'fashion show with a difference', we would like you to be careful to steer away from the following negative fashion issues – fashions that:

◆ promote the 'cult of skinniness' either through choice of models or styles: we are looking for healthy teenagers of all shapes and sizes and the aim is to look and feel good

◆ use animal fur or fur trim in any form

◆ promote the products or use of sweatshop brands.

(N.B. Any entries that have or promote these will not make it to the final competition.)

So, what is likely to impress judges? Here are some examples that have impressed our judges in the past:

◆ innovative designs that fuse cultural concepts with modern, practical twists

◆ colours and textures that are thrown together in new and exciting ways

◆ designs and styles for all body types between 14 and 21 (feel free to enter different designs for different age groups)

◆ designs that promote fair employment and fair trade for all producers

◆ green designs that use natural and biodegradable fabrics and materials

◆ designs that have an international, multi-cultural feel.

2 Now that the formalities are over, here's what you need to do to get cracking on your own fashion show.

● Get your design team together – four designers are ideal for four to six design ideas. Sign up as above.

● Draw or sketch your fashions or put them together for real.

● Write your own commentary/voiceover for the show, describing and explaining your design/fashion item. Each entry must include the following:
  – a descriptive statement about the outfit
  – an explanation of what inspired it
  – why it is innovative/versatile/practical.

Check your progress

Here are the Reading, Writing, Speaking and Listening skills you learnt about in Chapter 10.

Use this table to decide how good you are at the different skills, and make a note of what you need to be able to do in order to move up a level.

READING I can …		WRITING I can …	
Higher	consistently and accurately locate facts and details in complex texts containing graphics understand and use a wide range of graphics accurately	**Higher**	make effective use of a good range of vocabulary, including comparatives and superlatives, in my writing consistently use formal or informal vocabulary appropriately according to reader and purpose
⬆ **Middle**	sometimes find facts and details in a range of texts containing graphics understand and use different kinds of graphics	⬆ **Middle**	use a fair range of vocabulary, including comparatives and superlatives, in my writing distinguish formal and informal vocabulary and attempt to choose the right word according to reader and situation
⬆ **Lower**	find a few facts and details in straightforward texts containing basic graphics understand a few basic kinds of graphics	⬆ **Lower**	use a limited vocabulary, including basic comparatives and superlatives, in my writing use informed vocabulary, but do not adapt my choice of words according to reader and purpose

SPEAKING I can …		LISTENING I can …	
Higher	use a good range of specialist vocabulary accurately and confidently when speaking	**Higher**	consistently listen thoughtfully to other students and can understand and select information accurately from what they say usually understand what is implied but not actually said in a conversation
⬆ **Middle**	use some specialist vocabulary correctly when speaking	⬆ **Middle**	listen to other students attentively, so that I can understand and select information from what they say understand some of what is implied but not actually said in a conversation
⬆ **Lower**	use a basic range of vocabulary when speaking	⬆ **Lower**	listen to other students politely, so that I understand and pick out a few details correctly from what they say understand what is said during straightforward conversations

The big picture

In this chapter you will:

- think about what you do to amuse yourself.

- hear about, read about and write about all your favourite pastimes!

- consider other people's pastimes.

Thinking big

1 In pairs, look at the photographs and discuss them.

- What forms of entertainment do they show?

- Create a list of all the forms of entertainment you can think of.

- Which forms of entertainment are the most expensive?

- Which forms of entertainment are the most popular in your country?

2 In pairs, explain your usual forms of entertainment. Give details of:

- what you like to do

- when you do it

- why you like it.

3 Draw a pie chart to show your own work/play life balance. It should look something like this.

30% play
music practice
football practice
70% school

4 In groups, discuss whether you agree with this quote when you think about your work/play life balance.

> *Anyone who tries to make a distinction between education and entertainment doesn't know the first thing about either.*

Marshal McLuhan, **Educator, Writer and Social Reformer, 1911–1980**

Chapter **11**

Entertainment

In this section you will learn to:
- understand and select relevant information
- identify points for and against a point of view in a text
- recognise a point of view when it is implied and not stated.

Getting started

The way we buy and listen to music is changing quickly. Thinking and reading about what this might mean for musicians and the music industry is going to be your focus. In pairs, discuss what types of music you enjoy listening to yourself. Do you play an instrument?

Exploring the skills

Articles for magazines and newspapers often try to build a **balanced argument** by giving both **reasons for and against** an issue. When you are reading it is useful to be able to:

- identify the reasons given
- decide if they are for or against an issue
- decide yourself whether the reasons given are valid.

1. Although it is against the law, lots of people download music for free. In pairs, discuss the following questions. Find out where you agree and disagree with each other.
   - How do you usually get your music?
   - How much is a CD in your country? How much does it cost to download a CD? Are either of the prices 'too expensive'?

2. You are going to read a newspaper article about downloading music without paying. Before you read, with your partner, brainstorm and then copy and complete the table below with all the reasons you can think of:
   - **for** downloading and sharing music without paying
   - **against** downloading and sharing music without paying.

For	Against
People can copy CDs quickly and easily	Denying songwriters and musicians money for their work

3 Read the article and answer the questions.
- Which paragraph introduces the discussion, which argues for and which against?
- Write down the main idea (the main reason for or against) of each paragraph.
- Add the reasons for and against to the table you created in task 2.

To download or not to download?

Downloading music from the internet is a popular way of buying and accessing music. Consumers armed with their mp3 players or phones or computers can copy CDs at the click of a mouse button. But every time you copy a CD you deny the musician any money for his or her work. Hence downloading and filesharing is a contentious issue.

The most serious drawback is that downloading music without paying is illegal. Music is covered by copyright law: the musician who writes and/or plays the music owns it. This means that every time the music is played or sold, the musician or band has the right to a small payment. It is widely maintained, therefore, that taking music without permission is a criminal act that is the equivalent of stealing.

In contrast, those arguing in favour of downloading and sharing music state that many young independent bands are in favour of filesharing. Such bands think filesharing enables more people to listen to their music, and allows them to build up a wider and bigger fan base. For many new bands, punishing their fans is the last thing they want to do.

Developing the skills

There are some signals that a writer is giving you a reason to support or oppose an argument. Often they will use phrases which structure the reasons. For example:

Reasons supporting	Reasons opposing/against
On the one hand	In contrast
Moreover	However
Furthermore	On the other hand
Firstly, secondly	
Since	
In view of the fact that	

4 You are going to read a newspaper article which discusses whether classical music is still relevant to young people today. Before reading, in pairs:
- Discuss and choose the best two synonyms for 'relevant'.
  - meaningful
  - useful
  - significant
  - important
  - practical
  - popular.
- Discuss your experience of classical music. Talk about opportunities to:
  - take part in an orchestra or choir at school
  - listen to classical music.

5 Read the article below. Identify the paragraphs (labelled A to G) which give reasons for and against. Complete the diagram with the reasons.

A Many people believe that classical music is not relevant to young people today. However, this issue frequently generates heated debate.

B On the one hand, many people say that classical music is associated only with small numbers of people from privileged backgrounds and older people. For instance, if you look at the audience at a classical concert, the majority is over the age of fifty.

C In contrast, others say it is more popular than we first imagine. Many young people listen to classical music without realising. It is often used in films and advertisements. For example, a famous piece of classical music was used as the theme music for the 1990 Fifa World Cup. Not many people could have given its name – 'Nessun Dorma' – but millions recognised it and, more importantly, enjoyed it.

D Also, some people point out that young people reinvent classical ideas to produce new music: for instance, it is said that rap music was first invented by a classical composer, Schoenberg, in 1912, but it is now used by young people in pop music.

E However, young people point to the fact that classical music has been outstripped by technology. To play a classical instrument, such as a violin or cello, you need to study hard and practise for hours. Nowadays, you do not need to get aching arms and blisters on your fingers from practising. A teenager can write and produce a professional-sounding track using a computer program in the comfort of their own bedroom.

F A final point to bear in mind is that the term 'classical music' is used to refer to a dazzling variety of music, from jazz to pieces for large orchestras. This makes it even more difficult to say whether classical music is relevant to young people.

G So, it may be only a minority of young people who play classical instruments, but when it comes to enjoying classical music – well, it depends on the piece of music. It may be more relevant to young people in the modern world than they realise!

Reasons against

Associated with privileged backgrounds and old people classical music is still relevant to young people today

Reasons for

More popular than realise

IS CLASSICAL MUSIC RELEVANT TO YOUNG PEOPLE?

6 In pairs, copy three reasons from task 2 – it doesn't matter whether they are for or against – into the table and complete with the supporting evidence.

Reason	Supporting evidence
More popular than people realise	Classical music is often used in films and advertisements – used as the theme music to the World Cup in 1990

7 In pairs, discuss:
- if you think the article gives a 'balanced' view
- which of the reasons given were the most persuasive for you and why.

Going further

We often need to be able to work out someone's opinion even when they do not state it. For example:

The band strutted on stage but only managed to sing three songs.

Poor opinion: the word *only* implies that three songs is not enough.

Here is another example:

The band strutted on stage and wowed the audience from the first minute with the stunning power of their guitar playing.

Good opinion: the words *wowed* and *stunning* are strong positive words.

8 Read this series of texts from friends about a karaoke evening.

What is the opinion of each friend about the following?
- the singing
- the venue
- the food
- overall

Hi. Last night's karaoke evening. What did you think?

Had such a laugh. Nearly died laughing trying to sing Fantasy.

But I didn't get a go!

How come?

Not sure. None of my favourites on playlist. But still enjoyed it!

What did you think of the venue?

Too many people chatting. It put me off performing.

Yes, but then everyone was dancing.

Yes. I could have danced till dawn.

And food?

Yum! Verdict?

Ten out of ten! When can we go again?

Writing skills in focus (W5)

In this section you will learn to:
- punctuate speech correctly
- use a wide range of punctuation correctly and effectively.

Getting started

1 On your own look at the photographs on this page. As a class, brainstorm and create a list of all the different types of reading texts you know.

2 In pairs, discuss the following questions. Listen carefully to what your partner says and make notes.
- When do you read?
- Where do you read?
- What do you read the most frequently?
- What do you like reading?

3 In groups of four, share what you have found out about your partner's reading habits.

Exploring the skills

Quotation marks are used to show the exact words that people say.

- You put the quotation marks around the words that someone says. For example:

  "I prefer non-fiction," said Lara.

- When the spoken words come first, put a comma or question mark **inside** the speech marks after the last word spoken. For example:

  "What happened?" she asked.

- When the spoken words come last, put a comma before the first quotation mark.

- The speaker's first word uses a capital letter. For example:

  The sorceror proclaimed, "Let the magic begin!"

- When a new person starts speaking, start a new line.

I prefer graphic novels.

4 Write out these sentences, inserting quotation marks where necessary.

  a) This book really inspires me said Hassan.

  b) My best friend asked why don't you read this book?

  c) Amina maintained books are better than television any day.

  d) I cried at the ending because I found it so sad admitted my brother.

  e) Bao Zhi added the suspense nearly killed me I couldn't put the book down.

5 You are going to write a short story about the world's most successful spy. Imagine the spy goes into an underground car park of an abandoned office block to meet the leader of a criminal gang. Describe what happens, writing two sentences about each of the following:

  ● what the gang members look like
  ● what the gang leader says to the spy (using direct speech)
  ● what the gang members say to each other (using reported speech)
  ● what the gang members decide to do with the spy (using direct speech)
  ● how the spy feels
  ● what the spy does next.

> **Language booster**
>
> What people actually say is called **direct speech**. You put what people say inside the quotation marks.
>
> When you tell what people said (for example, *Lara said that she prefers graphic novels*) this is called **reported speech**.

Developing the skills

Apostrophes are used to show that letters have been missed out (apostrophe for omission). For example:

> *We are reading a book.*
> *We're reading a book.*

The apostrophe is also used to show that something belongs to someone (apostrophe for possession).

Use *'s* for a singular owner. For example:

> *The girl's writing is neat.* (To show that the writing of one girl is neat.)

Use *s'* for plural owners. For example:

> *The girls' writing is neat.* (To show that the writing of all the girls is neat.)

6 Put the apostrophe in the correct places in the following sentences.

  a) Well write up our science experiment.

  b) Borrow Yousefs textbook to read all the punctuation rules.

  c) Mum says she cant take the book back to the library. Shes at work.

  d) The girls writing is very similar to her brothers.

  e) The boys bedrooms are very tidy. Theyve put all their clothes away.

7 Alex Rider is a boy who is the world's most successful international spy. Copy the passage below, which comes from the Alex Rider Series, where Alex discovers a dead man but is then kidnapped by a criminal gang. Insert quotation marks and apostrophes where necessary.

> And then there was a man standing in front of him. Alex looked up.
> Come with me the man said.
> What?
> The man opened his jacket, revealing a gun in a holster under his arm. You heard what I said.
> A second man had crept up behind him and dragged him to his feet. Both of them were in their thirties, clean-shaven with sunglasses. The man with the gun had spoken with an American accent.
> We have a car. We're going to walk you there. If you try anything, well shoot.
> Alex didnt doubt them. There was a seriousness about them, a sense that they knew exactly what they were doing. For a brief moment he considered a countermove. Right now, before it was too late, jabbing with an elbow then swinging round to kick out.
> But the first man had been expecting it. Suddenly Alexs arm was seized and twisted behind his back. Dont even think about it the man warned.
> Alex was bundled into the waiting car.
>
> Extract from *Scorpia Rising*, Walker Books

Going further

Mistakes in punctuation and spelling make your writing difficult to read. In examinations you may lose marks for incorrect punctuation and spelling. If you are aiming for a top-level grade, you also need to show that you can use a wide range of punctuation marks, from full stops and capital letters to colons, brackets and pairs of commas. You will need to show that you are using punctuation to help you express your ideas clearly.

The **colon** is used to introduce a list of items. For example:

I like the following types of entertainment: TV, film, music and board games.

Colons are also used to introduce people's words in a dialogue or interview. For example:

Reporter: What kind of things do you write?

Author: I usually write adventure or mystery stories.

Pairs of commas can be used to add more information to a sentence. The information between the commas is not essential, but adds more detail. For example:

Her father, who is retired, spends hours every day reading the newspapers.

Brackets (or **parentheses**) are also used to give extra information in a sentence. They set the information apart more strongly than commas do. For example:

The journalist wrote articles (often more than four a day) at an astonishing rate.

In this sentence the basic information is that the journalist wrote quickly. The fact that he wrote more than four articles a day is the extra information and is put in parentheses.

8 Rewrite the sentences below using colons, commas and full stops.

a) The following authors have won the Nobel Prize for literature Naguib Mahfouz, Doris Lessing and Orhan Pamuk

b) Literature covers a wide range of genres poetry drama novels and non-fiction

c) After writing the following need checking punctuation spelling and number of words

d) There are many types of fiction romance thriller science fiction horror historical fiction and the graphic novel

9 Write your own lists, introducing each list with a colon. Use full sentences.

a) Four recent books I have read   **c)** Games I play

b) Four recent films I have seen

10 Insert pairs of commas or parentheses around the extra information in the following sentences.

a) What is the value if any of studying literature?

b) The teacher told me in an excited voice that the *Theory of Code* was an excellent book.

c) The numbers of books available in schools, in libraries, on the internet is beyond counting.

11 As a class, create a list of recent reading. Then:

● Write a 100-word review of something you have read recently outside school. It can be long (e.g. a novel) or short (e.g. a football report).

● Add a comment at the bottom of your review. For example: The Hunger Games *by Suzanne Collins: "I was obsessed with this book," says Bassem.*

● Make a class display of all your recent reading.

12 Write a 250-word imaginary interview with your favourite writer.

● First, think about the type of books/texts your author writes.

● Decide what questions you want to ask. Use the key question words:

      What   When   How   Why   Where

● Imagine the answers your author gives.

● Write up the interview, using colons to show each speaker. For example: *Reporter: What inspired you to start writing?*

● Finally, check your work for:

      punctuation   spelling   number of words used

In this section you will learn to:
- disagree politely in a conversation
- keep a conversation going by rephrasing what the previous speaker has said.

Getting started

1 As a class, find out the most watched TV programmes in the class.
- First, make a list of five popular TV programmes in your country.
- Each person in the class should tick the programme they watch the most.
- Make a class bar chart showing the most popular TV programmes in the class, like the example below.

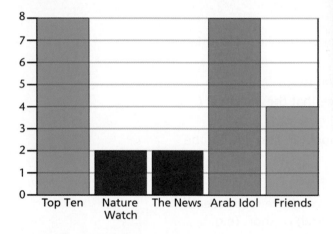

Exploring the skills

When disagreeing, try not to say 'no'. People will think you are impolite.
Try instead to use one of the many polite ways of disagreeing.

2 Read the list of phrases below which express disagreement. In pairs, sort them into either 'polite' or 'impolite'.
- I take your point, but that's not the way I see it.
- Perhaps, but I can't help thinking that …
- You must be joking!
- No thank you. I'd rather not.
- I see what you mean, but I'm not convinced that …
- That's rubbish.
- I'm not sure about that; however, what about …

3 Listen to the following short conversations. For each one:
- Write down the phrase used to disagree.
- Decide together whether you think the phrase is polite or not.
- Add any new phrases to your list from task 2.

(11.1)

4 It is 5 o'clock. On your own, read the TV programme listing on page 220. Scan the schedule quickly and decide what you would prefer to watch after you have done your homework this afternoon or this evening.

5 Scan the listings again. Identify:
- a news programme
- a dance programme
- a charts programme
- a film
- a soap opera
- a football highlights programme
- a chat show
- a documentary
- a natural history programme.

Developing the skills

Remember that when you want to disagree or introduce your own (different) idea, there are many phrases you can use to disagree politely. Refer to the list you created for tasks 2 and 3.

6 Imagine four young people who are flatmates and all like watching TV.
- In groups of four, take on the role of person A, B, C or D.
- Look at the TV listing on page 220 and decide what you would like to watch.
- Hold a polite conversation where you try to watch your chosen programme.

Person C

Age: 18
Interests: Current affairs
Notes: Prefers to catch up on the news on the internet

Person A

Age: 19
Interests: Sport
Notes: Going out at 7pm

Person B

Age: 21
Interests: Nature and wildlife
Notes: Comes in from work at 6.30pm

Person D

Age: 17
Sex: Male
Notes: Has band practice from 3–5pm

7 In groups of four, repeat task 6 but as yourselves. What would you like to watch when you come in from school?

8 In pairs, role-play a scene between a mother and young person disagreeing politely about watching television in the evenings. Arrive at a solution which works for both of you. You could use these prompts or develop your own ideas for the role-play.

Mother

Thinks child watches too much TV.
Would prefer child plays football/does homework/practises his/her instrument.

Child

Has homework to do.
Has Grade 5 piano exam next week.
Wants to watch 1 entertainment programme.
Must watch 1 TV programme for homework.

	Channel V	Gulf International	Nature watch	Sports	Movie 2	News daily	Pop TV
17:00	**Koffee with Karan:** this week costume designer and couturier, Manish Malhotra, in the chat show chair	**Cancer sell:** People and power goes undercover to investigate the bogus clinics offering cancer patients little but false hope	**Jellyfish Invasion:** it has no bones, blood or brains but the jellyfish has survived for millions of years. Now its numbers are exploding.	**Australian Open Tennis:** the first day live	**King Fu Panda 2:** animation's fiercely funny follow up to the original	**World Business Today:** looks at the breaking business news stories and financial headlines, with special report on China	Hong Kong's pop charts
18:00	**VCD:** the unique countdown show of all the biggest hits	**News:** live breaking and in-depth news from Asia, Africa, Europe and the Americas	**Mystery of the murdered saints:** for the first time the Catholic Church will allow scientific experts to test the veracity of the remains of reported saints	**English football:** highlights from the day's Chelsea v Man Utd match	**Swades (2004):** award-winning performance from Bollywood legend Shahrukh Khan	**Back story:** brings you the stories behind the stories you see on the news; the emotions and experiences of people involved in the news.	**10 on top:** this week's most texted and talked about young celebs
19:00	**The Bold and the Beautiful:** episode 1517: more from South Africa's longest-running soap	**Focus Asia:** this week the investigative news programme looks at the recent phenomenon of kidnapping	**How to build a beating heart:** scientists are beginning to harness the body's natural powers to grow skin, muscle, body parts and vital organs – even hearts	**Football managers:** five of the best managerial legends	**The Matrix (1999):** Seminal science fiction movie	**African Voices:** the Bard of Nigeria: Whether it's through music, dancing or his art, Nigerian Jimi Solanke has a story to tell.	**Music in the Gulf:** A look at how the music industry is flourishing in the Gulf
20:00	**Videoscope:** a look at the rise and fall of American Idol	**Khawater:** daily show for Ramadan with engaging host Ahmed Al Shuqeiry; today looking at how history of Science and Technology was born within the Islamic faith	**World's most dangerous shark:** our correspondent, Ilsa Ling, goes underwater to investigate how and when Great White sharks attack.	**Swimming World Champion–ships:** today the 100m freestyle	**The Great Magician (2011):** drama and mystery with Tony Leung Chiu-Wai and Zhou Xun	**Piers Morgan Tonight:** in-depth interview with the platinum-selling rapper 50 cent	**America's Best Dance Crew:** the five former champions return to perform

Going further

Remember, you can keep a conversation going by:

- Listening carefully and then asking questions to find out more.
  For example:

    English was my best class today.

    Oh really. What did you do?

- Agreeing and then giving your opinion. For example:

  I read a lot more non-fiction than fiction.

  Oh yes, we read a lot of non-fiction in school, for instance …

- Rephrasing (saying what the other person has said in similar words) to show you have understood. For example:

  <u>*I can't afford*</u> *to get satellite TV.*

  Mmm, yes, the monthly subscription is <u>very expensive</u>.

9 Listen to two people discussing what they saw on TV last night and answer these questions:
- What do their mothers want them to watch?
- What alternative phrases or **synonyms** are used to describe 'The Big Bang Theory'?

10 Listen again and answer the questions.
- What phrase does the boy use to mean the same as 'educational'?
- In the end, what programme does the girl want to watch and why?

11 Read this section from the listening passage. Identify any techniques used to maintain the conversation that are listed in 'Going further'.

> **Girl:** Do you watch 'The Big Bang Theory'? I do. It's so funny.
>
> **Boy:** Yes. I agree, it makes me laugh a lot, but it gets boring in the end because they are all repeats.
>
> **Girl:** True, the repeats are tedious. But I like to watch something light at the end of the day. So what do you watch?
>
> **Boy:** I tend to watch the sports highlights because I can watch it on the computer in my room – I just watch it when I want.
>
> **Girl:** Good point, although …

12 Discuss TV-watching habits with a partner. If they don't watch television then they can invent when, where and what they would like to watch.

Prepare for your conversation.
- Write down at least five questions you would like to ask.
- Write down two prompt phrases you can use to agree with your partner.
- Write down two prompt phrases you can use to disagree politely with your partner.
- Plan what you will say about your TV-watching habits.

Hold the conversation.

Maintain the conversation for at least five minutes. Both of you should try to use different techniques to keep the conversation going.

11.4 Film

Listening skills in focus (L2 and L3)

In this section you will learn to:

- understand and select facts in both formal and informal spoken texts
- recognise and understand opinions and attitudes in a more formal dialogue.

Getting started

1 On your own, think of a film. Take turns asking and answering other students in your class if they have also seen the film. If yes, ask them what they thought about it.

Exploring the skills

Most texts mix both fact and opinion. It is important to be able to tell facts from opinions so that you can decide for yourself whether you believe something or someone.

As you have learnt in earlier chapters:

- a fact is something you can prove to be true, whereas
- an opinion is what someone thinks or feels about a subject and cannot be proved.

2 Shahnaz and Swayam are deciding which film to see and where to eat afterwards. Listen to what they say. Identify the facts and opinions to complete the table below.

Fact	Opinion
At 7 o'clock there's Don 2	He makes a gorgeous villain

Developing the skills

You have just listened to a conversation between two friends and identified some facts and opinions. Now you are going to hear a more formal text. It is a talk about a serious subject – film-making in Nigeria. Here, you will have to listen a little more closely to identify some facts and opinions.

Match the words to their definitions.

Word	Definition
a) (on) location	**A:** record/make a film
b) prolific	**B:** a room where a film company makes films
c) (at an astonishing) rate	**C:** very fast
d) shoot a film	**D:** making a lot
e) (in a) studio	**E:** outside/in the real world

3 Listen to the talk about Nollywood, Nigeria's Hollywood. Write down any facts you hear and how you could prove each one. Watch out – you should not write down opinions. **11.4**

Nollywood fact bank	How can I prove this?
second largest film industry in the world	find out how many films made in Nollywood, Hollywood and Bollywood and compare

4 Now listen again. How does the speaker describe Nollywood?

Listen carefully. Copy the sentences and fill in the gaps with the correct information (the gaps are often more than one word). Which of the sentences are facts and which are opinions?

- Nollywood is _____ – so that it is now the second largest film industry in the world.
- Nollywood usually makes about _____ films annually.
- Movies are not produced in film studios but _____.
- Because there are no _____ in Nigeria, Nollywood films go straight to DVD.
- Discs are _____ for most Nigerians.
- You can buy Nollywood DVDs from _____ traffic.

5 Now listen to a radio interview in which a film critic is discussing whether an Indian Bollywood film, *Bombay*, should be included in a top 100 all-time best movies list. Listen a first time and make notes on the questions the radio presenter asks.

6 Listen again. Complete the sentences (the gaps can be filled with up to four words) and then decide whether the sentence is a fact or an opinion.

Bombay

a) *Bombay* was made in _____.

b) It was _____ Rani Matnam.

c) It is about a Hindu man who _____ a Muslim woman.

d) The film _____ Mumbai during a time of rioting and violence.

e) The best thing is the _____.

f) The film was a bit too _____ for me.

g) The director and editors _____ some of the romance scenes _____.

h) Manisha Koirala, _____, was the best for me.

i) The film won _____.

j) The _____ sold 15 million CDs.

k) It was one of the biggest grossing films _____.

l) It is a must-see from one of the most _____.

m) If you want to go and see a great _____ movie then you should go and see *Bombay*.

n) Five stars _____ five.

7 Listen again and answer these questions in writing.

a) Give **two** facts that the guest knows about the film.

b) Give **three** opinions that the guest holds about the film.

c) Give **two** reasons the guest gives for including *Bombay* in the top 100 films.

d) Do you think these are good reasons?

8 In groups, discuss if you would you like to go and see *Bombay*. Make sure you give a reason for your answer.

Going further

Sometimes one word can change a fact into an opinion, for instance, an adjective can change a fact into an opinion. For example:

> *It's got fighting scenes.* (fact)
> *It's got thrilling fighting scenes.* (opinion)

Films are often described using extreme adjectives and often they are hyphenated.

Example: Bombay *is a great all-singing, all-dancing movie.*

Read the following adjectives and then discuss the questions below in pairs.

star-studded   *action-packed*   *nerve-wracking*
slow-moving   *jaw-dropping*   *laugh-out-loud*

Think of:

- a film with a star-studded cast. Who played in it?
- an action-packed movie. What happened?
- a nerve-wracking movie. Why was it frightening?
- a slow-moving film. Why was it slow?
- a jaw-dropping moment in a film. What happened?
- a film that was laugh-out-loud funny. Why was it funny?

9 In pairs, talk about your favourite film or your imaginary favourite film.

- ● Make notes and then copy and complete the table below with one fact and two opinions on your favourite film.
- ● Listen carefully to what your partner says. Add details to the table about their favourite film.
- ● Compare your notes with your partner's. Are they the same?

Item	What	Fact	Opinion	Opinion
My favourite film	The Monkey King	The budget was 400 million yen	Chow Yun Fat makes an awesome Jade Emperor	It's got gripping fighting scenes
My partner's favourite film				

10 In groups, discuss the last film or TV programme you saw. Take turns to speak giving your film a rating in stars as shown on the right.

> ★ = Deadly dull and boring
>
> ★ ★ = Okay
>
> ★ ★ ★ = Good
>
> ★ ★ ★ ★ = Great
>
> ★ ★ ★ ★ ★ = Fantastic – an all-time great

11 Make a film or audio recording of your discussions (using a mobile phone if you have one). Play back the recording listening carefully to what each person said about their film. Was it mostly fact or opinion?

The big task

In groups of four, hold a debate that TV plays a positive role in society.

Group 1: **argue for** the role of TV being positive

Group 2: **argue against** this, i.e. that the role of TV is negative and/or changing

(1) **First prepare for the discussion**
- Choose roles.
- In your group, sort these facts and arguments into *for* and *against* TV playing a positive role in society. Throw out any arguments that are irrelevant.

> ○ The average person watches three hours of TV per day.
> ○ TVs are redundant. You can now watch shows and films where and when you want on your computer and mobile phone.
> ○ Spending time watching TV takes time away from sports which keep you active and healthy.
> ○ The variety of programmes on offer is astonishing.
> ○ Going out with your friends is a more sociable thing to do.
> ○ TV is a comparatively cheap form of entertainment.
> ○ Radio keeps you informed better than TV about current events.
> ○ I don't watch much television.
> ○ Many programmes are worthless entertainment.
> ○ Television series popularise many great novels.
> ○ Television provides enormous possibilities for education.

- Add any further arguments of your own.
- Allocate arguments to each person and decide the order in which people will speak. Usually the strongest arguments are presented first and last.

(2) Now write up each argument, adding an example. For instance:

> *The average person watches three hours of TV per day – I certainly do. I watch in the morning and before supper. It all adds up and it seems that the adage is true – time flies when you are enjoying a good TV programme!*

(3) Now hold your debate in front of the class. Take turns so that a person from Group 1 speaks first, followed by a person from Group 2, then the next person from Group 1 followed by the next person from Group 2, and so on.

> **Top tip**
>
> Introduce your opinions using one of the phrases for disagreeing politely.

(4) Now take a vote in class. Which side won? Do you think that TV has a positive role in society?

Check your progress

Here are the Reading, Writing, Speaking and Listening skills you learnt about in Chapter 11.

Use this table to decide how good you are at the different skills, and make a note of what you need to be able to do in order to move up a level.

READING

I can ...

Higher	consistently and accurately locate facts and details in complex texts
	identify most of the points for or against a point of view, even when they are implied and not actually written
Middle	find some facts and details in a range of texts
	identify some points for or against a point of view, including some implied but not actually written
Lower	find a few facts and details in straightforward texts
	identify a few obvious points for or against a point of view

WRITING

I can ...

Higher	use a wide range of punctuation in my writing, securely and to good effect
Middle	use a fair range of punctuation in my writing and with a reasonable degree of accuracy
Lower	use a basic range of punctuation in my writing

SPEAKING

I can ...

Higher	disagree politely and confidently in a conversation
	sustain a conversation for some time and can use rephrasing effectively
Middle	disagree politely and clearly in a conversation
	take part in a two-way conversation and sometimes make use of rephrasing
Lower	disagree in a conversation
	take part in a conversation, but will need support from the other speaker to keep it going

LISTENING

I can ...

Higher	consistently understand and pick out details accurately from a range of spoken texts including the more complex
	usually understand opinions and attitudes in a formal spoken dialogue
Middle	confidently understand and pick out details correctly from a range of spoken texts
	understand some opinions and attitudes in a formal spoken dialogue
Lower	understand and pick out a few details correctly from some straightforward spoken texts
	understand a few simple opinions and attitudes in a formal spoken dialogue

The big picture

In this chapter you will:

● think about what it means to be young, and what it means to be old

● research, think, talk and write about what young people and old people do, what they want and how people change as they get older.

Thinking big

1 Look at the photographs and make notes on what they show about different stages in life.
   ● What do you think are the advantages and disadvantages of each stage of life?
   ● How does age change your attitude to learning new things?

2 In pairs, look at the photos and then discuss these questions:
   ● In what ways do different cultures differ in their attitudes to children and very old people?
   ● What do you think about each of the activities shown? Talk about the differences between people's abilities when they are young, and when they are old.

3 On your own, note down ideas about the following points. You will come back to these later in the unit.
   ● What do you think are the best things about being young?
   ● Are there any problems or difficulties with being young?
   ● Think about how much your life has changed since you were a young child. What can you do now that you couldn't do before? Are there things you can't do now that you used to enjoy?
   ● In what ways do you think that getting older will make your life easier? In what ways could it make life more difficult?
   ● Consider your own culture's attitude to childhood. What childhood experiences do you share with other cultures? In what ways might they be different?

12.1 Power for the young and the old

In this section you will learn to:
- recognise both facts and opinions in different types and lengths of text
- understand how the use of language may suggest a viewpoint.

Getting started

1 Read the questions below and discuss your ideas about them with a partner.
- Do you help to make decisions about things that affect you at home and at school? Think of examples.
- In what ways can young people play a part in the decisions which affect their lives?
- Do you think that young people should be involved in political decisions?

Exploring the skills

When you read a formal text, such as a newspaper report, you need to be able to tell the difference between facts and opinions, and also to identify the author's viewpoint. Articles that you read in newspapers, magazines and websites often express the **viewpoint** of the author. This is the main belief that the author wants to convey, and he or she will use facts and opinions to present his or her viewpoint.

2 Read the introduction to an article about voting rights for young people in Africa. What is the main idea in this piece of text? Choose one of the answers below.

A More young people in Africa should vote.

B More young people in Africa should be allowed to vote.

C Young people in Africa are not interested in voting.

One of the most important issues in African politics is to match the voting system on the continent with the age of the general population. One way to do this is to lower the voting age to 16. This would increase opportunities for young people to help shape their own future.

Africa has the youngest and fastest-growing population in the world. Over 40% of the population are under the age of 15. More than 20% are between the ages of 15 and 24. Three out of five of Africa's employed are young people. Young people account for 36% of the overall working-age population.

There are two steps Africa can take that could help convert the 'youth bulge' from a threat into a development opportunity. The first is including more people in the political process by lowering the voting age, and the second is increasing opportunities for technical training and job creation.

When we read an article like this, it is important to realise that the writer has researched the topic and formed a viewpoint based on what they have discovered.

Consider the viewpoint of the author, given in paragraph 1.

Then notice the facts the author uses to support his or her viewpoint:

Over 40% of the population are under the age of 15.

More than 20% are between the ages of 15 and 24.

Young people account for 36% of the overall working-age population.

3 In pairs, read the rest of the article and discuss the questions on page 232. Explain your ideas in your own words.

A Most African countries have set the minimum voting age at 18. This is because of tradition more than social, economic and political realities. Decision-making among Africa's youth has been significantly improved by changes in community structure, increased political awareness, and access to education, information and technology.

B The minimum voting age is 21 in Central African Republic and Gabon, and 20 in Cameroon. But people between the ages of 12 and 18 work, participate in political discussion through social media, and make household decisions. Yet they cannot vote. In Kenya, for example, which has a population of 38 million, about 4 million people are aged between 12 and 18, most of whom are socially, economically and politically active.

C Lowering the voting age to 16 for all African countries would not only be a better reflection of the general age of the population, but it would also improve political participation. Austria, Brazil, Cuba, Ecuador and Nicaragua have lowered the voting age to 16. In Bosnia, Serbia and Slovenia, 16-year-olds can vote if they are employed. The voting age in Indonesia, North Korea, Timor-Leste and the Seychelles is 17.

Lowering the voting age continues to be discussed in many countries. One of the main arguments against it is that people at the age of 16 cannot be relied upon to make informed decisions. This argument is usually made by older people who ignore the many decisions that young people already make. But people at 16 have much more at stake in regard to the future than many of those holding power today.

E It is true that lowering the voting age will not necessarily increase political participation by young people. It has to be accompanied by formal and informal political education. However, education about the political role of young people is even more urgent for older leaders whose worldviews were shaped by more traditional societies. Many of them do not realise the extent to which modern technologies and education have moved power from centralised authorities to groups of people of a similar age and with similar viewpoints.

From 'Why Africa needs to lower its voting age to 16' by Calestous Juma, *The Guardian*, 9 February 2011

4 Reread paragraph A.

a) Why has the voting age been set at 18 in most African countries?

b) What factors have improved the decision-making abilities of young people in Africa?

5 Reread paragraph B.

a) What does the text say people aged between 12 and 18 can do in African countries?

b) Is the writer stating a fact or an opinion here?

6 In paragraph C, how does the writer support his opinion that the voting age should be lowered?

7 a) In paragraph D, the writer says, 'people at the age of 16 cannot be relied upon to make informed decisions'. Is this the opinion of the writer, or of somebody else?

b) What argument does the writer give about why people should be able to vote at 16?

8 Read paragraph E.

a) What will young people need if the voting age is lowered?

b) What will older leaders need if the voting age is to be lowered? Why?

9 With your partner, discuss the following questions.

● At the moment, in your own country, are you able to vote?

● Do you think it is important to vote, or do you think it does not make much difference?

● Is the voting age in your country correct, or should it change? Should it be higher or lower?

Developing the skills

Online newspapers often let readers express their points of view about material published on the site. This means readers can respond to and engage with topics they read about.

10 Read these comments about the voting age article.

'I disagree with the idea that the voting age should be lowered. I think that people of 16 are too young to vote.'

'People can get married, have babies and fight in the army before the age of 18, so why shouldn't they be able to vote?'

'Young people have great responsibilities – they often work and earn money, and pay taxes, all before they are able to vote. This doesn't make sense to me.'

'Surely voting isn't important – there are more important things to think about, such as healthcare and ending poverty and disease. We should be worrying about this instead.'

11 In pairs, discuss what you think about each of the comments.

12 Working individually, write a short comment like those on page 232, expressing your opinion about the age at which people should be allowed to vote.

Going further

Just as **adjectives** can give you a strong impression of the writer's opinion (for instance, 'The *spectacular* scenery...' tells us the writer loves the scenery), so **nouns** and **verbs** can also tell us about the writer's attitude. Each word can have an emotional connection. For example:

Nouns: a *crowd* of people, might be a *mob* or an *audience* or a *congregation*.

Verbs: the man *walked*, might mean he *swaggered boastfully* or *marched smartly*.

13 Discuss the words in the examples above with a partner and look them up if necessary. Which is positive, negative, neutral?

14 Read the texts below. What problem do they highlight?

> In my town I see a lot of young people hanging around aimlessly on street corners, wasting their time idly chatting to friends, kicking balls around and talking rudely to other, more respectable members of society. And then they complain that there is nothing for them to do. My retort to this is that they should find something to do – find some more useful way to pass the time.

> I was disgusted to read the letter and felt I had to reply. I am a young person and I feel insulted by the way this reader dismisses all young people. I believe that the vast majority of young people in this town are hardworking, conscientious and courteous. The school has an excellent record, and we try hard to be responsible members of the community.

15 What type of texts are these – factual accounts or expressions of opinion?

Identify the words and phrases which express the emotions in each text. Copy and complete the table.

	Positive	Negative	Neutral
Letter 1		hanging around	
Letter 2			

16 Sum up the viewpoint of each writer.

Setting the tone

Writing skills in focus (W6)

In this section you will learn to:
● choose the correct tone and style for different readers and different situations.

Getting started

1 Read the questions below and discuss them with a partner.
● Describe any websites or blogs you have read recently.
● Do you ever write material such as reviews or news stories for websites?
● What is the difference between formal newspaper articles and informal blogs?
● What different reasons can you think of for writing websites and blogs?

Exploring the skills

When writing an informal text, it is important to use the correct tone and style to suit your reader. Think about who your text is for. If you are writing in a formal situation, for example to your employer, you need to use the formal writing techniques covered in Chapter 6. If you are writing in an informal situation, to your friend perhaps, you will use a very different style. You might use different vocabulary, as well as different sentence structures.

2 Read this blog about Maria Amelia Lopez, 'the world's oldest blogger' and then do the 'Language booster' on page 235.

As a blogger myself, I was very touched to read about Maria Amelia Lopez, a Spanish grandmother who started to write a blog on the internet when she was 95 years old.

On her 95th birthday, Maria's grandson gave her a blog. At first she had no idea what this was – she thought it was a kind of paper notebook – and thought he was being very stingy. However, once she started writing, she quickly became hooked, and so did her readers.

Her blog postings were soon read by people, young and old, all around the world, and attracted the attention of politicians and leaders, as well as ordinary folk. So the great-grandmother in her nineties was changed overnight from being completely web-illiterate to being a cyber superstar. Her blog allowed her to communicate with people all over the world, and chat away to them as if they were in the room with her.

At one point, Maria had over 60 000 regular readers, who all wanted to read about her memories. She was surprised by how interested the younger generation were in her blog. She had felt that nobody would be bothered about what old women thought or felt, but she was wrong.

So, you're never too old to learn something new. You CAN teach a dog new tricks!

Look at some of the phrases from the blog. Are they formal or informal? What do you think these words mean? Match them to their meanings.

a) *hooked*   A unable to use the internet
b) *stingy*   B a person who has become famous because of the internet
c) *web-illiterate*   C enjoying something and wanting to do it again
d) *cyber superstar* D not very generous with money

Language develops to fit new experiences in the world. New words and phrases, such as *web-illiterate* and *cyber superstar* develop to describe new situations.

3 Read an article about internet use in Spain and answer the questions.

Internet use

In Spain, only one in ten people over the age of 65 use the internet. This is slightly below the European average. This figure has nearly doubled over the last two years, but it still shows that older citizens are missing out on the digital revolution. This is despite the fact that they make up a growing percentage of the population.

'Age is more important (to determining internet use) than income, gender ... or level of education,' said Domingo Laborda, an official in Spain's Industry Ministry.

After the age of 65, the proportion of internet users decreases even more steeply. Only 2.7 per cent of over-74s have ever used the internet.

However, technology is a useful method for breaking down the isolation often experienced in old age.

'Although nothing can make up for affection, the internet can help communication, with mail, chat or messaging, and it's fun and always available,' said the ministry's Laborda.

4 How is the tone in the blog different from the article? Why do you think it is different?

5 Domingo Laborda works in the Spanish government. How does his tone and style differ from the tone and style Maria used when she wrote her blog, addressing her readers as friends?

6 Maria said that the internet had given her new life. In one of her last posts she wrote, 'When I'm on the internet, I forget about my illness. The distraction is good for you – being able to communicate with people. It wakes up the brain, and gives you great strength.' Discuss these questions in pairs. Can the internet change older people's lives?

a) How have computers or the internet affected the lives of some older people you know?

b) Can older people where you live feel isolated, or are they part of the community?

c) What can older people gain from using the internet?

Developing the skills

Remember to think about your reader and use the appropriate style.

7 Imagine that you are going to start a blog. Consider the points below and make notes.

a) Who are you writing your blog for?

b) Will your blog have a serious topic, such as your views on politics, education, or global issues? Or will it be informal and deal with more personal issues?

c) How will your choice of topic affect the tone you use in your blog?

8 Decide how to create the tone you want to use. For example, in Chapter 6 we looked at formal writing conventions, such as using full forms rather than contractions. Match the features across the two sides of the table.

Formal writing (e.g. a letter to/from a teacher)	Informal writing (e.g. an email to a best friend)
1. Full forms: 'I have written a letter to your father'	A Friendly language to end: 'Best wishes from '
2. Formal language to start: 'Dear Sir, Thank you for '	B Contracted forms: 'I've written a letter to your dad '
3. Formal language to end: 'Yours faithfully'	C Use idioms: 'It was blazing hot today'
4. Avoid using idioms 'It was extremely hot weather '	C Friendly, conversational start: 'Hi, Thanks a million for …'

9 Write two letters, one to your teacher and one to your school friend, explaining why you were away from school yesterday.
Try to use the different techniques shown in the table.

Going further

Just as you need to adjust your tone for different readers, you need to think about the purpose of what you are writing. Here we will look at how to write instructions.

The internet is a very useful learning tool at any age. Imagine that you have to write a set of instructions for a young person who is new to using the internet. These must give advice about the best way to proceed, what to do and what not to do.

Read the extracts below and decide which is the most suitable introduction to those instructions:

> *The internet is an international network of computers linked up to exchange information through high-speed connections, which are either wireless or use cables. You can access information almost instantly using a web browser.*

> *The internet is a bit like a giant library inside your computer. Ask the right questions, look in the right places, and you can find out all sorts of things.*

The second extract is a better introduction for a young person who is new to the internet. The writer:

- uses a friendly, direct tone
- uses less sophisticated vocabulary
- writes about the experience in an accessible way, making comparisons with familiar settings (a library) rather than using unfamiliar technical language.

When you write instructions, it is important to present the information in the correct sequence, using clear language.

10 Choose your reader. Will you write instructions for a young child, or an elderly person? Your tone and style will be different depending on your reader. In pairs, read the phrases in the box and put them into the correct columns in the table. Some words will fit in both.

> clear simple words   more sophisticated language
> short sentences   variety of sentence types
> not too much technical language   fun and interesting

Young reader	Older reader

11 Now work individually to write your instructions about using the internet. Remember to adjust your language according to your reader. You should write about 150 words.

12.3 Growing up

Speaking skills in focus (S6)

In this section you will learn to:
- speak clearly and use the correct stress when speaking
- vary your tone to interest your listener.

Getting started

1 Discuss the questions in pairs.
- At what age do you think people become adults? Is this because of what you are allowed to do, or because of how mature you are?
- Is there a clear moment at which you become an adult in your society, or is it a gradual process?
- In your country, are there any traditions which you associate with the change from being a child to being an adult?
- Do you think the step from being a child to being an adult is exciting, or is it something that makes young people nervous?

Exploring the skills

In situations where you want to tell a story or talk in a way which will interest your listener, there are different techniques you can use to make your speech more exciting, or to convey your emotions more clearly. For instance, you might:
- emphasise particular words and use a wider range of expression
- pause before some words to build up greater dramatic expression
- repeat certain words, or vary the volume of your voice.

Remember – it is not just *what* you say, but *how* you say it, that conveys your ideas.

2 Listen to Carmen, Adil and Keiko describing how children become adults in their country. How do you think they feel?

3 Listen to the extract. What techniques from 'Exploring the skills' do you hear being used here?

Listen to the whole thing again. How does each speaker show their emotions? Consider *what* they are talking about and *how* they present their stories.

4 Think about a time when you first felt that you were being treated like an adult. What happened, and how did it make you feel? Practise describing this situation in pairs, using the three techniques on page 238 to make your story sound interesting. Then present your ideas to the class.

5 Look at the photographs on this page and read about more ceremonies from around the world. Note down ideas about how you might feel in each situation. Use the words below to help you.

> excited   proud   nervous   happy   scared

Land diving – South Pacific

On Pentecost Island in Vanuatu in the South Pacific, there is a ceremony that started a world-famous sport. When young boys are ready to become men, they take part in a land-diving **ritual** called Naghol. A 20–30 metre high tower is made from wood. Then local men and boys jump off the tower, with only a **vine** attached to their legs. The vine takes them all the way down to the ground – to complete the ritual, they have to brush the ground with their head! The vine doesn't stretch, so if the length isn't right, the diver could be seriously injured, or killed.

This ritual influenced bungee jumping, but the festival has a strong spiritual significance for the islanders, as it is thought to make the land **fertile**.

Initiation by bullet ants – the Amazon rainforest

The bite of the bullet ant of the Amazon rainforest is said to be the most painful bite of any insect in the world. Its name shows that the bite from this ant is like being shot. But young men from the Satere Mawé tribe of the Amazon have to experience bites from the bullet ant as part of their **initiation** into adulthood. The pain can make them unable to move their arms for a while, and they may **shake uncontrollably**. If they can cope with the pain, they are seen as men.

Glossary

ritual – a series of actions performed in the same way, often as part of a religious ceremony
vine – the long stem of a climbing plant
fertile – (for land) able to grow a lot of food
initiation – the act of becoming part of a group, often through a ceremony
shake uncontrollably – to be unable to stop moving part of your body

6 Talk about the two ceremonies in pairs. Imagine you are going to take part in one of them. What would you be thinking and feeling?

Developing the skills

(7) In 'Thinking big' on page 228 you made notes about being young: what was good about it; what you can do now that you couldn't do as a child; how your life changes as you get older. Did any of these topics come up in your notes?

> *learning to drive*　　*leaving home*　　*marriage*

In pairs, discuss what each of these things means to you, and your hopes and plans for the future.

Language booster

When talking about the future, you can use phrases such as 'I hope', 'I can't wait', and 'I'm looking forward to' to describe your hopes and plans.

(8) Read these comments from young people about their experiences. Are they similar to or different from your ideas?

> *I'm so excited about learning to drive – I've been saving up money for lessons, and my parents have helped me too. I'm starting lessons on my seventeenth birthday, and hopefully I'll pass my test soon! I'm looking forward to having more freedom. I won't have to ask my parents to take me to places any more!*

> *I can't wait to leave home. My parents are great, but I'm 19 now and I think I'm ready to have my own space. I'd like to live with friends, I think that would be really, really good. I'm looking for a job at the moment, and when I find one, I'll think about moving out.*

> *My parents want me to get married and maybe start a family. But I think I'm too young for that! I'd rather go travelling, see the world, just ... do what I want for a bit! Then I want to find a really interesting job.*

(9) Are these people excited about the topics they are discussing or are they nervous about the future? How can you tell what emotions they are feeling? What spoken techniques for adding interest have they used? Discuss your ideas in pairs.

(10) Listen to a conversation between two friends. Why is one of them very excited?

(11) Listen to the conversation again. How can you tell Eliza is excited?

Going further

Telling a story to one person or a group of friends is one thing, but what about talking to a large group of people? Giving a presentation is an important and useful skill, and you can use many of the same techniques to interest your listeners.

12 Read the question and note down your ideas.
  ● How do you feel about the changes in life you will experience as you grow older?

13 a) On your own, read the topics below. Think of any other important life stages or events.

work	**leaving home**	**university**	**travelling**
having a family	**learning to drive**		**responsibilities**

b) In pairs, describe what you hope to do in the future. Using the ideas above, decide what you will do first. How do you feel about the life stage you have chosen to discuss? For example, are you looking forward to having more responsibility, or not? What expectations do people around you have?

c) Carry out your conversation. Take time to listen to each other's points of view, and be prepared to offer advice, if appropriate. For example:

  A *I really want to learn to drive, but it's so expensive.*

  B *Well, you could get a part-time job. Then you could save money for lessons.*

14 Prepare a presentation about coming-of-age ceremonies in your country, or about a ceremony in another country that interests you.

Research information about it, then give your presentation to the class. Remember to use your tone of voice to help you express your ideas and emotions. You may have a mixture of factual information and your own opinions and emotions, so think about how your tone of voice should change.

> **Top tip**
>
> Record yourselves preparing your ideas and having your conversation, then listen to it. Does your speech sound interesting, and have you used the techniques for expressing emotion? Can you think of ways to improve it?

Listening skills in focus (L3 and L4)

In this section you will learn to:
- recognise and understand ideas, opinions and attitudes
- answer multiple-choice questions about ideas
- recognise connections between ideas
- understand what is implied but not actually said in a formal interview.

Getting started

1. In pairs:
   - Tell one another about a young person who has achieved something amazing.
   - Do you think young people should be encouraged to try dangerous activities? Why or why not?
   - If a young person has a talent for a particular sport or activity, how far should they go with this? Should it be more or less important than their education and social life?

Exploring the skills

Sometimes when you are listening, you have to pick out specific information in order to answer questions or follow instructions. Check that you understand what you need to know. If you have to choose between two or more options, there are steps you can take to help you answer the questions correctly.
   - First, make sure you read and understand all of the options.
   - Then, reject any which are obviously wrong.
   - Think about key words you should listen for. Think of synonyms for these words – words with the same meaning – as the text may not be identical.

2. Read the question and the answer options.
   Why is this person famous?

   A He is the youngest person to pass his A levels.

   B He is an Olympic swimming champion.

   C He is a record-breaking English diving champion.

Once you have read and understood the question and options, listen to the text. We can reject option A, because we hear that he is working towards his A levels.

The key words we need to listen for are 'swimming' or 'diving' and 'champion'. We hear 'diving', so we can reject option B, and when we hear the word 'star' – a **synonym** for champion – we know option C is correct.

3 Look at the photos. Listen to the passage and match the photos to the descriptions.

> *Youngest person to sail around the world*
>
> *Youngest world champion ever in any sport*
>
> *Youngest person to climb the Seven Peaks*

4 Listen to the recording again and answer the questions.

i) What has Jordan Romero achieved to win a new world record?

    A He has climbed seven high mountains.

    B He is the youngest person to climb Mount Everest.

    C He is the youngest person to climb the highest mountain on each of the seven continents.

ii) When did Jessica start her journey?

    A October 2009

    B May 2010

    C October 2010

iii) How does Fu Mingxia feel about her success now as she looks back?

    A that she still thinks it was amazing

    A that she was too old to enjoy it

    A that she was too young to be pushed so hard

Achievements of youth and old age

Developing the skills

In an exam situation you may also have answer question about longer listening pieces. With these, it can be more difficult to follow the main ideas. The technique is the same: read the questions and options, and listen for key words. These will help you focus on what you hear and enable you to answer the questions successfully.

5 Discuss the questions in pairs.
- What achievements are important to you? If you live to be 100, what would you like to do before then?
- Do you think people are more able to fulfil their ambitions when they are old, or when they are young?

Try using some of this vocabulary. Check that you know what these words mean:

> achievement marathon finish line exhausted
> dehydrated energy blood sugar levels
> concentration record breaker personal best

6 Read this introduction to an article about a marathon runner. What is unusual about him?

World's oldest marathon runner completes Toronto race at age 100

Fauja Singh from east London finishes in 8 hours, 25 minutes and 18 seconds – ahead of five other competitors.

7 Answer the questions.
a) Which marathon did Fauja Singh run in this article?
b) How long did it take him to finish?

8 Listen to the rest of the article. Remember to read all the options before you listen, and use the pauses and replaying to check your answers.

i) Where does Fauja Singh live?
- A India
- B East London
- C Toronto

ii) When was he born?
- A 11 April 1901
- B 1 April 1910
- C 1 April 1911

iii) When did he run his first marathon?
- A when he was a farmer
- B when he was 89
- C in 1911

iv) What does Singh say makes him successful?
- A ginger tea and being happy
- B curry and cups of coffee
- C ginger curry, cups of tea and being happy

Going further

Sometimes you might have to answer questions about quite a complex text. In this situation, do not worry about understanding every word. Remember that sometimes the answers have to be 'worked out' from the text.

9 In this chapter you have looked at the different achievements and difficulties of young and old people. Now, in pairs, draw a timeline of life from birth to death, and mark on it what you think are the significant stages and developments which people experience. For example:

0	5
born	start school

10 Listen to an interview with Jago Philips. What has he done?

12.7

Language booster

Write definitions for these words. Use a dictionary.

adolescence	infancy	adulthood
responsibility	inadequacy	regret

11 Listen again and answer the questions.

i) What is the subject of Jago's book?

   A How his children have developed

   B His own theory of how life changes

   C An explanation of someone else's theory about how life changes

ii) What is important about the first stage, called Infancy?

   A We learn about love.

   B We become independent.

   C We are very confident.

iii) What can happen in Early Childhood?

   A Everyone starts saying 'No' to the child.

   B Children can do more for themselves.

   C Parents start to do everything for the child.

iv) What is the different between Play Age and School Age?

   A We play with different toys.

   B We don't learn anything in the Play Age.

   C We start to develop relationships outside the family in School Age.

v) What do we try to discover In Adolescence?

   A Our own identity

   B Who is in charge of the world

   C How the world works

vi) Why is young adulthood difficult?

   A We don't have as many friends.

   B We have a lot of new responsibilities.

   C It is difficult to find work.

12 Listen to the recording again and answer these questions in your own words:

a) Why did Jago decide to write this book?

b) What kind of a person is Jago? Choose one word to describe him and explain why you think this describes him well, by giving an example from the interview.

The big task

In this unit you have looked at the different rights and responsibilities of young and old people. Now you are going to prepare a presentation about the subject, choosing from the topics in the speech bubbles below.

1 In groups, read the following statements and discuss them. Note down some ideas about your opinions. Then choose one of the statements for your presentation.

> *The age of 18 is too young to vote. Young people need to learn much more about how the world works before they can be trusted to vote.*

> *The internet can be dangerous. Young people shouldn't be allowed to use it because they won't find out anything useful.*

> *Older people aren't capable of achieving success in the same way as younger, healthier people.*

> *It is dangerous for young people to attempt difficult activities such as mountain climbing or sailing, and parents shouldn't encourage it.*

> *There aren't any different stages to life – we just start young, then grow up gradually. We don't 'become' an adult at any particular age.*

2 Prepare a presentation about your chosen statement, giving your viewpoint on the subject. Remember to use facts and other people's opinions to back up your viewpoint and express it convincingly.

3 Once you have agreed on a topic, divide it up into different areas for each person in the group to work on individually. For example:
- one person can research famous people whose work is linked to the topic
- two others can find articles and other sources of information which support your point of view.

4 Once your research is completed, bring your work together and look at what you have found. Think about the best way to present your work – for example, a poster with images and text, or a presentation of images, key phrases and lists of arguments using PowerPoint. You should try to produce a combination of written work with images, and oral presentation.

5 Prepare your presentation. Think carefully about your audience, and use an appropriate style and tone. Remember to express your views clearly.

Check your progress

Here are the Reading, Writing, Speaking and Listening skills you learnt about in Chapter 12.

Use this table to decide how good you are at the different skills, and make a note of what you need to be able to do in order to move up a level.

READING	
I can …	
Higher	consistently and accurately recognise and understand facts and opinions in a range of texts including complex ones understand how the choice of language may suggest viewpoint
Middle	recognise and understand some facts and opinions in a range of texts sometimes understand how language may suggest viewpoint
Lower	sometimes recognise and understand more obvious facts and opinions in straightforward texts

WRITING	
I can …	
Higher	consistently and effectively adapt the tone and style to the reader and purpose of my writing
Middle	sometimes choose the right tone and style according to the reader and purpose of my writing
Lower	write for different readers and purposes but use the same tone and style

SPEAKING	
I can …	
Higher	consistently speak confidently and clearly, using the correct stresses in my pronunciation and varying the tone of my voice for effect
Middle	speak clearly, using appropriate stresses in my pronunciation and varying the tone of my voice so that I can be understood quite easily
Lower	express some simple ideas but do not always use the correct stresses; I tend to use the same tone all the time

LISTENING	
I can …	
Higher	consistently understand ideas, attitudes and opinions in quite complex spoken texts and then answer multiple-choice questions accurately usually understand what is implied but not actually stated in a formal interview
Middle	understand ideas, attitudes and opinions in spoken texts and then answer some multiple-choice questions correctly sometimes understand what is implied but not actually stated in a formal interview
Lower	understand ideas, attitudes and opinions in straightforward spoken texts and then answer a few multiple-choice questions correctly understand straightforward ideas stated in a formal interview

13 Answering reading questions

A short text reading question

Essential information

What you have to do: from a short text, pick out details to answer questions. Your answers should be single words and phrases – they do not need to be full sentences.

The kinds of text: advertisement, brochure, leaflet, guide, report, manual, instructions.

To go one step further: find extra details.

The reading skills you will use – the ability to:

1 skim and scan to find details.

A short text reading question: step by step

STEP 1 Skim read the text

This will give you a quick idea of how the information is organised. Do not worry too much if there are words you do not understand – you may not need them for the answers anyway!

- You learnt and practised the skill of skim reading in Chapter 1 on pages 10–13).

STEP 2 Read all the questions through

This will give you a quick idea of the information you will need to find.

STEP 3 Find the detail

Answer the questions one at a time, and find just the information you need. Use the scanning skills you practised in Chapter 1. In Chapter 3 you also learnt about using the question words (who, what, why, where, when, how) to help you decide what kind of information is needed. Remember that the answers are to be found in the text in the same order as the questions.

Now that you understand what to do, and the order in which to do it, you are ready to do a complete set of reading questions, in the style of an IGCSE examination paper.

Checklist for success

✔ Skim read the text and read the questions before you start writing.

✔ Underline key words in the questions to help you focus on the information you are looking for.

✔ Scan the text to find the details you need.

✔ Keep your answers brief and concise.

Practice reading question 1

Read the following extract from a leaflet, which gives the events taking place in the town of Melton this week. Then answer the questions below.

The List: a guide to what's on where in Melton

MUSIC Rock ON! returns to your local Community Theatre. This is a great talent show where you can hear the latest sounds from local groups such as Future Sound, The Lazy Bones and The Crazy Antics. It starts at 9pm on Saturday, for one night only. Make sure to phone and reserve a place so you don't miss out! Phone 01334 671 298 to book.

THEATRE We are really lucky to be able to go and see Romeo and Juliet written by William Shakespeare, performed by the Sydney Touring Company. As usual from this company, you can expect some spectacular lighting effects in a highly imaginative production. But this production is simply out of this world – literally! It's set in the future on the planet Venus. We don't think you'll have ever seen anything like it before! There are plenty of opportunities to see it. It runs every night this week at 7pm, with an afternoon performance at 3pm on Wednesday.

FOOD Why not have a meal out with a difference at Gnashers? This is a modern restaurant specialising in vegetarian dishes which appeal to everyone. There is an unmissable opening offer – buy one meal, get a second meal at half price. You can find it at 278 High Street, Melton Town.

ALPACAS Why not take the family to Melton Zoo this weekend? Special attraction for the holidays: rides on alpacas for the under-5s. Show this advert at the gate to get the special discount of 50% on a family ticket. This offer is only available this week, during the school holidays.

ART Exhibition of art by Daniel Hargreaves, a portrait artist who has started producing water colour landscapes which have won critical acclaim. You can find it In Melton Town Hall until the end of the month.

a) Give the names of two of the rock bands you could go to hear on Saturday. [1]

b) What is very unusual about the production of the Shakespeare play? Give two details. [2]

c) If you want to see the Shakespeare play this week, but cannot go in the evening, when exactly would you be able to go? [1]

d) What is the name of the restaurant which has just opened in town, and what kind of food does it offer? [1]

e) What exactly is the special deal offered by the zoo during the school holidays? [1]

f) What kind of paintings can you see in the town hall this month? [1]

g) *Extended only*: What does this artist normally paint pictures of? [1]

h) *Extended only*: How can you tell that the paintings are likely to be worth going to see? [1]

[Total: CORE – 7 marks]

[Total: EXTENDED – 9 marks]

A longer text reading question

Essential information

What you have to do: select details from a slightly longer, more demanding text to answer questions. Then write concise answers – each one as a single word or phrase, not a sentence.

The kinds of text: a report, a newspaper article or a magazine article which will include a graph or diagram of some kind.

To go one step further: find extra details and infer meaning, i.e. understand what is implied but not actually written, for example, draw conclusions or explain reasons.

The reading skills you need: the ability to

1 read closely for details

2 have a basic understanding of graphs and diagrams

3 understand what is implied but not actually written.

A longer text reading question: step by step

STEP 1 Skim read the text

Find out quickly what the text is about. Look at the subheadings or, if there aren't any, focus on the first sentence of each paragraph to give you an idea of how the information is organised.

STEP 2 Read all the questions through

This will give you a quick idea of the information you will need to find.

STEP 3 Find the detail

Answer the questions one at a time, and find only the information you need. Use your skim reading skills to find the section of text that is likely to contain the information you need. Then scan the section for any key words. Remember that the answers are to be found in the text in the same order as the questions. You learnt and practised the skill of scanning for key words in Chapter 4, pages 70–71.

STEP 4 Double-check the graphics

In this question you will have to show that you understand a graph or other kind of diagram. Check that you have really understood how the graph organises its information, and exactly what the question is asking for. You learnt about understanding graphics in Chapters 4 and 7.

STEP 5 Check your answers

Check that the information you have found is exactly what is asked for, without any extra unnecessary information.

STEP 6 Read 'in between the lines'

You need to be ready to show that you have understood what is implied but not actually stated – usually in the last question. You learnt this skill and practised it in Chapters 1 and 7.

Now you understand what to do, and the order to do it in, you are ready to do a complete set of reading questions in the style of an IGCSE examination paper.

Checklist for success

✔ Skim the text and read through the questions. Underline key words in the questions to help you focus on what you need to find.

✔ Read for detail, and underline the information you need for your answer.

✔ Check you give the right number of points in answer to the last question, and that you have understood what was implied in the text.

✔ Check all your answers are as brief as possible and that they make sense.

Practice reading question 2

Read the following newspaper article about the problems faced by American beekeepers, and then answer the questions on page 252.

Richard Ford, a beekeeper in California, got the shock of his career last month when he examined his bee boxes and found that about 50 million bees (half of all the bees he owns) were missing. Standing in his almond orchard, Richard said, 'I have never experienced anything like this.'

Other beekeepers in 24 states across the USA have had similar shocks. Bees have been disappearing alarmingly quickly and for no apparent reason. This threatens not only the beekeepers' livelihoods but also the production of a variety of crops, including the most profitable, Californian almonds.

The inexplicable disappearance of so many bees highlights the importance of honeybees in the successful production of the fruit and vegetables that feed people across the country. Although there have been regional bee crises before, this is the first time there has been a national crisis. Bees are flying off in search of pollen and nectar and simply not returning to their colonies.

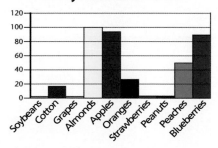

Percentage of crops pollinated by honey bees in the USA

Bees are not the only way that plants are pollinated – but some plants are more dependent on bees than others, as this bar chart shows.

Worried beekeepers met with researchers in Florida this month to try to find out what is causing the problem and how to cope with it. They discussed a range of possible causes, including viruses, a fungus and poor nutrition in the bees.

Another problem is that queen bees are spawning fewer worker bees and only living half as long as they did a few years ago. This is thought to be because insecticides used to kill mites that threaten bee colonies are also harming the queen bees.

Producing honey is not, in fact, the main way beekeepers earn money. They make much more from renting out their bees to pollinate crops. Over the past ten years, the costs of fuel, equipment and even bee boxes have doubled and then trebled, as has the cost of controlling mites. In addition, the price of queen bees has gone up from $10 each three years ago to $15.

a) What gave Richard Ford the biggest surprise of his career last month? [1]

b) In how many American states have beekeepers had the same experience as Richard? [1]

c) Give **two** reasons why beekeepers are alarmed at the sudden disappearance of so many bees. [1]

d) Which valuable crop is under threat by the disappearance of bees? [1]

e) What is different in this new scare about the bees' disappearance? [1]

f) According to the bar chart, name two crops that are not likely to be seriously affected by the disappearance of so many bees. [1]

g What are the bees looking for when they fly off? Give **two** details. [1]

h) Apart from the use of insecticide, give **two** possible reasons for the sudden loss of so many bees, according to the experts in Florida. [2]

i) Give **one** negative effect of the insecticide intended to help the bees? [1]

j) How else do beekeepers earn their living, apart from selling honey? [1]

k) *Extended only* Give four reasons why beekeepers are finding it hard to keep their businesses going. [4]

[Total: CORE – 11 marks]
[Total: EXTENDED – 15 marks]

Answering information transfer questions

Essential information

What you have to do: from a short text, pick out details. Write the details exactly as you find them, transferring them onto a form of some kind, following instructions carefully.

The kinds of text: factual accounts, for example, a short life story; an account of a real-life scenario; forms of different kinds, for example, application forms, competition entry forms.

To go one step further: find extra details and be prepared to understand what is implied but not actually written, for example, draw conclusions or explain reasons. **E**

The reading skills you will use – the ability to:

1 skim and scan to find exactly the right details
2 follow form-filling instructions accurately
3 understand what is implied but not actually written **E**
4 write clear and accurate sentences.

Approaching the question step by step

STEP 1 Get the general idea of the text and the task

Skim read the whole text quickly, including the form, to understand what the text is about and how it is organised – this will help you later with scanning to find the details you need. Then skim read the form, so you can understand what sort of information you are going to have to look for.

> You have had practice at transferring information and completing forms in Chapter 2 on pages 31–33.

STEP 2 Study the form carefully

Now look at the form again, and this time read it very carefully so you know exactly what information you need.

STEP 3 Double-check instructions on the form

You must make sure you know what all these instructions mean:

- circle
- tick
- put a cross by
- underline

- delete (means cross out the one which does not apply, so you are left with the right answer showing)
- use block capitals (means every letter must be a capital letter).

These instructions may seem straightforward, but it is important to follow them accurately and correctly.

> **Top tip**
>
> When you are asked to give an address on a form, do not use prepositions, such as *in*, or *by*, or *near*, for example: in the text: *He lives in Apartment12A, found at the bottom of Rue Lazare in Paris, France.*
>
> on the form you write: *ADDRESS: Apartment 12A, Rue Lazare, Paris, France.*

STEP 4 Find the exact details

Scan to find the exact information you need to copy and write. It might help you to focus if you underline the word or phrase in the text when you find it. Think of it like 'cut-and-paste' on a computer.

Here is an exercise to practise these four steps:

Read this paragraph then follow the instructions after it.

Marcella di Paola has always wanted to have a career on the stage as a singer or dancer – or maybe even a combination of the two. She started out at an early age, taking part in a local singing contest and winning first prize at the age of only six. When she was 11 she took ballet lessons at a special Dance School in her town, and took several ballet exams. This lasted until she was 18. During this time, she also took part in school plays. At the age of 19, in 2009, she managed to get a place at the Royal Drama School in Rome. This is where she is now, following a three-year course in Acting and Dancing. She works hard, practising her dancing routines from 8am until 8pm every day. She enjoys the physical challenge of dancing, and loves the excitement of taking part in live performances, when she enjoys the thrill of hearing audiences clapping and cheering for her. On the other hand, she has to put up with antisocial hours as she has to work late during the week and most weekends as well. Her email address is mdipaola@fastermail.com and www.dancespot.com/MarcellaD is her webpage.

Imagine you are Marcella and you have to fill out this application form for a place with a dancing company.

Full name (IN BLOCK CAPITALS):...

Email address: ....

Website address (if you have one): ....

Age of starting ballet lessons: ....

Year of starting present course: ....

Name of present place of education: ....

Length of current course (delete as necessary) 1 year / 2 years / 3 years / 4 years

Career aims (circle as necessary any that apply)

       dancer   actress   singer   teacher

Check your answers with a partner. Did you follow the instructions exactly? Did you use capital and lower-case letters correctly? *Hint*: Check the website address especially carefully.

STEP 5 Write one or two sentences correctly

Further questions may ask you to read information and then write about it, usually within a set number of words, in one or two sentences.

Remember that you are writing, not as yourself, but as the person described in the text. So, if you are asked for your opinion, you must remember that you are supposed to be someone else – do not give your personal opinion. This is not a piece of creative writing. Look for the information in the text!

STEP 6 Check

Make sure you have followed all the directions carefully. Check:
- that you have written the correct number of sentences
- that you have written no more than the set number of words (if there is a word limit)
- all grammar, spelling and punctuation.

If you make any mistakes in any of these things, you will lose marks

STEP 7 Get the length right

Now you have a chance to practise steps 5 and 6 and complete the last section on Marcella's form. Ⓒ Ⓔ

In this instance, for practice, you should aim to write between 12 and 20 words.

a) Imagine you are Marcella. Write one sentence explaining your practice routine.

b) Write one sentence about your experience as a dancer before you went to Drama school.

c) Write one sentence explaining what you enjoy about being a dancer and what you find difficult about a dancing career.

Some hints:

First look at your answer to a).

Did you underline some of the sentence starting *She works hard … every day*? Did you remember to change the subject to *I*, and *her* to *my*? Did you change the verb from *practising* to *I practise*? You could have written:

> *I practise my dancing routines from 8am until 8pm every day.*
> (13 words)

Now look at b).

Did you read the question carefully and write only about her dancing experience? You could have written:

> *Between the ages of 11 and 18, I took ballet lessons and some ballet examinations at a local Ballet School. (20 words)*

Look at these example answers in response to b):

> *Marcella loved dancing at her ballet school and she took ballet exams, too.*

> *I always wanted to be a dancer and now I go to dancing school.*

> *Ballet lessons for about 7 years ages 11 to 18 and exams in ballet*

> *from 11 to 18 I have took lessons and pass exams in balet*

None of these answers would have got any marks. Can you see why? Discuss this with a partner.

Now look at c).

Did you start each sentence with a capital letter and end with a clear full stop?

You could have written:

> *I love the physical challenges of dancing and the excitement of live performances, although I find the antisocial hours difficult.*
> *(20 words)*

Look at these further example answers to c):

> *Marcella loves practising every day and the excitement and the clapping but she finds late nights at weekends and in the week very difficult*

> *Marcella loves the physical experience of dancing and the excitement of hearing audiences clapping her and she hates the unsocial hours.*

> *I love challenges, I hate lateness.*

> *I adore the challenges of dancing and the audience's appreciation but I hate late finishes to the working day.*

Discuss with a partner whether you think any of them could have got full marks. If not, why not?

> **Top tip**
>
> Sometimes you can save words by replacing a phrase with a single word. For example, 'she enjoyed the audience's clapping and cheering' could become 'She enjoyed the audience's applause'. This technique for saving words is really useful when writing summaries – see Chapter 5, pages 92–97.

STEP 8 **Understand what is implied**

If you are an Extended-level student, you may have to use some inference to answer the last section. Be ready to show you can understand what is implied but not actually written down. **E**

> You learned about inference in Chapters 1 and 7.

Imagine you are Marcella and write one sentence of between 12 and 20 words about how you are showing real determination to become a successful dancer.

Practice information transfer question

You are now ready to do a complete information transfer question, just like in your IGCSE exams.

Checklist for success

✔ Skim read the text and the form before you start to write.

✔ Read for detail and underline the key detail, the golden nugget, you want to transfer.

✔ Copy it over carefully. Double-check that the spelling, capital letters or punctuation are clear and **exactly** as in the text.

✔ Read all the instructions very closely, for example, if the form asks for two details, check that you give only two details, even if there are many others in the text; if it asks you to circle the answer, circle it.

✔ Make sure your handwriting is clear, and that capital letters are larger than lower-case letters.

✔ Check that your answers make sense.

✔ In every section of the information transfer question, spelling and punctuation mistakes will stop you getting the mark. You must check these very carefully.

✔ Expect to use inference skills.

Exercise 3

Kwame Annan was born in Kumasi, a city in the south of Ghana, about 250 km north of the capital, Accra, on 30 August, 1995. He still lives here, with his parents at 28, Royal Palm Road. The landline number of his home is 00-233-51-896151. He played football every day with his friends, in the streets, and on any patch of open ground that he could find. At school, Kumasi Junior High, he was well-liked and popular, and did reasonably well in his lessons, passing his examinations so well that he received a scholarship to a private international school, the Kumasi Academy. While studying here for his A levels, his passion for football has developed even further. He played for his school in regional matches and was noticed by the trainer–manager of the national youth team. He played football for this team during the 2012–2013 season, and was able to travel to Europe, visiting Spain, Germany and France for the international youth events. He made a great impression in this team and on his return was offered the chance to play for the national youth team for a further two years. He scored two goals during the final round of the competition, and was given a special 'Man of the Match Award' for his outstanding performance, although the team was only able to be runner-up, which was a bit frustrating for the team. Now that he has left school, he is part of the national team hoping to take part in the new competition, the Africa–Asia Cup. This will take place in Shanghai, China from 10 to 17 October 2015. The plans are that they will stay at the Imperial Hotel, 208 Pusan Road, Shanghai, arriving at Shanghai International airport, two days before the start of the tournament and then staying on for two days after it to do some sight-seeing. They will be in China from the 8th to the 19th October. He wants to become a recognised member of the adult national team for Ghana, and hopes to become as famous as Michael Essien, a fellow Ghanaian who played in France and England, and who won the coveted 'African Footballer of the Year Award' for his amazing football skills.

Imagine that you are Kwame. You have been sent a form to complete by the manager of the Ghana Youth Team, so that he can apply for visas for the team to travel to China, and also get to know you a little better.

Fill in the form, using the information above.

Section A Personal details (BLOCK CAPITALS)

Full name: ....

Date of birth: ....

Home address (include town): ....

....

....

....

Home telephone number:: ....

Name of last school attended: ....

....

....

Section B Travel history

Country of birth (delete as necessary):

      Ghana   other country in Africa

         other country in Europe

Please circle any of these countries that you have visited in the last three years:

    United Kingdom   Germany   France

      Belgium   Italy   Spain   China

Section C Visit to China

Name of football competition: ....

City to be visited: ....

Dates when you will be in the country: ....

Name of hotel where you will stay: .... Ⓔ

....

Hotel address: .... Ⓔ

....

....

EITHER Section D Core

In the space below, write **one sentence** about what you achieved, and **one sentence** about what caused you disappointment during the last international tournament you took part in.

....

....

....

....

....

....

OR Section D Extended

In the space below, write **one sentence** saying what you achieved and what caused you disappointment during the last international tournament you took part in. Your answer should be between 12 and 20 words long.

....

....

....

[Total: Core – 14 marks]

[Total: Extended – 8 marks]

15 Answering a note-making question

Essential information

What you have to do: from a short text, select details in order to make notes and organise them under given headings.

The kinds of text: brochures, articles, reports or imaginative writing.

To go one step further: find some extra details, for example: under an extra given heading.

The reading and writing skills you will use – the ability to:

1   select relevant details

2   recognise the difference between facts, ideas and opinions

3   find and organise related details.

Approaching a note-making question step by step

STEP 1 Make sure you understand the task

A little extra time spent checking that you understand the task can save you time and marks in the long run. First, use your skim reading skills to get an idea of the text's content, what it is about and how it is organised. Read the first sentence of each paragraph to help you do this, if the text has no subheadings to help you. Then, carefully read the headings that you are asked to use in the question, before going back to the text to start selecting the details you need.

STEP 2 Find the related details

It is a good idea to use different colours to underline the information you think you are going to need. If there are two headings, use different colours to underline the two different kinds of information. Sometimes the information you need will be all together in the text and you may have to sort out the points. Other times the information will be spread through the whole text. Make sure you put the detail under the right heading!

Here is an exercise to practise these steps. It is similar to the kind of task you might find on the examination paper. Remember, you are not to write anything yet – you are just going to read and underline the points you need. (You will need to have a copy of it so you can write on it.)

If you are an Extended-level student, there is an extra heading and some extra points to find and you will need a third highlighting colour. Be extra careful to put the detail under the right heading. **E**

Read this speech which was read out at a school assembly and then follow the instructions carefully.

Imagine you have to write an account for the weekly Parents' Newsletter. Prepare some notes to use as the basis for your article.

JOIN OUR GREEN CLUB

We are a group of four students in Grade 12 here at Stocklea High School. We have decided that our school needs to play a much bigger part in helping to improve the environment – not just in our school itself, but in the area around it.

It all started when we heard that the council had sent leaflets to everyone in the town, explaining that the cost of collecting all the rubbish from households – the wages, the transport costs, etc. – has doubled in the last two years. We thought this was a shocking statistic. This is despite a 5% improvement in recycling used cardboard boxes, newspapers and unwanted office papers. They said that people are still throwing away plastic bottles, yoghurt pots, takeaway food containers and other things like these, instead of recycling them, which adds to the landfill problem because we are running out of places to bury it all. The situation is getting out of control – it's like a monster on the loose!

It's not just how people deal with their household waste that's the problem. We noticed for ourselves how the town is being spoilt by rubbish being discarded without any thought for the consequences. It really makes us feel so unhappy and ashamed. Why can't we all look after our town properly? The town centre is left filthy after Saturday afternoon shopping – food wrappers, drink cans, cardboard cups, newspapers … that sort of thing. It's so unhygienic. The river flowing through our town has got empty glass bottles floating in it; there are old rusty cans and even a broken shopping trolley. The riverside walk should be a colourful and attractive place to walk with your family, but now it's quite unsightly, and hazardous, too.

So we wanted to do something to improve matters. First of all we asked our Form Tutor, Mr Hussein and our English teacher Mrs Heywood, if they would help us and give support. We all know how keen they both are on the environment from their classes. We were really pleased when they agreed. Unfortunately, as you know, Mrs Heywood was taken ill and has been off school, so she has not been able to join us, but she has sent us a good luck card.

Now we are asking all of you in Grade 9 and 10 to come and help. We intend to have Saturday afternoon collections in the High Street, starting this weekend. We plan to go round with black sacks and collect the empty sweetpapers, chip packets and cans, and take them to the recycling centre. We are lucky because some parents are going to supervise and drive us and take the heavier items. And we will go down to the river in the afternoon and fish out all the broken bottles and tin cans, and just generally clean it up and make it safe at the same time. If you have some gardening tools, like shears, clippers, spades and rakes, be sure to bring some with you. You'll need to wear old clothes, and be ready to get your shoes wet! Wear boots if you have them. And bring some thick gloves, too, to protect your hands. We also want to tidy up the footpaths, picking up any newspapers and wrappings; we want to cut some of the overgrown branches – and get rid of some of the weeds from the paths, which are difficult to walk down in places especially for parents pushing prams or strollers.

Please come and help. The more of us there are, the quicker we can get the job done. Meet us outside the Market Coffee Shop at 10am. The weather forecast is overcast – so it may be a good idea to bring a raincoat or anorak.

Make your notes under the following headings.

Core and Extended: **Members of the Green Club going into town on Saturday**

- ....
- ....
- ....

Extended only: **The problems the Green Club has seen in the town**

- ....

- ....

- ....

- ....

Core and Extended: **Actions the Green Club will carry out this weekend**

- ....
- ....
- ....
- ....
- ....

STEP 3 Make your notes

Read the headings again carefully as you make your notes. Double-check that each detail is one you *really* need. Remember, notes do not need to be full or proper sentences – save time and keep them brief. The bullet points tell you how many points you need to make; the lengths of the lines give you an idea of how long each one should be. Extended-level students will be expected to find more details than Core-level students. Make sure you have not written the same point twice.

STEP 4 Keep the notes brief

Imagine you had to use paragraph 2 of the speech to produce a poster to inform people about the facts of the situation in the town.

> **Top tip**
>
> Remember, you can always neatly cross out an answer and write in the correct one if you need to. Whiteout fluid is not allowed in IGCSE examinations.

Here are one student's notes:

i)   the cost of collecting all the rubbish from households – the
     wages, the transport costs, etc. - has doubled in the last
     two years. We thought this was a shocking statistic

ii) despite a 5% improvement in recycling used cardboard boxes,
     newspapers and unwanted office papers

iii) people are still throwing away plastic bottles, yoghurt pots,
     takeaway food containers and other things like these,
     instead of recycling them

iv) adds to the landfill problem because we are running out
     of places to bury it all. The situation is getting out of
     control – it's like a monster on the loose!

Top tip

You do not have to use your own words for these notes, but sometimes it can save you space and time.

There is not enough room for all this. How can you cut it down?

Some hints

You can:
- delete all the examples
- miss out any unnecessary detail
- omit any irrelevant opinions, emotions or comparisons
- use one word which sums up a longer phrase.

And so **i)** becomes:

i) *cost of household rubbish collections has doubled in two years*

Look back and see what has been left out and why. Now reduce notes **ii)** **iii)** and **iv)** in the same way.

Then, with a partner, compare your reduced notes and see if you can make them even briefer. Each one should be between 7 and 10 words.

Finally, use steps 3 and 4 to complete your notes on the Green Club.

Checklist for success

✔ Skim through the text first; then read the headings carefully before you start to select the details you need.

✔ Read the headings carefully again as you make your notes. Double-check that each detail is one you really need.

✔ You do not need examples, details and comments – unless you are asked for them!

✔ Remember, notes do not need to be in sentences – save time and keep them brief.

✔ The bullet points tell you how many points you need to make; the lengths of the lines tell you how long each one should be.

✔ Check that you have not written the same detail twice.

✔ You do not need to use your own words for these notes.

Practice note-making question

You are ready to do a complete note-making question, in the style of an IGCSE examination paper.

Read the following magazine article about the Inuits. Then copy out and complete the notes that follow.

The Inuits are a fascinating group of people who have always lived in the Arctic region. They always used to be called 'Eskimos' by outsiders, but now are known as 'Inuits', the name they call themselves, which literally means 'the people'. It is really remarkable how they have spread from a small region, across such a huge geographical area including many different countries from Greenland to Russia. Today, for example, there are more than 40 000 Inuits living in Canada and over 55 000 in Greenland. But despite all these changes, they have amazingly managed to maintain their own values, traditions and beliefs.

They hunt for their food, and traditionally eat sea mammals, such as seals, walruses and whales and fish, such as salmon. They also hunt and eat birds such as geese and ducks. Even today, their main food source is the sea, though of course they can use more modern weapons such as guns, rather than the traditional spears and fishing lines.

In the areas of the frozen north where the Inuit live, there are few building materials. Obviously no trees grow there, so houses cannot be constructed from wood; the ground is so hard frozen that no bricks can be made from mud or stone. However, the Inuit discovered a skilful way of building out of the compacted snow and ice around them. They hacked out large blocks of ice, and then cleverly carved them into the right shapes to build a circular 'igloo', completely enclosing them and protecting them from the snow and blizzards. In the summer, after the ice had melted, the Inuit lived in tents made out of animal skins stretched over a frame. To travel, the Inuit used sleds pulled by teams of dogs. Nowadays, the traditions of igloo building and using dog sleds are still alive, but they are able to live in more solid buildings, designed as more permanent homes. They can use petrol-driven vehicles for transport.

Art is very important to the Inuit people. In ancient times they used stone or bone to make sculptures and small figures that they believed had magical powers, as well as useful everyday items such as pots and weapons. Nowadays, art is important for a different reason. They produce beautiful rings, necklaces and brooches – still out of of bone or stone – to sell around the world and generate an income.

What does the future hold for the Inuits? Although Inuit life has changed so much over the past century, many of their traditions show no sign of changing. Radio and TV programmes using the Inuit language will ensure it continues into the future. Inuit artists and film makers will produce films reflecting the Inuit values and ways of life. The Arctic Winter Games, held every two years, will continue to keep the Inuit sense of identity strong in the future. Perhaps, however, a more negative aspect is that many younger Inuits will find themselves torn between their cultural heritage and the demands of modern society. Many will have to leave the traditional way of life behind as they seek ways of earning a living in the cities of Canada and other industrialised countries.

Core students

Prepare some notes for a short article about the Inuits for a class Geography magazine. Copy out the heading given below. Make your notes under this heading.

Inuit way of life in the past

- Lived in the arctic
- ....
- ....
- ....
- ....
- ....
- ....
- ....

[1 mark each up to 7]

Extended students

Prepare some notes for a short article about the Inuits for a class Geography magazine. Copy out the headings given below. Make your notes under each heading.

Inuit way of life in the past

- Lived in the arctic
- ....
- ....
- ....
- ....
- ....

[1 mark each up to 5]

How present way of life is different from the past

- ....
- ....
- ....
- ....

[1 mark each up to 4]

[Total: 9 marks]

16 Answering a summary-writing question

Essential information

What you have to do: a summary-writing question on the Core paper is a test of writing skills. Using your notes from the note-making task, link them together into a short summary following a given word limit.

The writing skills you will use – the ability to:

1 write clear sentences and punctuate correctly

2 use appropriate vocabulary

3 write in paragraphs, using a variety of grammatical structures

4 use words and phrases to link paragraphs.

Approaching a summary-writing question

Let's look at an example of a summary-writing question, which uses the notes you made for the note-making question in Chapter 15 (pages 260–63):

> **Write a summary of 70 words for the weekly Parents' Newsletter. You have to tell the parents a) who in the Green Club will be going into town on Saturday and b) the actions the Green Club will carry out this weekend.**

STEP 1 Understanding the task

In the note-making task you made your notes under the heading or headings you were given. In the examination, there may be one, two, or even three of these headings. In the summary-writing task you have to write a summary **using these notes**. You should never add any ideas of your own at all – this is not a test of imagination (that comes in the later writing questions – see Chapter 18). This is a test to see if you can:

- organise your ideas
- show that you have understood the text from the note-making question by using your own words
- write clear sentences with correct spelling and punctuation
- use paragraphs
- keep to a set word limit.

STEP 2 Using the notes

Now you have a clear idea of what you have to do in the summary-writing task, you can make a start. The first step is to check that the notes you made are properly organised. Read them through and check that they are under the correct headings.

> **Top tip**
>
> Never be tempted to add any ideas of your own when writing a summary. Use only details from the text, put into your own words.

Let's go back to the Green Club's speech and the notes you were asked to make in Chapter 15.

For practice, take the notes listed below and write them under the correct headings:

The Green Club members (3 points)

Actions the Club will be taking this Saturday (5 points)

Note: there are four extra points here which you should not include.

- Town centre is unhygienic and the river has empty glass bottles floating in it
- Meet at 10am
- Grade 12 Form Teacher is called Mr Hussein and helps
- Town centre spoilt and left filthy by rubbish discarded without any thought for the consequences after Saturday shopping
- Members are school students in Grades 9 and 10
- Go down to the river in afternoon and fish out all the bottles and tin cans
- River – old rusty cans and even a broken shopping trolley in it
- Four people studying at school in Grade 12 decided to do something and get others to help
- Riverside walk should be a pretty place but now is hazardous
- Go with black sacks and collect empty wrappers and cans in the High Street to improve this dire situation
- Taking the empty food wrappers and cans to the recycling centre
- Go to river and fish out bottles and cans

You should now have some well-organised notes and be ready to start writing.

STEP 3 Using your own words

Remember that when you write a summary, you should try to use your own words as far as possible. Obviously some of the basic key words will be the same, but you should try to reword the text to show that you have really understood it, and that you are not just copying it out word for word. You did some work on vocabulary in Chapter 4 which will have helped prepare you for this.

As a practice, look at the following words from the notes in Step 2. Write down a word or a phrase that means the same as (is a **synonym** for):

a) unhygienic

b) filthy

c) discarded

d) fish out

e) hazardous

f) improve this dire situation.

STEP 4 Write in paragraphs

You have learnt that you can organise your ideas by putting them together in paragraphs. Each heading could become a topic sentence, that is a sentence that introduces or sums up the paragraph. Then you have to link your ideas together. Do not write strings of short sentences always joined together with *and* and *but*. Find some different ways of joining the sentences instead.

> You learnt about and practised the different ways of joining ideas and sentences in Chapters 3 and 9.

For example, a one-paragraph summary of 'The Green Club members' might be as follows:

> *The Green Club has members of all ages. Four people studying at school in Grade 12 decided to do something and get others to help, and the Green Club members are all school students in Grades 9 and 10 and the Form Teacher for the students in Grade 12 is called Mr Hussein and he is helping.*

This has a **topic sentence**, but is rather muddled and could be better organised. There is an overuse of *and*. The details about Grade 12 appear in two different places.

For practice, work with a partner to put the ideas in a better order and have a better variety of sentence structures.

STEP 5 keep to the word limit

Remember that there is a word limit. You must stay within the word limit, so make sure you count your words.

Sometimes a few words will do the work of a long phrase or even a whole sentence. Using shorter phrases can be a great way to write **concisely**. You can be cunning and use synonyms (or re-wording), not just to show you have understood the text, but also to save words.

> **Top tip**
>
> Writing **concisely**, means writing in as few words as possible but still getting the meaning across.

As a practice, find one word or a short phrase that means the same as:

a) without any thought for the consequences

b) old rusty cans and even a broken shopping trolley

c) empty wrappers and cans

d) colourful and attractive.

Now write the practice task:

> **Write a summary of 70 words for the weekly Parents' Newsletter. You have to tell the parents a) who in the Green Club will be going into town on Saturday and b) the actions the Green Club will carry out this weekend.**

Write your summary, making sure you use only the notes that are relevant to the question.

Afterwards, with a partner, work together to make your summary as clear and concise as possible, following the five steps. When you have finished, count up your words and make sure you are within the word limit. Cross out any unwanted words neatly.

> **Top tip**
>
> Remember to have a final read through to check that it all makes sense after you have made any alterations to your summary.

Checklist for success

✔ Check your notes from the note-making question closely and ensure that you have not noted the same detail twice – you can neatly cross out an answer and write in the correct one if you need to.

✔ While you do not need to use your own words for the notes in the note-making task, you *should* try to use your own words for the summary-writing task.

✔ When you finish your summary, check that you have not used more than the set number of words or you may lose marks.

Practice summary-writing question

You are ready to do a complete summary-writing question, in the style of an IGCSE examination paper.

You need to look at your answers to the note-making question – the notes that you made about the Inuits (page 264–65) – and use these to write your summary.

> **Use the notes you made in the note-making question to write a summary of the Inuit way of life in the past.**
>
> **Your summary should be no more than 70 words. You should use your own words as far as possible.**
>
> ....
>
> ....
>
> ....
>
> ....
>
> ....
>
> ....
>
> ....
>
> ....
>
> **[Total: 5 marks]**

17 Answering a summary-writing question Ⓔ

Essential information

What you have to do: an extended-level summary-writing task involves another text, slightly longer or slightly more complex than the one you read for the note-making task. You have to pick out details and organise them in order to produce a summary about **one**, **two** or **three aspects** of this new text. You will be given a set word limit for your summary.

The summary-writing task is a test of the same reading skills as you used in the note-making task, AND a test of writing skills.

The kinds of text: brochures, articles, reports or imaginative writing.

The reading skills you will use: the ability to:

1 select relevant details
2 recognise the difference between facts, ideas and opinions
3 find and organise related details.

The writing skills you will use – the ability to:

1 write clear sentences and punctuate correctly
2 use appropriate vocabulary
3 write in paragraphs, using a variety of grammatical structures
4 use words and phrases to link paragraphs.

Approaching a summary-writing question Ⓔ

Let's look at an example of a summary-writing question, to see the steps you will need to take.

> **Read the following email from Fathima to Wahida about her new hobby, scuba diving. Write a summary about the benefits and the costs of scuba diving.**
>
> **Your summary should be about 100 words (and no more than 120 words).**
>
> **You should use your own words as far as possible.**
>
> *Hi Wahida*
>
> *You asked me to tell you more about my new hobby, scuba diving. Well, the first thing to tell you is that it's absolutely amazing – it's really great and I'd really recommend it to you. It's quite a costly hobby, I*

admit – I've had to pay $100 to take my latest diving exam – but I get out into the clean, fresh air and feel revitalised. It's just fantastic after living in the city and breathing in all the car fumes. Not only that, it is a very effective aerobic workout. It burns up those calories and keeps me on top form physically. You get so captivated by all the wonderful sights – the different coloured fish, the corals, the colourful sea plants and sea anemones – that you don't stop to realise that you have been using your arms and legs to keep you going forward. Last time we went out, we saw a conger eel. It was beautiful and so enormous. I was quite scared because they have rows of very, very sharp teeth and it was my first instinct was to get away from it as fast as I could. Then curiosity got the better of me, and the creature just ignored me totally.

Of course, there are some other things to bear in mind. You have to be fit to start with – you need a medical certificate of fitness from a doctor before you can even start the training courses. I had to pay around $50 for that. You may also need to fork out for extra swimming lessons to bring your swimming skills up to scratch. And the training courses are not cheap. Find a really good instructor – that's essential, so you can be sure that you are learning all about the safety regulations, all the dos and don'ts. There is a lot to learn, and you have to pass some exams in diving. It is quite expensive too – not just the training, I mean, you need to buy an oxygen tank, a mask for your face , a special wetsuit and other bits and pieces. It all adds up. But when you weigh it up, and consider the fact that you learn so much about submarine flora and fauna, and have such fun socialising with new people, well – I'd recommend it to you totally. Come and join me soon!

Your good friend,

Fathima

STEP 1 Understanding the task

In the note-making task you prepared some notes under headings. For the summary-writing task, you need to do exactly the same except there are no headings or bullet points to help you find the relevant details; and then you have to **write** a summary.

However, you are marked on the final summary – there are no marks for any notes you might make in preparation. This means you must decide if you will have time to make notes, or whether it will be enough just to underline the key points in the text and write your summary from these.

Remember, when preparing to write the summary:

- Skim read the text first, then read the question carefully before you go back to the text and start selecting the details you need for your notes.
- To save time, you could just underline the key points, perhaps using two different colours if there are two different aspects to the question.
- Check that you have not identified the same detail twice.

Before you start writing the summary, you need to understand that you should never add any ideas of your own – this is not a test of imagination (that comes in the writing tasks – see Chapter 18). This is a test to see if you can:

- find and then organise related ideas
- show that you have understood the text by using your own words
- write clear sentences of different lengths and types, with correct spelling and punctuation
- use paragraphs and join your ideas in a variety of ways
- keep to a set word limit.

> **Top tip**
>
> Never be tempted to add any ideas of your own when writing a summary. Use only details from the text, put into your own words.

STEP 2 Finding and organising the related details

Although the summary-writing question may not mention paragraphs, it is a good idea to use two paragraphs rather than just one if two sets of related details are needed, as in this question. You could make notes under the headings 'Benefits' and 'Costs'. To save time, let's use the technique of underlining or highlighting the important points in two different colours. After you have tried this, try the exercise which follows for practice.

Which points have been highlighted in orange, and which in green – the benefits or the costs?

Hi Wahida

You asked me to tell you more about my new hobby, scuba diving. Well, the first thing to tell you is that it's absolutely amazing – it's really great and I'd really recommend it to you. It's quite a costly hobby, I admit – I've had to pay $100 to take my latest diving exam – but I get out into the clean, fresh air and feel revitalised. It's just fantastic after living in the city and breathing in all the car fumes. Not only that, it is a very effective aerobic workout. It burns up those calories and keeps me on top form physically. You get so captivated by all the wonderful sights – the different coloured fish, the corals, the colourful sea plants and sea anemones – that you don't stop to realise that you have been using your arms and legs to keep you going forward. Last time we went out we saw a conger eel. It was beautiful and so enormous. I was quite scared

---

because they have rows of very, very sharp teeth and it was my first instinct was to get away from it as fast as I could. Then curiosity got the better of me, and the creature just ignored me totally.

Of course, there are some other things to bear in mind. You have to be fit to start with – you need a medical certificate of fitness from a doctor before you can even start the training courses. I had to pay around $50 for that. You may also need to fork out for extra swimming lessons to bring your swimming skills up to scratch. And the training courses are not cheap. Find a really good instructor – that's essential, so you can be sure that you are learning all about the safety regulations, all the dos and don'ts. There is a lot to learn, and you have to pass some exams in diving. It is quite expensive too -, not just the training, I mean, you need to buy an oxygen tank, a mask for your face , a special wetsuit and other bits and pieces. It all adds up. But when you weigh it up, and consider the fact that you learn so much about submarine flora and fauna, and have such fun socialising with new people, well – I'd recommend it to you totally. Come and join me soon! Your good friend, Fathima

STEP 3 Making and using notes

For practice, write out a list of the points you want to include. Check the following:

- **Organisation:** make sure that you organise your notes properly and that you know which points will go under which heading. As in this case, the related points may not all come together – you may have to select them and then arrange them in a more logical order.
- **Relevance:** make sure that you do not include unnecessary details, opinions or feelings.
- **Keep it short:** make sure that your notes are as brief as possible.

Compare your final list with a partner's.

STEP 4 Using your own words

Remember that when you write a summary, you should try to use your own words as far as possible. Obviously some of the basic, key words will be the same, but you should try to reword the text to show that you have really understood it, and that you are not just copying it out word for word.

As a practice, write down a word or a phrase that means the same as (is a synonym for):

a) revitalised

b) aerobic workout

c) on top form

d) physically

e) captivated

f) fork out

g) submarine flora and fauna

h) socialising.

STEP 5 Write in paragraphs

Now that your notes are prepared, you are ready to link the ideas together into paragraphs. Remember to give each paragraph a **topic sentence** which sums up or introduces the paragraph. Try to make the topic sentence of the second paragraph link back to the previous paragraph in some way, so the whole summary reads smoothly.

Avoid writing strings of short sentences always joined together with *and* and *but*. Find different ways of joining the sentences.

You need to vary your sentence structures and write smooth-flowing paragraphs, with effective linking words. For instance, when you are writing a list of costs, you could use paired phrases such as *not only … but also*; or *as well as … you have to remember that… .*

When you have written your paragraphs, work with a partner to see if you can put even more variation into the way you have linked ideas within the two paragraphs.

> You learnt about and practised the different ways of joining ideas and sentences in Chapters 3 and 9.

STEP 6 Keep to the word limit

You must be careful to keep to the word limit. So, be cunning and use synonyms (or re-wording), not just to show you have understood the text, but also to save words.

> You learnt about different ways of linking ideas within paragraphs in Chapter 5 on pages 96–97.

As a practice, find one word or a short phrase that means the same as:

a) an oxygen tank, a mask for your face , a special wetsuit and other bits and pieces

b) the safety regulations, all the dos and don'ts

c) the fish, the corals, the colourful sea plants and sea anemones

d) a medical certificate of fitness from a doctor.

Now write the summary.

When you have finished, count up your words and make sure you are within the word limit. Cross out any unwanted words neatly. Afterwards, with a partner, work together to make it as concise as possible, following the five steps.

> **Top tip**
>
> Remember to have a final read through to check that it all makes sense after you have made any alterations to your summary.

For further practice, using the notes you made for the tasks on the Inuits in Chapter 15, page 265:

> **Write a summary on a) the facts about the Inuits in the past and b) how the Inuits' present way of life is different from the past.**
>
> **Your summary should be about 100 words (and no more than 120 words). You should use your own words as far as possible.**

Checklist for success

✔ Skim read the text to get a general sense of how the information is organised.

✔ Use the skimming and scanning skills (see Chapter 13) to find the details you need.

✔ Use two different colours to underline the two different kinds of information you need.

✔ Check that you have found **exactly** the right information – read the instructions at least twice, carefully.

✔ If you have time, write brief notes under headings.

✔ Check for repetition in your underlining or notes.

✔ Check that you have not used any unnecessary words. Can you reduce a phrase to one word?

✔ Use your own words as far as possible.

Practice Exercise 5

You are ready to do a complete summary-writing question, in the style of an IGCSE examination paper.

> **Read the article on pages 276–77 about left-handedness. Write a summary about the difficulties facing left-handed people and how those difficulties can be overcome.**
>
> **Your summary should be about 100 words (and no more than 120 words).**
>
> **You should use your own words as far as possible.**
>
> **You will receive up to 6 marks for the content of your summary, and up to 5 marks for the accuracy of your language.**

Do left-handed people have the upper hand?

About one out of every ten people reading this article is left-handed. That means that they prefer to use their left hand rather than their right hand for everyday activities such as writing or drawing. Over the years, many superstitions and myths have evolved about left-handed people – some positive and some negative. For instance, the ancient Incas thought it was a sign of healing power. Of course, nowadays we know that being left handed is neither good, nor bad; it's just the way some people are.

Scientists are still trying to fathom out what it is that makes some people left handed. It is known that babies start showing a preference for the left or right hand even when in the womb. From medical scans we can see babies prefer to put just one hand near their mouth, eventually even sucking that thumb, some weeks before being born. Then, as the baby grows it has been observed that that is the hand the child will go on to prefer in adult life.

Many left-handed people do face some inconvenience in their everyday lives. Perhaps the most obvious one is when writing English by hand. This is because in order see what they are writing, they often curl their hand around the top of the line where they are writing, which will smudge the ink. Obviously writing in pencil can get around this little problem. Avoiding spiral bound exercise books and ring binders may be another way of making life a little easier, as the metal rings can get in the way of the left handed writer. No doubt 'lefties', as they are sometimes called, welcome the use of computers nowadays for essay writing. But even here, problems can arise as the keyboards are designed for right handed people, for example the number pad usually being on the right hand side. Another common problem is the use of scissors, which left-handed people find almost impossible to use. In the kitchen, you may want to use a potato peeler. This would be impossible for left-handed people normally, but now we can all happily share the chore, as left-handed potato peelers are on the market. Scissors, cameras, fishing reels, golf clubs, even wrist watches … all items we want to use for our work or leisure, originally designed for the right-handed person and awkward for the left-hander, which can now be bought especially adapted.

Musical instruments are another area where left-handed people may feel at a disadvantage, as they are all designed for the majority of people, favouring the right hand. Nowadays you can buy left-handed guitars quite easily. No doubt Paul McCartney, perhaps one of the most famous left-handed musicians, has helped publicise these. Less well-known is that pianos have been manufactured with the left handed person in mind, with the deepest notes being at the top end, the right hand end of the piano instead of on the left, as normal.

Is there any advantage to being one of the special few? They will be pleased to hear that yes, there is – on the sports field. In baseball and cricket, the left-handed batsman can force the bowler to make errors. In soccer, tennis and basketball, the left-handed player can take his opponent by surprise with unexpected moves. We can understand why so many successful sportsmen and women are left-handed (and left-footed!) – John McEnroe being just one example and Lionel Messi, the Argentian footballer, another.

In any event, left-handers can be proud to be in the company of such 'lefties' as Albert Einstein, Bill Gates – and even the cartoon character Bart Simpson!

[Total: 11 marks]

18 Answering long writing questions

Essential information

Two types of task: the first long writing task will always have a different purpose and be in a different form from the second writing task.

Writing questions involve: a short composition which describes, reports or gives an opinion, using pictures and/or prompts as a guide. The question includes information on purpose, format and audience and there will be a set word limit. **C**

Writing questions involve: a slightly longer composition in which you develop your ideas further; adapt your style well to the reader and purpose; use more sophisticated vocabulary and structures; use very accurate grammar and punctuation. You will be given a set word limit. **E**

The writing skills you use – the ability to:

1. write to describe, inform or explain in response to pictures
2. write to express opinions in response to prompts
3. adapt your style according to the form, reader and purpose of the writing
4. use a range of grammatical structures
5. use a range of vocabulary and spell accurately
6. use paragraphs correctly
7. use punctuation correctly.

A long writing question to explain or describe

The first writing question asks you to produce a piece of writing to explain or describe something, or to give an account of something. You are asked to imagine you are in a particular situation and then you are given some guidance about what to include in the writing. There are usually some pictures to give you ideas. In this writing you have to be clear and write something which the reader will enjoy.

Let's look at an example of this type of question.

> ### The Grand Opening
>
> **Your school or college is about to open a large new building, and a special grand opening event is planned.**
>
> **Write an article for your school newsletter, telling people about the event and inviting them to come.**

In your article you should:

● describe the new building and what it will be used for

● explain what will happen at the opening event

● invite people to attend and explain why they would enjoy it.

The pictures above may give you ideas, but you are free to use any ideas of your own.

Your article should be between 100 and 150 words (Core) or 150 and 200 words (Extended).

You will receive up to 7 marks for the content of your letter, and up to 6 marks for the style and accuracy of your language. **C**

You will receive up to 10 marks for the content of your article, and up to 9 marks for the style and accuracy of your language. **E**

Answering long writing questions

STEP 1 Decide on the form, reader and purpose

Read the details of the task very carefully. The first things to check are:

- What **form** of writing are you being asked for? Is it an article, a speech, a letter, a blog?
- Who is the **reader** – the person you are writing for? Is it a head teacher, a close friend, an elderly relative, students your own age, young children?
- What is the **purpose** of the writing? Is it to inform? Is it to explain or describe something? Is it to persuade? Is it to convince someone of your opinion? Is it to give advice? Sometimes it may be a mixture of several of these.

All these things will affect the style of writing, and the level of formality you use. Aim for the highest marks by showing you can adapt your style according to the form, reader and purpose of the writing.

Before you write anything, underline the words and phrases in the question that tell you the form, reader and purpose of the task. Then discuss these with a partner and decide together how formal or informal your writing should be.

> You learnt about style and degree of formality in your writing in Chapters 6 and 12.

STEP 2 Use the pictures

In this question there are some pictures to help give you ideas – in this case, for the kind of buildings a school/college would have.

In pairs, answer these questions:

- What types of building do the pictures make you think of? Try to draw up a list of ten others types of building.
- Which one of these would you feel most able to write about? Why?
- What other school/college buildings could you write about? Can you think of a building which would really interest you, perhaps one where you could take part in your favourite leisure activity?
- If someone wrote about the opening of a big shopping mall, why would this gain only a few marks for 'Content'?

> **Top tip**
>
> You should try to come up with your own ideas, but make sure they are all relevant to the question. If you can't think of your own idea, then use one of the ones suggested. They have been provided because they could be successful, so there is nothing wrong with using one of them. You can still show some individual thought in the details you add.

STEP 3 Use the prompts

Imagine you have decided to choose a new indoor swimming pool. You may not know much about swimming, but at least you have seen an indoor swimming pool and can think what schools might use it for.

Now look at the three prompts. The question makes it very clear that in your article for the school newsletter you should:

- describe the new building and what it will be used for
- explain what will happen at the opening event
- explain why people would enjoy coming to the opening event.

Use these prompts as part of your 'concept map', just like the ones you have worked on in earlier chapters. Draw a line out from each statement to help organise your ideas.

Here is an example:

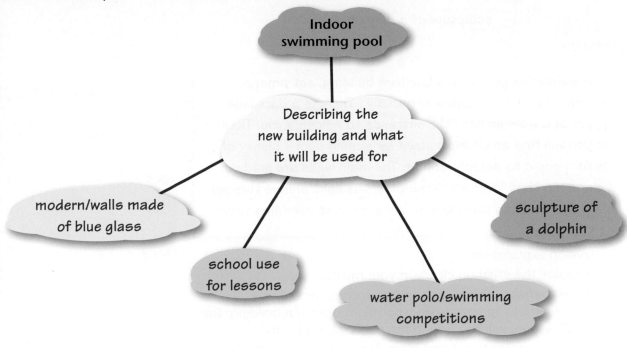

If you need more room, you can use a piece of rough paper or find a blank space on the page.

Now quickly do the same for the other two prompts. Under time pressure in an examination you may be short of time – so spend no more than five minutes sketching out your 'concept map'.

You can see now that all you will have to do later is develop these ideas and combine them into clear sentences.

Sometimes you may be able to use the prompts to help you divide your work into paragraphs – but some prompts may need more than one paragraph.

STEP 4 Develop your ideas

When you write your sentences describing the indoor swimming pool and what it will be used for, you must avoid just writing a list of points. You need to develop your basic ideas.

Here are some suggestions to help you develop your descriptions:
- Imagine you are there.
- Add some details to make it sound realistic.
- Use the senses of hearing, seeing, smelling, touching and tasting if it seems appropriate.

So, these notes:

indoor swimming pool   modern walls made of blue glass

sculpture of a dolphin

could become:

> The new swimming pool is in a low-level building, set among trees which have been planted especially . There is a dark blue sculpture of a dolphin near the entrance to welcome you. Then inside you will find an Olympic sized swimming pool – plenty of space for people to splash around. The main walls are made of blue glass, so that when you are inside, the light shines through. It is so beautiful and it make you feel good just standing there!

To help develop explanations:

- Try to imagine the situation clearly in your mind.
- Give details to make the explanation convincing, for example, the name of the famous sportswoman who might open the building; the detail that the pool will be open to the public at weekends.
- Give evidence/reasons to support ideas, for example, people who attend the opening will get a special discount.

In pairs:

- Compare the notes you made around the two other prompts.
- Discuss how these could be developed. What extra details could you use?

STEP 5 Use paragraphs correctly

Here are some connective phrases you could use to link ideas within or between paragraphs when writing to explain, describe or inform:

> *first of all   after a while   then   before this happened*
> *on the outside you can see ...   on the inside, however ...*

Add five more words or phrases to this list. Compare your suggestions with a partner or in a group, and see how many words you can find together.

Links in the first paragraph

Here is one student's first paragraph:

> *New Swimming Pool Opening*
>
> *I am writing to invite you all to the opening of an amazing new building at our college next Saturday afternoon: a new indoor swimming pool. I've had a look around it and I can tell you it is amazing! It looks fantastic from the outside. For a start, it is in a low-level building, set among trees which have been planted especially. Then there is a beautiful, dark blue sculpture of a dolphin near the entrance. Inside there is an Olympic-sized swimming pool – a huge space for people to splash around. The main walls are made of blue glass so that when you finally walk inside, the light shines through. It is so fantastic!*

On your own, write down some of the words and phrases the student has used to link the ideas in this paragraph.

Then work with a partner to identify the different ways the writer has linked the ideas together within this paragraph so that it flows smoothly.

Some of the methods you could use are:

- punctuation such as a **colon(:)**, a **semicolon (;)** or a dash (–), to show the link between the ideas at the start of the sentence and the ideas in the rest of it
- pronouns, for instance, *it* used to refer back to the previous sentence
- relative pronouns, for example, *which*, *this*
- connectives to show movement through time, for instance, *for a start … then …*

Did you identify any of these?

A long writing question including opinion or argument

The second writing question is usually a piece of writing which will include giving an opinion about something, and arguing for or against it. There may be some speech bubbles offering different points of view on the subject, to give you ideas to get started. In this writing you have to convince or persuade your reader.

Let's look at a possible second writing question.

> There is a problem of too much traffic in your local town and the town council is considering setting up a 'congestion charge'. This means that anyone who wants to drive their car into the town centre will have to pay a sum of money to do so. You decide to write a letter to the council to give your views.
>
> Here are some comments you have heard on the subject:
>
> *This will hit the poorest and weakest people the hardest – it's just not fair!*
>
> *I own a shop in the town centre and this change will mean fewer customers for me.*
>
> *This is a great idea – the town centre will be a safer place.*
>
> *It will cut down the pollution and noise in the town centre.*
>
> **Write the letter to the council, giving your views on the topic.**

Answering long writing questions

Your letter should be between 100 and 150 words long (Core) or between 150 and 200 words long (Extended).

The comments above may give you some ideas, but you are free to use any ideas of your own.

You will receive up to 7 marks for the content of your letter, and up to 6 marks for the style and accuracy of your language. **C**

You will receive up to 10 marks for the content of your letter, and up to 9 marks for the style and accuracy of your language. **E**

STEP 1 Decide on the form, reader and purpose

As in first writing question, the initial things to check are:
- What **form** of writing are you being asked for?
- Who is the **reader** – the person you are writing for?
- What is the **purpose** of the writing? Is it to explain or describe something? Is it to persuade them to do something? Is it to convince them of your opinion? Sometimes it may be a mixture of several of these.

> You learnt about style and degree of formality in your writing in Chapters 6 and 12.

Before you write anything, underline the words and phrases in the question that tell you the form, reader and purpose of the task. Then discuss these with a partner and decide together how formal or informal your writing should be.

Remember, all these things will affect the style of writing, and the level of formality you use. To gain the highest marks you will have to show you can adapt your style according to the form, reader and purpose.

STEP 2 Understand the prompts – the speech bubbles

The prompts for the second writing task may be in the form of speech bubbles. These may give different points of view about a topic, which you can explore and develop in your writing.

The prompts in this example give different viewpoints on the issue of whether or not the town should introduce a congestion charge. Unlike the first writing task, there is no hint as to the content of each paragraph – this is left entirely up to you. The question just says you have to write a letter giving your views. So you will need to do some more planning in this exercise, and decide what points to make in each paragraph.

In pairs, answer the following questions:
- Look at the speech bubbles – which ones are in favour of the congestion charge; which ones are against?
- Who do you think would agree with these points of view – any particular groups/types of people?
- Which point of view do you agree with, on balance, and why?

- Try to imagine what other people in the town might think, for example: parents with young children; people in wheelchairs; the elderly; shop owners. How could these ideas help you write your letter? Could you pretend to be someone else writing the letter?
- If someone spent the whole letter describing the council as foolish and the town centre as useless for shopping, why would this gain very few marks for 'Content'?

STEP 3 Use the speech bubbles

Let us imagine you decide to argue strongly *against* the plan to introduce a congestion charge. You are probably going to use one or both of the comments offering this viewpoint.

Use the comments as part of a concept map, just as you have in earlier chapters. Draw lines out from the first speech bubble and add the ideas which could develop this point of view. Here is an example:

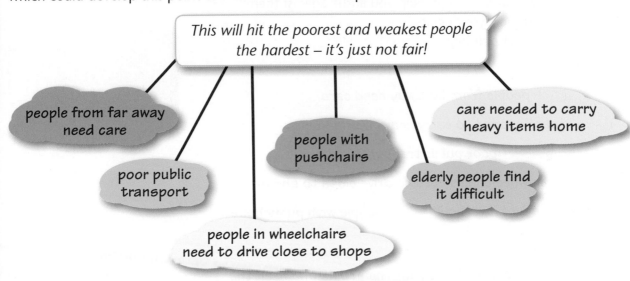

If you need more space than is available around the bubble, use some rough paper or a space on the page.

Now do the same for the other speech bubble which is against the congestion charge.

What about the points which are supporting the charge? Do you think they are true to any extent? You can use these ideas in order to support your point of view. Here is an example:

Now do the same for the other bubble supporting the congestion charge.

In pairs, compare your notes and see if you can add any more ideas. Can you think of any other reasons why you might be against the congestion charge? What about you, personally. How would it affect you?

STEP 4 **Develop your ideas**

When you write your sentences giving your point of view, avoid just stating your viewpoints in a list. You need to develop your ideas.

To help develop a point of view:
- Try to imagine the situation clearly.
- View it from different angles, so you can refer to other viewpoints – either to support your case, or to help you argue against them.
- Offer details to support your points.
- Give reasons for your opinions.

So, these notes:

people from far away need cars

cars needed to carry heavy items home

poor public transport

people in wheelchairs need to drive close to shops

elderly people find it difficult   people with pushchairs

could become:

> The congestion charge will be bad for the people who need the council's support the most. Many people won't be able to afford the charges. It will be very hard for people who live far away in country areas, without buses or trains to get them into town. They need their cars to get them into the town centre. Shopping can be very heavy – how are they meant to carry heavy things such as televisions to the car parks on the outside of town? The elderly and the sick will be very badly affected. They can hardly be expected to walk all the way into town. The same goes for parents with heavy pushchairs and energetic young children. They need the cars to get them into the centre as quickly as possible.

Top tip

Never simply copy out the words in the speech bubbles. If you want to include the idea, you must try to use your own words as far as you can.

Look at the example paragraph. Underline the reasons given for the viewpoint, and the examples.

Now write two more paragraphs: one using the notes you made around the other speech bubble against the congestion charge; one using the notes in favour of the congestion charge to support your viewpoint.

Top tip

Spend no more than 5 to 7 minutes planning or sketching out your ideas.

STEP 5 Use paragraphs correctly

Here are some connective phrases you could use to link ideas within or between paragraphs when writing to give an opinion and offer a clear line of argument:

after all this …   *as well as these points …*

in addition, I think that …   *on the other hand …*

another reason why …   *an alternative viewpoint …*

some people think that …   *first of all …*   *secondly …*

You can introduce your final paragraph with a phrase such as:

To sum up, I think that …   *On the whole, it is clear that …*

In brief, you must agree that …

Having weighed up the arguments for and against …

Think of five more connecting words or phrases. Compare your suggestions with a partner or in a group, and see how many words you can find together.

Read the paragraph below. Try to identify these five linking devices:

- a topic sentence introducing the main idea of the paragraph (there may be two topic sentences, working together)
- the word *them* used to refer back to the previous sentence
- three separate words/phrases linking ideas and showing the connection between them
- the word *also* to make a link within the paragraph
- one phrase to show how the final sentence is linked to the rest of the paragraph.

> *I feel so passionately about this topic that I have decided to write this letter to you. It would be very unjust to set up a congestion charge for anyone driving a car into the town centre. It will be especially unfair for the people who need the council's support the most. Many of them won't be able to afford the charges. For a start, it will be very unfair for people who live in remote areas without buses or trains to get them into town. They need their cars to get into the town centre. Shopping can be very heavy – how are they meant to carry heavy things to the car parks on the outside of town? Secondly, older people will be very badly affected. They can hardly be expected to walk all the way into town. Finally, the same goes for parents with heavy pushchairs and energetic young children (and we all know how difficult that can be). They also need their cars to travel into the centre as quickly as possible. In brief, this is all totally unfair.*

Checklist for success

✔ Read the question through carefully.

✔ Now read it again and underline key words or phrases which tell you the form, reader and purpose, so you know the level of formality to use.

✔ Look at any pictures/speech bubbles supplied. Remember, these are just ideas you can use if you wish. If you can think of your own ideas, so much the better. If you can't think of your own ideas, it doesn't matter – you can still get full marks using one or more of the ideas you are given.

✔ Make some very brief notes by each prompt – maybe use a quick concept map – so that you have an idea about what to include.

✔ You may be able to think of each prompt as one paragraph.

✔ Underline key words in the bullet points that you have to use.

✔ Start writing!

✔ Leave a few minutes at the end to check your work.

Practice writing question 1

Now you are ready to do a complete long writing question to explain or describe.

> **You and some friends have decided to hold a charity event to raise money. You want to make use of the school buildings, so need permission from the head teacher.**
>
> Write a letter to the head teacher, explaining:
>
> ● the charity you want to support and why
>
> ● the building or other area in the school you would like to use and why
>
> ● how you will make sure that the buildings will not be damaged in any way.
>
> The pictures opposite may give you ideas, but you are free to use any ideas of your own.
>
> **Your letter should be between 100 and 150 words (Core) or 150 and 200 words (Extended).**
>
> Do not write an address.

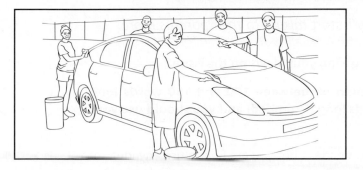

You will receive up to 7 marks for the content of your letter, and up to 6 marks for the style and accuracy of your language. **C**

You will receive up to 10 marks for the content of your letter, and up to 9 marks for the style and accuracy of your language. **E**

Practice writing question 2

Now you are ready to do a complete long writing question including opinion or argument.

Your local newspaper has a teenage magazine in it every weekend. There has been a suggestion in the paper that parents should not allow children under the age of 16 to play computer games at all. You have been asked to write an article giving your views on the issue.

Here are some comments you have heard on the subject:

This is so unfair – we can learn a lot from playing computer games!

We need to relax and unwind – and computer games are the best way to do it!

This is a great idea – young people need to do homework in the evenings, not play stupid games.

Good. Perhaps they'll start talking to their parents more.

Write the teenage magazine article, giving your views on the issue.

Your teenage magazine article should be between 100 and 150 words long (Core) or between 150 and 200 words long (Extended) and you should use your own words.

The comments above may give you some ideas, but you are free to use any ideas of your own.

Do not write in columns or add any pictures.

You will receive up to 7 marks for the content of your article, and up to 6 marks for the style and accuracy of your language. **C**

You will receive up to 10 marks for the content of your article, and up to 9 marks for the style and accuracy of your language. **E**

Responding to listening questions ⒸⒺ

Essential information

In all listening questions, you have to *listen carefully* to one or more people speaking, select details from what they say and then use them in some way. You may be asked to:

- simply listen out for a piece of information and then write it down as briefly as possible
- write information down in a different way, for example, on a form of some kind
- understand some information and then organise it in your mind to answer a matching question, a multiple-choice question or a gap-filling question.

In the following pages we shall be looking at different sorts of listening questions, one at a time.

Approaching shorter listening questions ⒸⒺ

What you have to do: listen to some short spoken extracts by individuals, or brief conversations between two people, select details to answer two questions, and then write concise answers – each one is a single word or phrase, not a sentence. In fact, you should use no more than three words for each answer. Each recording is played twice.

The kinds of text you will hear: travel announcements, answer phone messages, brief dialogues.

To go one step further: all students answer the same questions.

The listening skills you use – the ability to:

1. listen carefully for details.

Checklist for success

✔ Remember to make good use of every pause in the recordings.

✔ Underline key words in the questions to help you focus.

✔ Can you tell where the conversation is likely to be taking place and what kind of language you will need to use?

✔ Can you tell what kind of detail you should be listening for, for example, is it a weight? A time?

✔ Use the second playing of the question to check that you have selected the right details.

✔ Check that your spelling is as accurate as possible.

✔ If you don't know the word, you can still have a guess by writing the sounds you hear.

Practice listening questions 1–4

For questions 1 to 4 you will hear four short recordings. Answer each question on the line provided. Write no more than three words for each detail.

You will hear each recording twice.

1 **a)** Where are the students going on their school trip?

.... [1]

b) At what time will the school bus leave to take the students on the trip?

.... [1]

2 **a)** What is the class about to make in the experiment?

.... [1]

b) How much of the white powder should the students use?

.... [1]

3 **a)** Why is Bernice unable to get to work on time today?

.... [1]

b) If her employers want to speak to her, how should they contact her?

.... [1]

4 **a)** What does the waiter give Ali so he can choose what to order?

.... [1]

b) What two fruits does Ali decide to have in his fruit juice cocktail?

.... [1]

[Total: 8]

Approaching listening gap-filling questions

What you have to do: listen to a longer text spoken by a single person, and select details to complete gaps in a form or chart. You must write very concise answers – only one or two words in each gap. You will hear the recording twice.

The kinds of text you will hear: speeches, radio talks, lectures.

To go one step further: all students answer the same questions.

The skills you need – the ability to:

1. listen carefully for details
2. understand exactly which detail you need to complete gaps in a form.

Practice listening question 5

You will hear a radio talk about Josh Waitzkin, a young man who became one of the world's leading chess players while still a school student. Listen to the talk and complete the details below. Write one or two words only in each gap. You will hear the talk twice.

Chess master

Josh Waitzkin: career in chess

1. Chess titles: twenty-one times .... Champion and twice World Champion.   [1]

   Six years of age: started playing chess.

2. At 9: National Junior High Champion

   Age 11: drew against Kasparov, the adult World Champion.

   At 16: became .... Master.   [1]

Josh's teaching about chess

3. Title of his first book about chess: .... Chess.

   Title of educational ....: 'Chess Starts Here'.   [1]

4. Title of popular .... about chess: 'Chessmaster'.   [1]

5. Josh is .... to teaching chess and making his ideas available to everyone.   [1]

Josh's career in Tai Chi

6. Attracted to Tai Chi Chuan because of his interest in .... philosophy and because he wanted to learn something new.

   Won title of Middleweight World Champion in Taiwan in 2004.   [1]

Josh's worldwide career as a speaker

7. Talks about:
   - how we learn
   - the mental attitude needed to ....
   - psychology of competition.   [1]

Latest book

8. Explains we have to take .... if we are to develop.

   Book title.: The .... of Learning.   [1]

   [Total: Core and Extended – 8 marks]

Approaching listening questions: matching speaker to statement Ⓒ Ⓔ

What you have to do: listen to six short extracts spoken by six different speakers about the same topic. You are given a list of speakers and a list of statements that they could have said. You have to match each speaker to the correct statement, based on what you hear in the recording. You will hear the set of recordings twice.

The kinds of text you will hear: short monologues spoken by a variety of people of different ages.

To go one step further: all students answer the same questions.

The skills you need – the ability to:

1. listen carefully and understand ideas, opinions and attitudes
2. understand the connections between related ideas
3. understand what is implied but not actually stated, for example, feelings, intentions.

Checklist for success

✔ Use the pauses between the speakers in exactly the same way to prepare yourself as you did for the earlier listening questions.

✔ Use your pre-reading skills, just as you did in Questions 1–5. Look at the statements carefully. Make sure you really understand them, to prepare yourself for the sorts of information or clues you need to listen out for.

✔ Underline any key words in the statements which might help you focus and identify the clues you need to answer the question.

✔ After you have heard the six speakers for the first time, there is a short pause. Use this time to think quickly and decide which speakers you will really want to check or consider again.

✔ In the pause after the second playing, check that you have not put the same letter down twice.

✔ Remember that one of the letters will not be used – there is an extra one to make you think hard.

✔ Never leave a gap – you can always have a guess.

Practice matching speakers to statements: question 6

You will hear six people talking about sport. For each of Speakers 1 to 6, choose from the list A to G, which opinion each speaker expresses. Write the letter in the box. Use each letter only once. There is one extra letter which you do not need to use.

You will hear the full recording of all six speakers twice.

19.3

Speaker 1 [ ]

Speaker 2 [ ]

Speaker 3 [ ]

Speaker 4 [ ]

Speaker 5 [ ]

Speaker 6 [ ]

A I enjoy sport because it keeps me fit and helps me make friends.

B I love my sport and want to play in international competitions.

C I am really lucky because I am earning my living doing the sport I love.

D I have always enjoyed sport but it is definitely just a hobby for me.

E I am sorry that I do not do as much sport now as I did when younger.

F I used to hate sport but now I am really keen and will never stop.

G I have never liked sport, not when I was young, and not now.

Approaching listening questions: multiple-choice questions Ⓒ Ⓔ

What you have to do: listen to a discussion or conversation between two speakers and then choose one correct answer out of three possible answers.

The kinds of text you will hear: semi-formal discussions and conversations between two speakers, sometimes with a host to introduce them.

To go one step further: all students answer the same questions.

The skills you need – the ability to:

1. listen carefully and understand ideas, opinions and attitudes
2. understand the connections between related ideas
3. understand what is implied but not actually stated, for example, feelings, intentions.

Checklist for success

✔ Use the pauses in exactly the same way to prepare yourself as you did for the earlier listening questions.

✔ Use your pre-reading skills, just as you did before. Look at the questions and their three possible answers very carefully. Make sure you really understand them, to prepare yourself for the sorts of information or clues you need to listen out for.

✔ Underline any key words in the questions which might help you focus and identify the clues you need to answer the question.

Practice multiple-choice questions: question 7

You will hear a radio interview with Liang Chen, a travel writer, about pearls and pearl diving. Listen to the conversation and look at the questions.

For each question, choose the correct answer, A, B or C and put a tick (✔) in the appropriate box. You will hear the interview twice.

a) How can we tell that pearl divers have been at work for at least 2000 years?

    A The divers have found 2000-year-old pearls ☐

    B There is a 2000-year-old book that describes pearl diving ☐

    C People have admired pearls for at least 2000 years ☐

b) **What quantity of pearls do you need to give you about 4 good pearls?**

    A 2000 tonnes ☐

    B 20 tonnes ☐

    C 3 tonnes ☐

    D 1 tonne ☐

c) **Why were people willing to face death by diving down so deeply?**

    A They loved diving. ☐

    B They thought the pearls were beautiful. ☐

    C They knew the pearls were valuable. ☐

d) **In Japan, why are women thought to be better than men at diving for pearls?**

    A their bodies are able to keep warm better ☐

    B they are older than the men ☐

    C they are more active than the men ☐

e) **How does Ms Sakai feel now about her life as a pearl diver in the old days?**

    A sad

    B angry

    C proud

f) **What did the divers use to help them dive down as quickly as possible?**

    A a heavy basket

    B an oxygen tank

    C a big stone

g) **Why do the women pearl divers in Toba dive nowadays?**

    A to find pearls to sell to tourists

    B to give tourists an idea of the past

    C to show tourists how people still risk their lives

h) **In the last hundred years, the number of pearl divers in Toba has**

    A gone down

    B gone up

    C stayed about the same

[Total: 8]

Core: end of test

Extended only

Approaching listening questions: note-completion questions ⓔ

What you have to do: The question is in two parts:

a) Listen to a talk and then complete short notes.

b) Listen to a short conversation about the talk and complete short sentences.

For this question you will only hear the talk ONCE, so you will need to listen very carefully indeed.

The kinds of text you will hear:

a) a formal talk, lecture, presentation

b) an informal discussion based on the same topic.

To go one step further: only Extended students have to do this question.

The skills you need – the ability to:

1. listen carefully and select exactly the right detail
2. understand ideas, opinions and attitudes
2. understand the connections between related ideas
3. understand what is implied but not actually stated, for example, feelings, intentions.

Checklist for success

✔ Use the pauses in exactly the same way to prepare yourself as you did for the earlier listening questions.

✔ Use your pre-reading skills, just as you did before. Look at the notes and the sentences very carefully. Make sure you really understand them, to prepare yourself for the sorts of details or clues you need to listen out for.

✔ Underline any key words in the questions which might help you focus and identify the clues you need to answer the question.

Practice note-completion questions: question 8

Part A

You will hear a talk given by a member of an Arctic exploration team about the preparations they made for an expedition. Listen to the talk and complete the notes in Part A. Write one or two words in each gap.

You will hear the talk ONCE.

Preparations for Arctic trip

Accommodation

Will be staying in special .... designed for survival in cold weather.

Safety

Prepared for attacks from ....

Took for defence: flares, personal ...., a trip-wire fence and trained dogs.

Different kinds of ice

white ice: 6 to 12 inches thick – safe to walk on

.... ice: 4 to 6 inches thick – could be safe

black ice: new and very thin – very dangerous

Return home

Not prepared for big changes

From smell of fresh air to different smells of city

From white snow to the bright colours

From silence to city sounds

Together: an .... on the five senses. [Total: 5]

Part B

Now listen to a conversation between two students about preparing for an expedition, and complete the sentences. Write one or two words only in each gap. You will hear the conversation ONCE.

Preparing for an expedition:

The Year Group Activity Expedition involves walking for a distance of ....

....

When you pack a rucksack it is a good idea to put the .... items in first of all.

It is important to try to make the rucksack weigh as .... as possible.

To prevent blisters, before using new boots for a long hike, do short walks first and use ....

On their expedition, the speakers are looking forward to it getting away from the hustle

and bustle of ....

[Total: 5]

20 Responding to the oral assessment test

Essential information

A special note: Syllabus 0510 has what is called 'Oral Endorsement'. This means that your performance in the oral test is shown as a separate grade 1 (high) to 5 (low) on your certificate.

Syllabus 0511 has what is called a 'Count-in oral'. This means that the mark you get is added in, and is included in your final grade on the certificate.

What you have to do: have a conversation on a particular topic with an examiner, who may or may not be your usual teacher. The whole test lasts about 15 minutes, and will follow the same pattern for everybody, everywhere in the world. The conversation is marked out of 30 marks.

The kinds of topic: based on a wide variety of topics considered to be of interest to a broad range of people.

To go one step further: all students take the same test, normally following all five prompts provided for each topic of discussion. If you are aiming for a top-level grade you must use a variety of structures accurately; use a range of words precisely to express subtle shades of meaning; take an active part in helping to develop a conversation.

The speaking and listening skills you use – in order to give an account or description, or express opinions clearly in the test situation, you will need to be able to:

1. understand how the topic card is designed
2. use your preparation time effectively
3. respond effectively in a conversation
4. develop the conversation with the examiner.

What happens in the oral assessment

The oral assessments are all recorded. The centre can then send some of the recordings to the exam board, where they will be checked thoroughly to ensure fairness.

There are four steps in taking the test.

STEP 1 An introduction by the examiner

The examiner will welcome you into the exam room, and explain very briefly what will happen in the test. Then the examiner will read out your name and candidate number for the recording.

STEP 2 Non-assessed warm-up period of 2 to 3 minutes

The examiner will ask you a few questions about yourself, just to help you relax and get used to the examination situation. This section of the test is not marked in any way at all. At the end of the warm-up time the examiner will tell you the topic you are going to talk about. You cannot ask the examiner to change the topic – this is decided by the examiner. You are not offered a choice of the topics available to the examiner, but the examiner will do his or her best to select one to match your interests.

STEP 3 Preparation time

You will now have 2 to 3 minutes to prepare for the conversation. We will be considering this in more detail. The recording will be paused during this section of the test. You are not allowed to make any written notes at all. If there are any words or ideas on the card that you do not understand, you are allowed to ask the examiner about them. You can also ask if there is anything you do not understand about what is going to happen next.

STEP 4 An assessed conversation of about 6 to 9 minutes

This is the part of the test which will be marked. We will also be considering this in more detail. The examiner may start the conversation, or may invite you to begin. He or she is responsible for making sure that you use all the prompts on the topic card. You have to respond to the examiner and then help develop the conversation for 6 to 9 minutes. You must not give a speech or a monologue at any point. If you do, the examiner will stop you and lead you back into a conversation.

The assessment of the conversation

When you are marked during the conversation, you will get a separate mark for each of these three things:

- **Structure** – this means how well you can use a variety of well-structured sentences, with your ideas clearly grouped and organised.
- **Vocabulary** – this means how well you can use a good range of words and phrases to express exactly what you want to say.
- **Development and fluency** – this means how well you can respond to the other person and move the conversation forwards.

> **Top tip**
>
> Practise having a recorded conversation with another person. Get used to having a microphone between you, and learn to ignore it. You could use your mobile phone or a laptop to help you practise outside the classroom.

The oral assessment test: step by step

STEP 1 Understand the topic card

It helps to understand how the topic cards are organised. As an example, look at this topic card:

Prompt 1 asks about *you*, personally – a chance to talk about yourself, to give an account and/or give a description of when you have eaten fast food. If you have never eaten any fast food, talk about other people or even films or pictures where you have seen people eating fast food.

Modern eating habits

Nowadays many of us eat fast food, ready prepared meals and takeaways – so-called junk food.

Discuss the topic of modern eating habits with the examiner.

Please use the following ideas to help develop the conversation:

- times when you have eaten 'fast food', or seen other people eating it

- occasions when you have taken your time to eat, for example, home-cooked meals at home

- reasons why takeaway meals are more popular nowadays than ever before

- the idea that fast food is unhealthy food

- the suggestion that family life is being destroyed by modern eating habits.

You are free to consider any other **related** ideas of your own.

Remember, you are not allowed to make any written notes.

Prompt 2 again asks you to think about *your own experience* – but this time you have to think beyond yourself – in this case, to describe a time when your family or friends have eaten together at home. If you do not do this very often, think around the subject and talk about a special occasion in the past, or about people sharing meals in pictures or films.

Prompt 3 is starting to move away from personal aspects of the subject – asking you to think about the subject more widely. You could use people you know as examples. Are they typical and, if so, in what ways? If they are untypical, how do they compare with the majority of people?

Prompt 4 is now asking you to think about an idea – you should not give an account or a description. Think carefully about how healthy (or unhealthy) fast food is. You are free to argue either for or against the idea. You are being asked for your opinion, but make sure you support it well. Use general knowledge, for example, too much fat is unhealthy: comment on the amounts of fat/artificial colourings, etc. in fast food or compare it with home-cooked meals. (You do not need to show any scientific knowledge or statistics.)

Prompt 5 expects you to look at the issue from an even wider perspective. It is not about you, your immediate family or neighbourhood: you are being asked to consider the topic in relation to your country – even globally.

All the topic cards follow this pattern.

STEP 2 Use the preparation time effectively

The preparation time lasts between 2 and 3 minutes. It is very important to make the best possible use of this time. Remember that you are not allowed to make any written notes at all during this time. It would only slow you down if you did, and you would do worse, not better in the assessed conversation.

- You should read the card carefully. Check if there are any words, phrases or ideas you do not understand, and ask the examiner for help if you need it.
- Look at each prompt in turn, and think silently what you could include in your response to it. What is your opinion or attitude to the topic?
- For each prompt, start to think about the sorts of vocabulary you will need to use.

2.1 Deciding what to talk about

For this practice exercise you are going to make notes, just so that you can see the thought processes you will need to go through. Of course, in the test, you are not allowed to write any notes and all this will be done silently, in your head.

Look again at the sample topic card 'Modern eating habits' on page 302. Work through each prompt and note down some ideas. Remember, you do not have to agree with the statements on the card. You are being asked for your personal opinions but, also remember, you will be expected to support your opinions with reasons, details or examples. Copy the following chart to complete the notes under each heading and add your own ideas.

Prompt	Notes I could …	Useful vocabulary Add five other words/phrases to each lists
Prompt 1: times when you have eaten 'fast food', or seen other people eating it	Give an account of the time I … And the time I … Describe the time when I saw … And when I saw …	Beef burger Pizza Delicious
Prompt 2: times when you have taken your time to eat, for example, home-cooked meals at home	Describe my family meal times at weekends when … Talk about a special meal – a birthday celebration …	Special food Table manners Knives and forks
Prompt 3: reasons why takeaway meals are more popular nowadays than ever before	Explain mothers and fathers long working hours, for example … Explain that pizzas are cheap and children like them because …	Working parents Time pressure Convenience food
Prompt 4: the idea that fast food is unhealthy food	Agree because fast fried food is unhealthy – chips full of fat … Disagree because salads are a form of fast food, for example, as a side dish to a pizza …	Protein Saturated fat Obesity
Prompt 5: the suggestion that family life is being destroyed by modern eating habits	Disagree because family eats and watches TV together, for example … Say it's true because families do not talk to one another as in my grandparents' day …	Social breakdown Conversation Relationships

2.2 Working without notes

In the last exercise, you used notes to help you get started. Of course, in the examination you are not allowed to make any notes. Here is another topic card for you to work on.

Working for a living

Most people have to work to earn money and make a living for themselves and their families.

Discuss the topic of 'Working for a living' with the examiner.

Please use the following ideas to help develop the conversation:

- the job or career you might want to do in later life

- another job or career you know you definitely do not want to do

- the reasons why someone you know, or have heard about, really loves his or her work

- which is more important: a good wage or job satisfaction, and the reasons for your view

- the idea that in the future there will be fewer jobs and what this means for the world.

You are free to consider any other **related** ideas of your own.

Remember, you are not allowed to make any written notes.

Spend about 3 minutes looking at the five prompts in turn: around 30 seconds for each prompt. Ask your teacher to time you and let you know when you should move on to the next prompt.

As you consider each prompt, imagine the kinds of things you could talk about. Remember:

- Prompts 1 and 2 will most likely expect you to give a personal account or a description.
- Prompt 3 will expect you to talk about more general matters and other people's experiences or views, looking further outwards towards your family or wider circle of friends, or even famous people you know about.
- Prompts 4 and 5 will expect you to consider a suggestion, opinion or idea, and give your own views, supporting it with reasons or examples. They will ask you to consider the topic in a wide, even worldwide context.

In pairs, tell one another what you would have said about each of the prompts. If one of you is stuck for an idea, make suggestions or ask more questions to help the other think of ideas.

STEP 3 Respond effectively in a conversation

The conversation will probably start with the examiner asking you a question connected to the first prompt. A good way to keep the conversation going is to make sure you answer the questions – but go one step further and offer a little more, if you can.

Think of the conversation as a football. You have to keep it moving between the two of you. As you are the one being tested, you have to show how good you are at moving the ball onwards, with tiny pushes and kicks, or a long pass to the other person. But never let it stop. Remember, the examiner will be helping you keep the ball rolling, so you're not on your own.

3.1 Effective responses

Look at the **transcript** below. The examiner and the student are talking about receiving a large amount of money and what it would mean for the student.

Remember that people do not talk in proper sentences all the time – so there are a lot of pauses, and 'ers' as the student speaks. This is quite usual. No one expects a perfectly formed paragraph and perfect sentences in a conversation.

> **Glossary**
>
> **transcript** – a written record of what is said.

Examiner:	How do you think a large amount of money might help you personally?
Student:	Well... not much really ... I think ... er ... that I'm fortunate right now ... er ... and I think I've got everything I need actually. I'll be travelling next year as well ... er ... and I think a large amount of money wouldn't really change anything because I've got everything I need.
Examiner:	I like that. I mean, it seems you appreciate what you have already.
Student:	Yeah, I do ... er ... and ... er ... the only thing I think I'd do with more money would be ... er ... give it to charity ... er ... I mean or just not spend it anyway.

Looking at the transcript, find one place in the conversation where the student:

- answers a question, but then goes a step further to make the conversation move on
- picks up on a point made by the examiner and does not wait for an actual question to continue the conversation
- introduces a new idea into the conversation.

If you were the examiner, where would you take the conversation next? Predict what the examiner might have said or asked.

Here is a more from the transcript of the conversation, towards the end.

> Examiner: So, do you think society could function if we didn't have any money at all in the world?
>
> Student: That sounds like a very good idea … er … it would be nice … but I think it's been proved that it doesn't work … and I think people wouldn't work … they wouldn't … people need to have something back for their hard work.

3.2 Ineffective responses

If you are asked a question where you could just answer 'Yes' or 'No', try to find a way to explain or give reasons for your answer. Avoid giving short answers that stop the conversation.

Look back at the last transcript. What might a weaker response to this question have been?

STEP 4 Develop the conversation

You now know that you need to keep the conversation active and moving along – to keep that football on the move. So let's look at a few of the ways you can do this, besides just answering any questions the examiner asks.

4.1 Adding details to develop accounts/descriptions

Prompt 1 is usually about you and your own experiences. For instance, the topic might be 'Living at home' and the examiner might start by asking: 'Tell me about the house where you lived as a child.' You could just give a simple answer:

> I used to live in a flat in the city.

And then wait for another question. Of course, this is perfectly acceptable, but you would not want to answer every question or prompt with such a short comment. If you want to develop your response, you could, for example:

- offer some detail:
  > modern/old   what it looked like from the outside
  > the room where you slept   who lived there with you
- add your thoughts or feelings about it:
  > happy memories   hated it
  > liked it much more than where I live now...
- give more details about your thoughts or feelings:
  > I liked it more than where I live now because …

- tell a short anecdote (a short account of an event) to explain your feelings:

> *I really liked it there. I have happy memories of when my brother and I used to play hide and seek. One day, we …*

As you can see, you do not need to add a lot – just enough to keep the ball rolling.

Top tip

Remember, you must not give a speech or presentation. The assessment is in the form of a two-way conversation.

4.2 Using details to develop explanations

Sometimes you might be expected to give an explanation of one of the prompts on the topic card. For instance, on the topic 'Living at home', prompt 3 might be: 'how people can make a house feel like a comfortable home'.

You could just give a simple answer:

> *By having nice furniture.*

Again, this would be acceptable and the examiner could go on to ask you more. But you could offer a little more detail yourself:

> *You need to have a good, comfortable place where you can relax and unwind … I have some lovely soft cushions in my room, where I can collapse at the end of a busy day. And my dad has his own special chair so he can take a nap … none of us are allowed in it!*

On your own and in pairs, look at the sentences below, which the examiner might use for the second or third prompt on the topic card.

- What else makes a house into a home?
- How do you become a nurse/mechanic/engineer/teacher?
- How do most people earn a living in your country?
- What makes someone good at a sport?

Note down some ideas of how you could develop your responses to these. Then share your ideas with a partner, before putting your notes away and asking each other the prompts. Again, record yourselves and see the timings. Be prepared to let the exchange of ideas turn into a short conversation of no more than 2 or 3 minutes.

4.3 Using reasons to support opinions

When you and the examiner reach prompts 4 and 5, you will probably be invited to offer your opinion about something. For example, the examiner might introduce this prompt: 'What do you think of the idea that governments should build more houses, even if it means destroying countryside?'

You could just give a simple answer:

> *I think they should because houses are important.*

This would be fine as a start, but the examiner will no doubt go on to ask 'Why?' So you must be ready to support your opinion with reasons and examples – just as you learnt to do when writing to express an opinion. In the preparation time, remember to think quickly about your point of view on the set topic, and have a few reasons to support that opinion.

Top tip

Just as when you are writing, you can consider alternative views in order to disagree with them when speaking. This gives you extra ideas to get you started.

In pairs, consider the following prompts asking for an opinion. In each case, work together to note down ideas and complete the table. The first one has been started for you. Can you add any ideas?

Remember that in the conversations you are not expected to offer facts and statistics as you might do in an essay where you have had time to look up information. Instead, you should use your general knowledge, what you have experienced yourself, what you have read or seen or heard about from others. This speaking task is not a test of knowledge!

What do you think about the idea that	My opinion	Reasons for my opinion	Some people might say that	But I think
Governments should build more houses even if it means destroying countryside.	A shame but necessary to build houses.	Shortage of houses, many people homeless and sleeping in the streets. Young people have to live at home longer. Children being brought up in crowded places.	Environment is precious and cannot be replaced.	People are more important than trees and flowers.
All armies should be banned throughout the world.				
Everyone should leave school at the age of 14.				
Animals should be treated with the same respect as people.				
Everyone should be paid the same wage, no matter what their job.				

4.4 Practise giving reasons to support your opinions

Now take it in turns to role-play the 'examiner' and the 'student'. The person role-playing the examiner uses one of the prompts from the table above to start the conversation. The student should not look at any of the notes you made. Can you keep the conversation going for 2 minutes?

Checklist for success

✔ After the warm-up, and during the preparation time, read the topic card carefully.

✔ Ask if there is anything on the card that you do not understand.

✔ Use your time effectively and think of some of the things you are going to say.

✔ During the conversation, respond to the examiner's questions/prompts with several ideas and sentences – not just single words or phrases.

✔ During the conversation, use details and examples to develop your accounts and descriptions.

✔ Use reasons and details to support your opinions.

✔ Respond quickly to any change in the direction of the conversation.

Practice oral assessment

Now you are ready to do an oral assessment task, in the style of an IGCSE examination.

Daily life in the future

Many think that with all the advances in technology, everyone's daily life in the future will be much better than it is now.

Discuss this topic with the examiner.

Please use the following ideas to help develop the conversation:

● ways in which your daily life is easy because of modern technology, e.g. transport, telephones

● ways in which daily life could be made even easier for you in the future, e.g. at home, at work

● the attitudes of some older people to the fast progress they have seen in their lifetimes

● the suggestion that modern progress does not always bring greater happiness

● the idea that too much progress will be dangerous for mankind.

You are free to consider any other **related** ideas of your own.

Remember, you are not allowed to make any written notes.

21 Sample student answers

This chapter contains example answers to all the exam-style questions given in Chapters 13–20. There are usually two example answers for each question.

Read and listen to the example answers. Then look at the marks and comments to help you understand the total mark each answer is given. Apart from the answers to the listening questions, which were written by the author, student answers are generally based on answers written by real students. The marks have been allocated and the comments written by the author – they have not been through any formal marking or grading process.

Chapter 13

Short text reading question

For these answers, you could try covering up the last two columns, and think what mark you would have given before checking. You can do this on your own or with a partner.

Student 1 (who attempted all questions)

	mark	comment
a) Future sound	0	Only one given: the question clearly asks for **two** band names.
b) it's in the future with spectacular lighting effects	1	The 'spectacular lighting effects' are usual for this company, so this part of the answer does not get credit. 'in the future' gets one mark.
c) Wendsay afternoon at 3	1	Although Wednesday is spelt wrongly, it is recognisable and all other details are correct.
d) Gnashers is at 278 High Street	0	The name is correct, but the wrong information was given about it. The question did not ask for the address.
e) Family tickets have 50% off	1	Good, concise answer.
f) paintings in water colours	0	The idea of 'landscapes' is not there; both parts were needed for the mark.
g) exhibitions	0	The student has not understood the question – you need to read the question very carefully.
h) it's only showing for a month	0	The text says this but it does not prove the paintings are good or bad.

Student 1 (Extended) got 3 out of 9 possible marks.

Student 2

	mark	comment
a) Future Sound, The Lazy Bones, Crazy Antics	1	Only two were needed. The student has given all three. This is a waste of time – and if either of the first two had been wrong, then the mark given would be 0.
b) set in the future and on Venus	2	Both given. Good concise answer.
c) 3pm on Wednesday	1	Both given. Concise answer.
d) The name is 'Gnashers' and it serves vegetarian food	1	Both parts are correct. The student is wasting time, though, and might not have enough time for later questions.
e) there is a special 50% discount on a family ticket	1	All correct, but rather long-winded.
f) water colour paintings of countryside scenery	1	Student has used their own words to explain 'landscapes'. This is correct, though 'landscapes' would also get the mark.
g) portraits of people	1	Correct, though again could be more concise.
h) the portrait artist has produced many water colour paintings. These have all got critical acclaim.	0	An overlong answer which does eventually answer the question. However, there are two answers here. The first one is wrong, so this response gets 0 marks.

Student 2 (Extended) got 8 out of 9 possible marks.

Longer text reading question

For these answers, you could try covering up the last two columns, and think what mark you would have given before checking. You can do this on your own or with a partner.

Student 1

	mark	comment
a) he found 50 million bees missing	1	Correct answer.
b) twenty four	1	Correct answer.
c) they are disappearing alarmingly quickly	0	First answer is incorrect.
they are threatening many lifes of crops		Second answer is correct (you can ignore the misspelling of 'lives').
		But both were needed for the award of the mark.
d) Californian almonds	1	Correct answer.
e) it has never happened before	0	It has happened before on a regional scale, but never before on a national scale.
f) grapes and apples and peanuts	0	The question asked for two crops. Mark the first two and ignore the last one. Grapes is right, but apples is wrong – so this response gets 0 marks.
g) bees fly off in search of pollen and nectar and simply never returning	1	Correct answer but time is wasted on unnecessary words.
h) They discussed a range of causes including viruses, a fungus and poor nutrition in the bees	2	A correct response which gets 2 marks, but was very long and wasted exam time.
i) The mites are killing the queen bees	0	This is not one of the reasons discussed in Florida.
j) rent out their bees to make honey	0	The bees are rented out to pollinate crops.
k) fuel costs and bee boxes have gone up	2	Only two out of the four given.

Student 1 (Extended) got 8 out of 15 possible marks

Student 2

	mark	comment
a) 50 million bees went missing	1	Good, concise answer
b) 24	1	Another concise, clear answer
c) livelihoods and crops	0	Both parts have been attempted, but here the answers were **too** short, and did not include the idea that these things were under threat / in danger.
d) almonds	1	Correct, concise answer.
e) first national crisis	1	Correct answer.
f) strawberries and grapes	1	Correct answer.
g) necter and pollen	1	Correct answer – you can ignore the spelling error when the word is clearly recognisable.
h) viruses and poor food for the bees	2	'food' is acceptable for 'nutrition' so this gets two marks.
i) queens are living half as long as they used to	1	Correct answer.
j) rent out the bees to pollinate crops	1	Clear, correct answer.
k) the queens do not live long fuel and equipment costs have risen costs to control mites is higher queen bees are more expensive	4	All four are given, although they appear in the last three answers. The first one is true, but it is irrelevant so it can be ignored. If it had been a wrong answer, this could only have scored 3 marks.

Student 2 (Extended) got 14 out of 15 possible marks.

Chapter 14

Information transfer question

For these answers, you could try covering up the last two columns, and think what mark you would have given before checking. You can do this on your own or with a partner.

Student 1

Core students score 1 mark for each question for Sections A, B and C.

	answer	mark	comment
Section A Personal details (BLOCK CAPITALS)			
Full name	KWAME ANAN	0	Spelling of ANNAN is wrong.
Date of birth	30. 09. 1995	0	Acceptable way of giving a date, but the month is wrong.
Home address (include town)	28, Royal Palm road, KUMASI	0	Not in capital letters.
Home Telephone number	233 – 51 – 896151	0	Omitted 00
Name of last school attended	KUMASI JUNIOR HIGH	0	This was his first school, not the last. Good use of capital letters – wrong answer.
Section B Travel History			
Country of Birth (Delete as necessary)	Ghana / other country in Africa / other country in Europe	0	Right answer – but it is underlined – the others should have been crossed out.
Please circle any of these countries that you have visited in the last three years:	United Kingdom ⟨Germany⟩ ⟨France⟩ Belgium Italy ⟨Spain⟩ China	1	Has correctly drawn circles around the 3 right answers.
Section C Visit to China			
Name of Football competition	Arica–Asia Cup	0	Africa spelt wrongly.
City to be visited	SHANGHAI	1	Correct spelling. Capital letters were not required – but there is no instruction saying they can't be used, so this is fine.
Dates when you will be in the country	10 – 17 October 2015	0	These are the dates of the competition, not the dates of the stay in China.

Section D Core students score up to two marks for each sentence in Section D

In the space below, write **one sentence** giving two things that you achieved, and **one sentence** about what caused you disappointment during the last international tournament you took part in.	I was Man of the Match for my outstanding performance and I scored two goals I was disapointed my team lost the tournament as well.	2	Gives two achievements – good. Sentence 1 gives information asked for. One error – no full stop. So 1 mark. Sentence 2 contains the required information, but there is one error of spelling, so 1 mark for Sentence 2.

Student 1 (Core) got 2 marks for Sections A, B and C; and 2 marks for Section D
   TOTAL: 2 + 2 = 4 out of 14 possible MARKS

Student 2 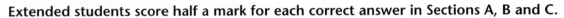 E

Extended students score half a mark for each correct answer in Sections A, B and C.

	answer	mark	comment
Section A Personal details (BLOCK CAPITALS)			
Full name	KWAME ANNAN	✓	Good answer.
Date of birth	30th AUGUST 1995	✓	Acceptable form of date.
Home address (include town)	28, ROYAL PALM ROAD,	0	Omitted town.
Home Telephone number	00 – 233 – 51 – 899151	0	Error in copying the number.
Name of last school attended	(the) Kumasi Academy	0	Correct answer, but forgot to use capital letters.
Section B Travel History			
Country of Birth (Delete as necessary)	Ghana / ~~other country in Africa~~ / ~~other country in Europe~~	✓	Good – has crossed out the required words.
Please circle any of these countries that you have visited in the last three years:	United Kingdom <u>Germany</u> <u>France</u> Belgium Italy <u>Spain</u> China	0	Did not draw a circle around the answers – underlined them instead. 0 marks for not following instruction exactly.
Section C Visit to China			
Name of Football competition	Africa-Asia Cup	✓	Exactly right.
City to be visited	Shanghai	✓	Exactly right.
Dates when you will be in the country	~~10–17 October 2015~~ 8–19 October 2015	✓	Has crossed out the wrong answer neatly and the new answer is very clear – and correct.

	answer	mark	comment
Section C Visit to China			
Name of Hotel where you will stay	Imperial	✓	It does not matter that 'Hotel' is not given.
Hotel address	208 Susan Road, Shanghai	0	Error in name of Road.
Section D			
Write one sentence saying what you achieved and what caused you disappointment (12–20 words)	He was Man of the Match and scored two goals but he was disappointed their team lost the tournament.	0	19 words; no errors in grammar or punctuation; gives all the required information; gives an extra achievement – no penalty for this. BUT not in the First Person – so 0 marks.

Student 2 (Extended) got 7 ticks for 7 right answers out of a possible 12. This becomes 4 out of 6 possible marks when it is divided by two, because any half marks are rounded up.

The student got 4 marks for Sections A, B and C and 0 marks for Section D.

TOTAL: 4 + 0 = 4 out of 8 possible MARKS

Chapter 15

Note-making question

For these answers, you could try covering up the last two columns, and think what you would have given that answer before looking. You can do this on your own or with a partner.

Student 1

	answer	mark	comment
Inuit way of life in the past	Called Eskimos	0	Not part of how they lived their lives – this is the name used by outsiders about them.
	Hunt their own food	1	It does not matter if the tense is in the present – not a test of grammar.
	Kill animals with spears	1	Correct.
	Catch fish with traditional fishing lines	0	This is not a separate answer.
	igloos	0	'Build igloos out of ice' is required.
	Magic powers of pots	0	Incorrect – the carvings were supposed to have magic powers.
	The Inuits live in tents made out of animal skin stretched over a frame	1	Correct, but too long – notes should be a few words, not a sentence. This wastes time.

Student 1 (Core) got 3 out of 7 possible marks for the note-making question.

Student 2

	answer	mark	comment
Inuit way of life in the past	Used traditional spears and fishing lines to hunt with	1	Both objects given, but only 1 mark.
	Made sculptures and small figgers believing they had magical powers	1	Correct, but too long – notes should be a few words, not a sentence. This wastes time. Wrong spelling of 'figures' does not lose marks.
	Lived in igloos	1	Correct.
	Made pots out of bone	1	We are not told what they are made of, but 'out of bone' does not make the answer wrong, so this gets the mark.
How present way of life is different from the past	Use more modern weapons like guns	1	Correct.
	Live in solid houses	1	Correct.
	Drive cars	1	This is a reasonable assumption from 'petrol-driven vehicles'.
	Make brooches to earn a living	1	Good clear answer.

Student 2 (Extended) got 4 marks for the first part, and 4 marks for the second part of the note-making question.

Total: 4 + 4 = 8 marks out of 9 possible marks

Chapter 16

Summary-writing question

Student 1

Wrong spelling of 'used'; 'use called' incorrect grammar.

Copied from text.
Starts in past tense, slips into present tense.

Wrong spelling of 'spears'.

Comma used instead of full stop.

Copied from text. Mix of present and past tense used but should be consistently past tense.

> The Inuits lived in the Arctic and they ~~use called~~ Eskimos and they hunt and traditionally eat sea mammals such as seals and whales and fish such as sammon for food, They use speers not guns like now they hacked out large blocks of ice cleverly carved blocks of ice and carve them into shape to build a circular igloo in summer they lived in tents made out ~~of animal skins stretched over a frame, to travel the Inuit used sleds made of animal bones and skins.~~

Wrong spelling of 'salmon'.

Full stop and capital letter are missed out which makes meaning unclear.

Over 70 words – the extra words have to be crossed out and ignored.

Student 1 (Core) gets only 1 out of 5 possible marks. The answer relies very heavily on copying out from the passage, but it still makes some sense, and the information is relevant to the question. There are several punctuation errors – not even one sentence has a clear capital letter and full stop. There is no real sense of organisation, and the word count is well over 70.

Student 2

Good – a topic sentence to introduce the summary.

Good – 'animals' to replace all the names of animals.

The Inuits used to live simple but hard lives. They hunted animals for food using their spears. They had to make homes out of hard ice, called igloos in the winter, but then in the warmer wether they made tents out of skins to live in. They used sleds and dogs for transport. They were clever artists, too, and made sculptchers which they thought had magik in them.

Wrong spelling of 'weather'.

Uses 'transport' – own choice of word to explain the use of the dogs and sleds.

Uses own words to explain igloos.

Uses own words to explain tents' construction.

Introduces the sentence with own words – 'clever artists'.

Incorrect spelling of 'sculptures'; 'magic' spelt wrongly.

Student 2 (Core) gets full marks – 5 marks. There is a good effort to organise the ideas, for example: starting with a topic sentence; using 'too' to link this sentence to the previous ones. There are several instances where the student uses their own words. Three spelling errors, but the many good qualities here outweigh these.

Chapter 17

Summary-writing question

The small numbers 1 to 8 refer to the content points in your teacher's marking guide. The letters in brackets refer to a point about style or grammar.

Student 1 Ⓔ

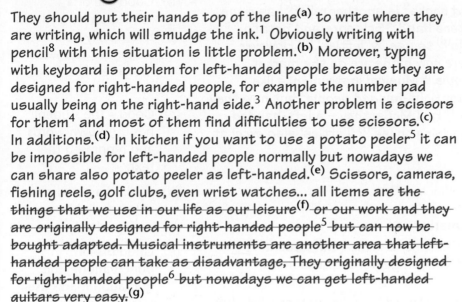

They should put their hands top of the line[a] to write where they are writing, which will smudge the ink.[1] Obviously writing with pencil[8] with this situation is little problem.[b] Moreover, typing with keyboard is problem for left-handed people because they are designed for right-handed people, for example the number pad usually being on the right-hand side.[3] Another problem is scissors for them[4] and most of them find difficulties to use scissors.[c] In additions.[d] In kitchen if you want to use a potato peeler[5] it can be impossible for left-handed people normally but nowadays we can share also potato peeler as left-handed.[e] Scissors, cameras, fishing reels, golf clubs, even wrist watches... all items are ~~the things that we use in our life as our leisure[f] or our work and they are originally designed for right-handed people[5] but can now be bought adapted. Musical instruments are another area that left-handed people can take as disadvantage. They originally designed for right-handed people[6] but nowadays we can get left-handed guitars very easy.[g]~~

(a) The meaning here is not clear – weak expression.

(b) The meaning is unclear again.

(c) Repeats the same idea twice, wasting words.

(d) Not a proper sentence – does not make sense on its own.

(e) Again this does not make proper sense.

(f) Very long-winded list – avoid examples like this.

(g) This is well over the word limit. All words after 120 are crossed out and ignored.

Student 1 (Extended) got 5 marks.

Difficulties: 4 marks   Ways to overcome: 1 mark   Language: 1 mark

This student's expression has many errors and is unclear at times. There is some lifting of words from the text (e.g. the list of items). There is some sense of order, but as the summary was not organised within the word limit, on balance the student scored 1 and not 2 for language.

Total: 4 out of 5 possible marks + 1 out of 2 possible marks + 1 out of 4 possible marks = 6 out of 11 possible marks

The small numbers 1 to 11 refer to the content points in your teacher's marking guide. The letters in brackets refer to a point about style or grammar.

Student 2

Many left-handed people face inconveniences every day.[a] When writing they curl their hand which can smudge the ink.[1] Using a pencil can overcome this.[8] Computers are a solution for these problems; however,[b] the keyboards are designed for right-handed people.[3] Avoiding spiral-bound books[9] is another relief[c] as rings can get in the way of the writer's hand.[2] Scissors and potato peelers [5] are found impossible[d] to use by 'lefties'.[e] However, these and other appliances are now made are on the market especially for left-handed people.[10] Musical instruments like guitars were generally made for right-handed people[7] but now they are available for left-handers.[11] Paul McCartney – a left-handed guitarist has helped in popularising these.[f] 'Lefties' also excel at sports.[g]

Student 2 (Extended) got 11 marks.

Difficulties: 4 marks   Ways to overcome: 2 marks (The student found all 4 points, but the most you can get for this section is 2 marks.)   Language: 4 marks

This student's expression is a little awkward , e.g. 'is another relief', but makes a good effort all the way through to use own words. Punctuation is excellent and showed some skill. The organisation is excellent, including a topic sentence. There were two irrelevant sentences at the end, which might have brought the language mark down to 4 – but on balance this deserved the full 5 marks.

Total: 4 + 2 + 5 = 11 out of 11 possible marks

(a) A good topic sentence – brief and sums up the paragraph well.

(b) Good use of a semicolon here to join two closely connected sentences; the word 'however' also links them well.

(c) Good – the student has used own words and rephrased the text.

(d) Again, has used own words to link 'scissors' and 'peelers'.

(e) Good use of punctuation – the quotation marks used to show that this is a slang word, as in the text.

(f) The last two sentences are irrelevant, but do not lose the student any marks.

(g) 117 words – within the 120 word limit.

Chapter 18

Long writing question

In this section there are sample answers for the first task only.

Student 1

Dear head teacher

Im[3] writing to you because Im interested in using our school hall for the concert. My plan is to raise money for a charity called 'Hot Lunch for All'. This charitys[3] aim is to get basic hot meal for eny child whos[1] parent cant[3] afford it at school in this country. I want to support them because it is very important that every child gets at least one proper hot meal a day.[4] It's quite shocking that in the 21st century there are famielis[1] that can't afford to pay for their children food in school.[2]

With your promition[1] I would like to use our school hall for the rock concert. The concert will be played by Metallica. There will be tickets that students, teachers and parents can buy and that's how I want to raise money. The concert will be 3rd February at 7pm but the hall is needed earlier because we need to set up the stage and let the band reherse.[1]

I will make sure there[5] will not be any damage to the building by asking 10 students from higher years to help me control the audience. I will be very thankful for your help.

Jason

Comments

Length: 201 words – this is longer than required for the Core-level response – the student will have less time for the second writing question now. No loss of marks for this though.

Content relevance: All the material is relevant, and essay covers all three prompts.

Good sense of reader – formal and respectful tone used, appropriate for a head teacher, for example, 'thankful for your help'.

Development: Some excellent realistic details to develop the ideas, for example the emotional appeal for the charity; and the need to set up earlier.

Top band – 7 out of 7 possible marks

Language

1. Spelling errors of reasonably common words. Permission was in the question and should have been copied correctly.

2. Good variety of structures used for sentences, e.g. first paragraph uses complex sentences with pronouns and subordinating connectives, then the last paragraph uses a shorter, simple sentence to good effect.

3. Some apostrophes were omitted, but sentences generally well punctuated.

4. Meaning is always clear.

5. Paragraphs used correctly.

Top band – 5 out of 6 possible marks

Student 1 (Core): 7 marks for Content and 5 marks for Language
Total: 12 out of 13 possible marks

Student 2 (E)

Dear Madam

I am a student representative on the School Council. I am writing to you to ask permission of using[1] the school football field in order to conduct a charity fun fair there.

The student representatives'[4] team and I have come up with[1] a fund raising fair for the 'Make A Wish Foundation'. We are willing to support[2] this foundation and raise money for it because we believe that every individual has the right to wish and to have their wish come true, especially the ones who are suffering[2] a severe illness or are in pain. I would like to have a fun fair on our field with different games to play, such as 'Hit the Coconut'. There would also be stalls where various accessories[4] – clothes and books - will be sold. I am sure we would make a good amount of money with having an entrance fee as well. I assure you that there will be no kind of damage to any school property as we will be having many students to volunteer to help about, and they will be in charge and take responsibility.[4]

I hope you let this fair take place[5] and give us the field for five hours on a Saturday morning.

Yours faithfully,

Ali Abdullah

Language

1. Slightly awkward expression – preposition error – but otherwise confident use of language throughout, for example, use of idiom: have come up with.

2. Good range of different tenses used confidently.

3. Variety of sentence structures – simple, compound and complex sentences all used correctly throughout.

4. Accurate punctuation and spelling even of unusual words.

5. Paragraphs clear and linked one after another.

Top band – 8 out of 9 possible marks

Comments

Length: 195 words – the correct length for an Extended-level essay.

Content relevance: Fulfils the task – covering all prompts.

          Excellent sense of purpose – very clearly explains what he wants from the head teacher.

          Good sense of the reader – uses a formal, polite style to ensure he is successful.

Development: All three prompts are developed with some convincing details, for example, the kind of games and the timing of the event. Prompt 3 could have a little more detail.

Top band – 9 out of 10 possible marks

Student 2: 9 marks for Content and 8 marks for Language

Total: 17 out of 19 possible marks

Chapter 19

Shorter listening questions

For these answers, you could try covering up the last two columns and decide what mark you would have give and why, before looking to see. You could do this on your own or with a partner.

Student 1

	answer	mark	comment
1a	Going to a museum	1	A bit long but correct
1b	The school bus leaves 6	1	An overlong answer, but correct
2a	ink	0	*Invisible* is required
2b	15 grams	0	Mishears 50 as 15
3a	Flat batry	1	Acceptable attempt at battery – word can be recognised
3b	phone	0	Must be mobile phone
4a	list of cocktails	1	Accepted
4b	strawberry	0	Omitted apple so no marks

Student 1 (Core) got 4 out of 8 possible marks.

Student 2 (E)

	answer	mark	comment
1a	museum	1	Correct – very concise and clear
1b	6 the next morning	1	Correct
2a	Invisible ink	1	Both required words so gets 1 mark
2b	50 gms	1	Correct
3a	Car stopped going	0	Incorrect
3b	mobile	1	Acceptable short form
4a	Drink menu	1	Correct – acceptable alternative
4b	Strawberry and apple cocktail	1	'cocktail' is not part of the answer but it does not contradict the right answer so it still gets a mark

Student 2 (Extended) got 7 out of 8 possible marks.

Listening gap-filling questions

For these answers, you could try covering up the last two columns, and think what mark you would have given, before taking a look. You could do this on your own or with a partner.

Student 1

	answer	mark	comment
	Josh Waitzkin: career in chess		
1	Chess titles: twenty-one times **Nashinall** Champion and twice World Champion.	1	Acceptable attempt at 'national'.
2	Six years of age: started playing chess.		
	At 9: National Junior High Champion.		
	At 11: drew against Kasparov, the adult World Champion.		
	At 16: became **intranashinall** Master	1	Correct.
	Josh's teaching about chess		
3	Title of first book about chess: **Attack** Chess.	1	Both are correct – misspelling of 'International' acceptable.
	Title of prize-winning instruction **video**: 'Chess Starts Here'.		
4	Title of popular **computer** about playing chess: 'Chessmaster',	0	'program' omitted so 0 marks.
5	Josh is **decoded** to teaching chess and making his ideas available to everyone,	0	Incorrect.
	Josh's career in Tai Chi		
6	Attracted to Tai Chi because of his interest in **east** philosophy and because he wanted to learn something new.	1	Close enough to 'eastern' to get mark.
	Won title of Middleweight World Champion in Taiwan in 2004.		

	answer	mark	comment
	Josh's worldwide career as a speaker		
7	Talks about: • how we learn • the mental attitude needed to **take part** • psychology of competition. Latest book	0	This does not mean the same as win, so 0 marks.
8	Explains we have to take **risks** if we are to grow and grow Book title: The **Book** of Learning	0	No mark as both had to be correct for the mark.

Student 1 (Core) got 3 out of 8 possible marks.

Student 2 (E)

	answer	mark	comment
	Josh Waitzkin: career in chess		
1	Chess titles: twenty-one times **international** Champion and twice World Champion.	0	Incorrect.
2	Six years of age: started playing chess. At 9: National Junior High Champion. At 11: drew against Kasparov, the adult World Champion. At 16: became **International** Master	1	Correct.
	Josh's teaching about chess		
3	Title of first book about chess: **Tack** Chess. Title of prize-winning instruction **video**: 'Chess Starts Here'.	0	The first is not acceptable and so no mark, although the second is correct.
4	Title of popular computer **game** about playing chess: 'Chessmaster',	1	'game' is acceptable alternative for 'program'.
5	Josh is **deddicayted** to teaching chess and making his ideas available to everyone, Josh's career in Tai Chi	1	Correct, although spelt wrongly.

	answer	mark	comment
6	Attracted to Tai Chi because of his interest in *easten* philosophy and because he wanted to learn something new. Won title of Middleweight World Champion in Taiwan in 2004.	1	Acceptable phonetic attempt.
7	Josh's worldwide career as a speaker Talks about: • how we learn • the mental attitude needed to *succeed* • psychology of competition. Latest book	1	Correct.
8	Explains we have to take chances if we are to grow and learn. Book title: The *Art* of Learning	1	Both correct.

Student 2 (Extended) got 6 out of 8 possible marks.

No example answers for Questions 6 or 7 are given as these are straightforward to mark.

For these answers, you could try covering up the last two columns, and think what mark you would have given, before taking a look. You could do this on your own or with a partner.

Student 1 Part A

answer	mark	comment
Accommodation		
Will be staying in special **place** designed for survival in cold weather.	0	Not the same as 'tents'.
Safety		
Prepared for attacks from **big animals**.	0	Not specific enough.
Took for defence: flares, personal **lams**, a trip-wire fence and trained dogs.	0	Unacceptable spelling of 'alarms'.
Different kinds of ice		
white ice: 6 to 12 inches thick – safe to walk on		
white ice: 4 to 6 inches thick – could be safe black ice: new and very thin – very dangerous	0	Incorrect answer.
Return home		
Not prepared for big changes		
From smell of fresh air to different smells of city		
From white snow to the bright colours		
From silence to city sounds		
Together: an **attack** on the five senses.	1	Acceptable alternative to 'assault'.

Total: 1 out of 5 possible marks

Student 2 Part A

answer	mark	comment
Accommodation		
Will be staying in special **tents** designed for survival in cold weather.	1	Correct.
Safety		
Prepared for attacks from **dangerous bears**.	0	Not specific enough – 'polar' is required.
Took for defence: flares, personal **alarming**, a trip-wire fence and trained dogs.	1	Acceptable form of 'alarm'.
Different kinds of ice		
white ice: 6 to 12 inches thick – safe to walk on		
grey ice: 4 to 6 inches thick – could be safe black ice: new and very thin – very dangerous	1	Correct answer.
Return home		
Not prepared for big changes		
From smell of fresh air to different smells of city		
From white snow to the bright colours		
From silence to city sounds		
Together: an **assort** on the five senses.	1	Acceptable spelling of 'assault'.

Total: 4 out of 5 possible marks

Student 1 Part B

answer	mark	comment
The Year Group Activity Expedition involves walking for a distance of **13 kilometres**.	0	30 misheard as 13.
When you pack a rucksack it is a good idea to put the **heavier** items in first of all.	1	Not exactly the same word but still conveys the correct detail.
It is important to try to make the rucksack weigh as **light** as possible.	1	Correct information, although wrong word.
To prevent blisters, before using new boots for a long hike, do short walks first and use **socks**.	0	Needs 'thick' to get the mark.
On their expedition, the speakers are looking forward to getting away from the hustle and bustle of the **shops**.	0	Incorrect.

Total: 2 out of 5 possible marks

Student 2 Listening Question 8 Part B

answer	mark	comment
The Year Group Activity Expedition involves walking for a distance of **thirty kilometres**.	1	Correct – numbers can be in word form.
When you pack a rucksack it is a good idea to put the **heavyest** items in first of all.	1	Spelling error but still conveys the correct detail.
It is important to try to make the rucksack weigh as **little** as possible.	1	Correct information.
To prevent blisters, before using new boots for a long hike, do short walks first and use **thik socks**.	1	Correct despite misspelling.
On their expedition, the speakers are looking forward to getting away from the hustle and bustle of the **town**.	1	Correct.

Total: 5 out of 5 possible marks

Chapter 20

Oral assessment test Ⓒ Ⓔ

The grid below shows how marks are awarded for 'Structure', 'Vocabulary' and 'Development and fluency'. Both Core and Extended students are marked using the same marking grid.

Marking grid

mark (out of 10)	structure	vocabulary	development and fluency
9–10	Variety of structures used accurately and confidently throughout the conversation.	Uses sophisticated vocabulary to explain complex and subtle ideas.	Keeps the conversation going and responds at some length to the other speaker. May introduce new ideas into the conversation.
7–8	Structures generally correct. Some errors in attempting complex sentences.	Uses a fair range of vocabulary to explain ideas clearly.	Responds to the other speaker well and takes part in a flowing conversation.
5–6	Uses straightforward structures well.	Uses straightforward vocabulary to convey simple ideas.	Responds to the other speaker but does not develop ideas. The other speaker has to keep the conversation going.
3–4	Very simple structures but with errors.	Uses a limited vocabulary and hesitates or searches for words.	Responds very briefly to the other speaker in a hesitant conversation. Some gaps and long pauses.
1–2	Attempts to take part but little clear meaning.	Uses a very limited vocabulary and cannot express ideas clearly at all.	Responds so briefly and says so little that no real conversation can take place.
0	No real response.	No real response.	No real response.

Listen to the recordings of three students who attempted the topic card headed 'Daily life in the future'. The grid opposite shows the marks they received for 'Structure', 'Vocabulary' and 'Development and fluency'.

Alternatively, you could listen to them and try to decide on the mark you think they should have received before you look at the comments opposite to help you understand why it got that mark.

Student 1

oral assessments	mark	comment
Structure (out of 10)	8	All straightforward structures are correct, but errors arise when more complex ideas are expressed, especially in response to Prompts 4 and 5.
Vocabulary (out of 10)	8	Some good vocabulary choices, though again some hesitation and errors when dealing with complex ideas.
Development and fluency (out of 10)	10	Excellent responses. Takes ideas and develops them; offers his own ideas without much prompting.
Total: marks (out of 30)	26	Very good. Bands 1–2.

Student 2

oral assessments	mark	comment
Structure (out of 10)	9	Some minor errors but overall a good range of structures is used throughout.
Vocabulary (out of 10)	9	Good range of vocabulary to express quite complex ideas, though perhaps not enough subtlety of meaning for full marks.
Development and fluency (out of 10)	10	Excellent responses. Develops ideas and includes own line of thought without prompting.
Total: marks (out of 30)	28	Excellent. Band 1.

Student 3

oral assessments	mark	comment
Structure (out of 10)	8	Overuses the colloquial isms 'like', 'and stuff', which makes some structures repetitive and hinders expression.
Vocabulary (out of 10)	8	A reasonable range of vocabulary used to convey straightforward ideas. No evidence of selection of vocabulary to express complex or subtle ideas.
Development and fluency (out of 10)	8	Responds well, but rather dependent on prompting from examiner to develop ideas.
Total: marks (out of 30)	24	Good. Band 2.

Acknowledgements

The publishers gratefully acknowledge the permission granted to reproduce the copyright material in this book. While every effort has been made to trace and contact copyright holders, where this has not been possible the publishers will be pleased to make the necessary arrangements at the first opportunity.

Text acknowledgements

Chapter 1: p 11: Extract from www.greatachievements.org © 2011 National Academy of Engineering, reprinted with permission; p 17: Extract from 'Dr Dillner's health dilemmas: should I limit my child's mobile phone use?' by Louisa Dillner, Guardian.co.uk 15 August 2001, copyright Guardian News & Media Ltd, 2011, reprinted with permission; p 19: Extract from www.sciencekids.co.nz, reprinted with kind permission of Rene Smith; p 21: DROPBOX is a trademark of Dropbox, Inc., reprinted with permission; SugarSync logo and description reprinted with permission; Memopal logo and description reprinted with permission; ADrive description reprinted with kind permission of ADrive.

Chapter 2: p 35: 'Why Explore Space?' From www.esa.int, reprinted with kind permission; p 45: origami boat diagrams from http://www.origami-fun.com/origami-boat.html, reprinted with kind permission of the author.

Chapter 3: p 53: Extract adapted from 'Pizza history' from www.inmamaskitchen.com, reprinted with kind permission; p 64: Extract from 'Teenage girls' junk food diet leaves them starved of vitamins' by Fiona MacRae, Daily Mail 9/7/2011, reprinted with permission of Solo Syndication.

Chapter 6: p 124 Extract from Sunday Times magazine, pp 49–53, Nov 6 2011, with permission © N. I. Syndication 2011.

Chapter 7: p 130 pie chart from www.uhv.edu/green/carbon_foot.aspx, reproduced with permission; p 131 Extract from 'A student's Guide to Global Climate Change', EPA, reproduced with permission; p 131 greenhouse effect diagrams reproduced by kind permission of Will Elder, US National Park Service; p 132 graph from http://www.climatechangeconnection.org/emissions/IPCC, reproduced with permission; p 136 letter 2065 first published in Chronica de los Tiempos, April 2002; p 140 from www.greenpeace.org reprinted under the Creative Commons License; p 140 from 'Carbon Monoxide' from Environmental Science in the 21st Century – an online textbook by Robert Stewart, found at http://oceanworld.tamu.edu/resources/environment-book/atmosphericpollutants.html, reprinted with kind permission of the author.

Chapter 9: p 173 Extract from www.trans-siberian-railway.co.uk © Clive Simpson

Chapter 10: p 192 Extract adapted from www.silk-road.com and www.madehow.com; p 195 from 'Get the look- White Heat!' by Xiaohan Shen, www.xssatstreetfashion.com/category/get-the-look, reprinted with kind permission of the author.

Chapter 11: p 216: from Scorpia Rising by Anthony Horowitz, copyright © 2011 by Anthony Horowitz, used by permission of Philomel Books, a division of Penguin Group (USA) Inc. and Walker Books Ltd (UK).

Chapter 12: p 231 From 'Why Africa needs to lower its voting age to 16' by Calestous Juma, The Guardian, 9 February 2011, © Guardian News & Media Ltd, 2011, reprinted with permission;

p 244 from 'World's oldest marathon runner completes Toronto race at age 100' by Caroline Davies, The Guardian, 18 October, 2011, copyright © Guardian News & Media Ltd 2011.

Photograph acknowledgements

The publisher would like to thank the following for permission to reproduce pictures in these pages (t = top, b = bottom, c = centre, l = left, r = right, f = far):

pp 8–9tcr ifong/Shutterstock, pp 8–9tr Marietjie/Shutterstock, pp 8–9c cobalt88/Shutterstock, pp 8–9bcl RubberBall/SuperStock, pp 8–9bl Supri Suharjoto/Shutterstock, pp 8–9tcl SSPL/Getty Images, pp 8–9tcfr Ferenc Szelepcsenyi/Shutterstock, pp 8–9br Cristi Matei/Shutterstock, pp 8–9bcl william casey/Shutterstock, pp 8–9tcfl Andreja Donko/Shutterstock, pp 8–9tl Pawel Gaul/iStockphoto, p 10c Martin Shields/Alamy, p 10l Seth Loader/iStockphoto, p 10r Andrew Buckin/Shutterstock, p 13 Image Courtesy of The Advertising Archives, p 14 dboystudio/Shutterstock, p 15 pkchai/Shutterstock, p 16 Nikifor Todorov/Shutterstock, p 17r Onoky/SuperStock, p 17l Felix Mizioznikov/Shutterstock, p 18 Pressmaster/Shutterstock, p 19 Tomislav Pinter/Shutterstock, p 20 FrancescoCorticchia/Shutterstock, p 21r Frank Gaertner/Shutterstock, p 22t Shawn Hempel/Shutterstock, p 22bl Vorm in Beeld/Shutterstock, p 22bc Mary Evans Picture Library/Alamy, p 22cl FotoSergio/Shutterstock, p 22cr Luis Louro/Shutterstock, p 22br elena moiseeva/Shutterstock, p 24 Blend Images/Shutterstock, p 26c incamerastock/Alamy, p 26l Sarunyu_foto/Shutterstock, p 26r kosam/Shutterstock, pp 28–29tr Richie Ji/Shutterstock, pp 28–29br NASA, pp 28–29tl Corbis Bridge/Alamy, pp 28–29tcl David Fleetham/Alamy, pp 28–29bc INTERFOTO/Alamy, pp 28–29cr christian keller/iStockphoto, pp 28–29bl Royal Geographical Society/Alamy, pp 28–29c amygdala_imagery/iStockphoto, pp 28–29cl Tom Grill/Shutterstock, pp 28–29tcr yuanann/Shutterstock, p 30 INTERFOTO/Alamy, p 31 Chris Hellier/Corbis, p 32 Arctic-Images/Alamy, p 33c Martin Hartley/Getty Images, p 33t North Wind Picture Archives/Alamy, p 33b GentooMultimediaLimited/iStockphoto, p 34br NASA Archive/Alamy, p 34l Keystone Pictures USA/Alamy, p 34tr Mechanik/Shutterstock, p 35 MARK GARLICK/SCIENCE PHOTO LIBRARY, p 37 ChinaFotoPress/Contributor, p 38bc jeremy sutton-hibbert/Alamy, p 38l U.S. Coast Guard/Handout, p 38tc Hybrid Images/Getty Images, p 40 Leo Francini/Shutterstock, p 41 Morgan Lane Photography/Shutterstock, p 42t Mariusz S. Jurgielewicz/Shutterstock, p 42b Mark Doherty/Shutterstock, p 43 JonMilnes/Shutterstock, p 44b NOAA/SCIENCE PHOTO LIBRARY, p 44t littlesam/Shutterstock, p 46r NASA, p 46c Leo Francini/Shutterstock, p 46l Andrew Jalbert/Shutterstock, pp 48–49bfl Philip Date/Shutterstock, pp 48–49br Aaron Amat/Shutterstock, pp 48–49bfr Alex Segre/Alamy, pp 48–49tr ElenaGaak/Shutterstock, pp 48–49cr Robert Pears/iStockphoto, pp 48–49tc Blend Images/Shutterstock, pp 48–49cl Dmitrijs Bindemanis/Shutterstock, pp 48–49tcr Maxisport/Shutterstock, pp 48–49bl Goran Shutterstock/Shutterstock, pp 48–49tl Jim West/Alamy, pp 48–49tcl Michelangelo Gratton/Shutterstock, p 51 travellinglight/iStockphoto, p 52 Levent Konuk/Shutterstock, p 53b Netfalls – Remy Musser/Shutterstock, p 53c Fernando Madeira/Shutterstock, p 53t Ableimages/SuperStock, p 54 David Grossman/Alamy, p 55 photofriday/Shutterstock, p 56 Jose Gil/Shutterstock, p 57b Cultura Limited/SuperStock, p 57t

gorillaimages/Shutterstock, p 58r Blaj Gabriel/Shutterstock, p 58l Kletr/Shutterstock, p 59 Alena Brozova/Shutterstock, p 60 Wutthichai/Shutterstock, p 62l maska/Shutterstock, p 62c Sean D/Shutterstock, p 62r Ken Tannenbaum/Shutterstock, p 63tr Nikola Bilic/Shutterstock, p 63tl Elena Elisseeva/Shutterstock, p 63bl Piotr Rzeszutek/Shutterstock, p 63br Matt Antonino/Shutterstock, p 66bl Kuttig – RF – Kids/Alamy, p 66tr Golden Pixels LLC/Alamy, p 66bc muzsy/Shutterstock, p 66tl Niko Guido/iStockphoto, p 66tc Pressmaster/Shutterstock, p 66br Jochen Schoenfeld/Shutterstock, pp 68–69tl Yawar Nazir/Getty Images, pp 68–69tcr Robert Kneschke/Shutterstock, pp 68–69bcr Rohit Seth/Shutterstock, pp 68–69bfl Falconia/Shutterstock, pp 68–69bfr Hung Chung Chih/Shutterstock, pp 68–69bl Zurijeta/Shutterstock, pp 68–69cl bikeriderlondon/Shutterstock, pp 68–69cr Design Pics/SuperStock, p 70 YAKOBCHUK VASYL/Shutterstock, p 71c StockCube/Shutterstock, p 71b Sergey Nivens/Shutterstock, p 71t Jeff Cameron Collingwood/Shutterstock, p 74t Popperfoto/Getty Images, p 74c Victorian Traditions/Shutterstock, p 74b chippix/Shutterstock, p 75 Jose Ignacio Soto/Shutterstock, p 76 The Stapleton Collection/Bridgeman Art, p 77 sellingpix/Shutterstock, p 79 MEHAU KULYK/SCIENCE PHOTO LIBRARY, p 80 Chris Schmidt/iStockphoto, p 82t michaeljung/Shutterstock, p 82l kali9/iStockphoto, p 82r Rehan Qureshi/Shutterstock, p 84 JO YONG-HAK/X90071/Reuters/Corbis, p 85 Monkey Business Images/Shutterstock, p 86tr KarSol/Shutterstock, p 86bl 35007/iStockphoto, p 86tc Zurijeta/Shutterstock, p 86tl auremar/Shutterstock, p 86br Robert Kneschke/Shutterstock, pp 88–89cr Image Source/Alamy, pp 88–89tcl i love images/business office/Alamy, pp 88–89tr Kim Karpeles/Alamy, pp 88–89bl Eye Ubiquitous/Alamy, pp 88–89cl Couperfield/Shutterstock, pp 88–89tcr Mark Bridger/Shutterstock, pp 88–89c Aspen Photo/Shutterstock, pp 88–89tr BlueMoon Stock/SuperStock, pp 88–89tc Science and Society/SuperStock, pp 88–89br andrea michele piacquadio/Shutterstock, p 90l Roberta Olenick/Getty Images, p 90r Mint Images Limited/Alamy, p 90c Gerrit_de_Vries/Shutterstock, p 91 Jim Agronick/Shutterstock, p 93cr jannoon028/Shutterstock, p 93cc Globe Turner/Shutterstock, p 93cl Globe Turner/Shutterstock, p 93b Biosphere Expeditions, p 93tl Biosphere Expeditions, p 93c Biosphere Expeditions, p 93tr Biosphere Expeditions, p 94 br Ian Walton/Getty Images, p 94c Quinn Rooney/Getty Images, p 94bl Tom Pennington/Getty Images, p 95 Popperfoto/Getty Images, p 96 Alexander Hassenstein/Bongarts/Getty Images, p 97 Portokalis/Shutterstock, p 98 MOHAMED OMAR/epa/Corbis, p 101c Gil Cohen Magen/Reuters/Corbis, p 101l Jose AS Reyes/Shutterstock, p 101r CREATISTA/Shutterstock, p 103 Goodluz/Shutterstock, p 104 Martin Shields/Alamy, p 106 B. O'Kane/Alamy, pp 108–109tc nikkytok/Shutterstock, pp 108–109c lisegagne/iStockphoto,
pp 108–109cl PKOM/Shutterstock.com, pp 108–109tl kataleewan intarachote/Shutterstock, pp 108–109br Dmitry Kalinovsky/Shutterstock, pp 108–109tcr Vasily Smirnov/Shutterstock, pp 108–109bl Blend Images/Shutterstock, pp 108–109bc Golden Pixels LLC/Shutterstock, pp 108–109tr Johnny Habell/Shutterstock, pp 108–109cr Monkey Business Images/Shutterstock, p 110 mykeyruna/Shutterstock, p 115 michaeljung/Shutterstock, p 116 Ann Worthy/Shutterstock, p 118 Monkey Business Images/Shutterstock, p 120 Rehan Qureshi/Shutterstock, p 122tc dboystudio/Shutterstock.com, p 122tl leungchopan/Shutterstock, p 122b Andresr/Shutterstock, p 122tr frantisekhojdysz/Shutterstock , p 123c Gunter Marx/AE/Alamy, p 123l Hank Morgan/Rainbow/Science Faction/SuperStock, p 123r

Todd Shoemake/Shutterstock, p 124 Yuri Arcurs/Shutterstock, p 125 Monkey Business Images/Shutterstock, p 126 Franck Boston/Shutterstock, pp 128–129br Remi Benali/Getty Images, pp 128–129bfl RainervonBrandis/iStockphoto, pp 128–129tr Rob van Esch/Shutterstock, pp 128–129tcr Jason Rothe/Shutterstock , pp 128–129c aluxum/iStock, pp 128–129tl NASA, pp 128–129cl Sergey Uryadnikov/Shutterstock, pp 128–129bfr erwinf/Shutterstock, pp 128–129cr iamanewbee/Shutterstock, pp 128–129bl Jamikorn Sooktaramorn/Shutterstock, pp 128–129tcl , p 131 Alex Staroseltsev/Shutterstock, p 134 Patrick Poendl/Shutterstock, pp 136–137 Bryon Palmer/Shutterstock, p 137 Tetra Images/SuperStock, p 138 U.S. COAST GUARD/SCIENCE PHOTO LIBRARY, pp 140–141 grynold/Shutterstock, p 142tl EcoPrint/Shutterstock, p 142tc Ronnie Howard/Shutterstock, p 142tr Paul Banton/Shutterstock, p 142b Serg64/Shutterstock, p 142c Mogens Trolle/Shutterstock, p 143b Iv Nikolny/Shutterstock, p 143t Dr. Morley Read/Shutterstock, p 144 Picture of Prerna Bindra reproduced by kind permission of Prerna Bindra, p 145 Nick Biemans/Shutterstock, p 146 pulsar75/Shutterstock, pp 148–149bc PhotoAlto/James Hardy/Getty Images, pp 148–149c Asia Images/Getty Images, pp 148–149bl Prisma Bildagentur AG/Alamy, pp 148–149br Peter Horree/Alamy, pp 148–149tcr Belinda Images/SuperStock, pp 148–149tcl Werner Forman/Universal Images Group/Getty Images, pp 148–149tcr gary yim/Shutterstock.com, pp 148–149cl fstockfoto/Shutterstock.com, pp 148–149tl Sergei Bachlakov/Shutterstock.com, pp 148–149tr Cedric Weber/Shutterstock.com, pp 148–149tc wong yu liang/Shutterstock, p 151 MARCO LONGARI/AFP/Getty Images, p 152 Alexander Yakovlev/iStockphoto, p 153 View Stock/Getty, p 154br Blaine Harrington III/Alamy, p 154bl Cora Reed/Shutterstock.com, p 154t Hulton-Deutsch Collection/CORBIS, p 156 Carsten Reisinger/Shutterstock, p 157 Pres Panayotov/Shutterstock.com, p 159 Tomohiro Ohsumi/Bloomberg via Getty Images, p 158r Anton Albert/Shutterstock, p 158l Patricia Malina/Shutterstock, p 161 OLIVER BERG/AFP/Getty Images, p 162b Lonely Planet Images/Getty Images, p 162t Seleznev Oleg/Shutterstock, p 163l Klaas Lingbeek- van Kranen/iStockphoto, p 163r Hung Chung Chih/Shutterstock, p 165t Zzvet/Shutterstock, p 165b Bjorn Stefanson/Shutterstock, pp 168–169bl Stock Connection/SuperStock, pp 168–169cl Pius Koller/imagebrok/imagebroker.net/SuperStock , pp 168–169tcl ben bryant/Shutterstock, pp 168–169tr NASA, pp 168–169c Fernando Jose Vasconcelos Soares/Shutterstock, pp 168–169tl Pichugin Dmitry/Shutterstock, pp 168–169br Thomas Nord/Shutterstock.com, pp 168–169bc Rob Byron/Shutterstock, pp 168–169tcr 1000 Words/Shutterstock, pp 168–169c Ajiro Bicycle image reproduced by kind permission of Alexander Vittouris, p 170 Michael Mihin/Shutterstock.com, p 171 SCIENCE PHOTO LIBRARY, p 172bl SCIENCE PHOTO LIBRARY, p 172t Hodag Media/Shutterstock, p 172br chippix/Shutterstock, p 173 Kaehler, Wolfgang/SuperStock, p 175t Steve Froebe/iStockphoto, p 175b Jorg Hackemann/Shutterstock, p 175c baki/Shutterstock, p 176r Steve Froebe/iStockphoto, p 176bl omers/Shutterstock, p 176br Ashwin/Shutterstock.com, p 178 Vitalii Nesterchuk/Shutterstock, p 179 Claudiu Paizan/Shutterstock, p 180t Brian Tan/Shutterstock.com, p 180b Devi/Shutterstock, p 182b E-volo multicopter reproduced by kind permission of http://www.e-volo.com/, p 182c Floating cloud image reproduced by kind permission of Tiago Barros, p 183 NASA/SCIENCE PHOTO LIBRARY, p 184tl Ajiro Bicycle image reproduced by kind permission of Alexander Vittouris, p 184tr Photo by Rex Features (1016836f), p 184b CAT water taxi Image reproduced by kind permission of Cal Craven, designer of the C.A.T (City Aquatic Transport) for his final degree project in Industrial Design at the National College of Art and Design, Dublin Ireland, p 186l Maurice Savage/Alamy, p 186c Transtock/SuperStock, p 186tr chungking/Shutterstock, p 186r ssguy/Shutterstock, pp 188–189tcl Keystone/Getty Images, pp 188–189br crystalfoto/Shutterstock, pp 188–189bfl Pete Niesen/Shutterstock, pp 188–189tc Anna Omelchenko/Shutterstock, pp 188–189c MAEADV/Shutterstock, pp 188–189tr Yuri Arcurs/Shutterstock, pp 188–189bfr Natali Glado/Shutterstock, pp 188–189tl lev dolgachov/Shutterstock, pp 188–189cr R. Gino Santa Maria/Shutterstock, pp 188–189tcr Dennis Albert Richardson/Shutterstock, pp 188–189cl Joe Seer/Shutterstock, pp 188–189bl Carlos E. Santa Maria/Shutterstock, p 192b Bai Yu/Xinhua Press/Corbis, p 192t Gerhard Zwerger–Schoner/imagebroker/Corbis, p 193t Ocean/Corbis, p 193b SuperStock/Corbis, p 194_8 Dennis Albert Richardson/Shutterstock, p 194_5 Alexander.Yakovlev/Shutterstock, p 194_3 Dana Ward/Shutterstock, p 194_7 John Springer Collection/CORBIS, p 194_1 NBC via Getty Images, p 194_6 Rick's Photography/Shutterstock, p 194_2 Neale Cousland/Shutterstock, p 194_4 CREATISTA/Shutterstock, p 196 Inga Marchuk/Shutterstock, p 197 David Bergman /Sports Illustrated/Getty Images, p 198_2 John Stanmeyer/VII/Corbis, p 198_3 Brendan Howard/Shutterstock, p 198_4 Thomas La Mela/Shutterstock, p 198_5 swissmacky/Shutterstock, p 198_1 jivan child/Shutterstock, p 199b Blend Images/Shutterstock, p 199t Kailash K Soni/Shutterstock, p 200b Massimo Calmonte (www.massimocalmonte.it)/Getty Images, p 200t Guo Jian She/Redlink/Redlink/Corbis, p 201r Rtimages/Shutterstock, p 201l Sergey Peterman/Shutterstock, p 201c cristovao/Shutterstock, p 202bl Bobbo's Pix/Alamy, p 202t Andrew Lichtenstein/Sygma/Corbis, p 202br Tim Wright/CORBIS, p 204 JEFFREY LEPORE/SCIENCE PHOTO LIBRARY, pp 208–209bl Lilyana Vynogradova/Shutterstock, pp 208–209c Media Union/Shutterstock, pp 208–209bc Wathiq Khuzaie /Getty Images, pp 208–209cr Lars Baron/Getty Images, pp 208–209tl & p 213 Herve BRUHAT/Gamma-Rapho via Getty Images, pp 208–209tr James Steidl/Shutterstock, pp 208–209br Nolte Lourens/Shutterstock, p 210 SAFIN HAMED/AFP/Getty Images, p 211 Fred De Bailliencourt/iStockphoto, p 212t MCales/Shutterstock, p 212b sharpner/Shutterstock, p 214tl INTERFOTO /Alamy, p 214tr Kevin Britland/Alamy, p 214b Jean-Baptiste Rabouan/Hemis/Corbis, p 214c Sebastian Crocker/Shutterstock, p 215 Tim Gander/Alamy, p 216t Alex Rider logo used by permission of Philomel Books, a division of Penguin Group (USA) Inc and Walker Books Ltd (UK), p 216b Brian Chase/Shutterstock, p 217 Kamira/Shutterstock.com, p 218 jeremy sutton-hibbert/Alamy, p 222 ARKO DATTA/Reuters/Corbis, p 223 PIUS UTOMI EKPEI/AFP/Getty, p 224 Catherine Karnow/CORBIS, p 226 Tomislav Pinter/Shutterstock, pp 228–229bc robert cocquyt/iStockphoto, pp 228–229tl Hill Street Studios/Getty Images, pp 228–229bl Jekaterina Nikitina/Getty Images, pp 228–229cl Martin Harvey/Corbis, pp 228–229br Catherine Yeulet/iStockphoto, pp 228–229c ZouZou/Shutterstock, pp 228–229cr Yuri Arcurs/Shutterstock, pp 228–229tr Iakov Filimonov/Shutterstock, p 231 SEYLLOU/AFP/Getty Images, p 233t Monkey Business Images/Shutterstock, p 233b Hill Street Studios/E/Blend Images/SuperStock, p 235 Paul Maguire/Shutterstock, p 237 Juice Team/Shutterstock, p 238br CREATISTA/Shutterstock, p 238bl Phil Date/Shutterstock, p 238t Zurijeta/Shutterstock, p 239t Robert Harding World Imagery/Corbis, p 239br Herve Collart/Sygma/Corbis, p 239bl Ryan M. Bolton/Shutterstock, p 240 Rimantas Abromas/Shutterstock, p 241 zhu difeng/Shutterstock, p 242 Action Plus Sports Images/Alamy, p 243t Getty Images, p 243br TORSTEN BLACKWOOD/AFP/Getty Images, p 243bl epa european pressphoto agency b.v./Alamy, p 244 JIM WATSON/AFP/Getty Images, p 246t Jack.Q/Shutterstock, p 246c William Perugini/Shutterstock, p 246b Rob Marmion/Shutterstock

Audio acknowledgements

Track 1.1: reproduced by kind permission of www.eBackpack.com

Track 3.2: Department of Health Press Release from 2010. Crown Copyright © 2010.

Track 4.2: 'How to make a Mindmap – the Basics' reproduced by kind permission of Susan Gregory; http://www.susangregory.ca

Track 4.3: 'Rules for mindmapping' reproduced by kind permission of ThinkBuzan, http://www.thinkbuzan.com

Track 6.7: Extract from *Sunday Times* magazine, pp49–53, Nov 6 2011, with permission © N.I. Syndication 2011, reproduced by kind permission.

Track 7.2: extract from 'The Plight of Endangered Species/Endangered Earth' by Craig Kasnoff. Reprinted with kind permission of the author.

Track 12.6: from 'World's oldest marathon runner completes Toronto race at age 100' By Caroline Davies, The Guardian, 18 October, 2011, copyright © Guardian News & Media Ltd 2011.

CD-ROM track list

Chapter 1:
1.1 (p 20); 1.2 (p 23); 1.3 (p 24)

Chapter 2:
2.1 (p 42); 2.2 (p 42); 2.3 (p 43); 2.4 (p 43); 2.5 (p 43)

Chapter 3:
3.1 (p 62); 3.2 (p 63); 3.3 (p 64); 3.4 (p 65); 3.5 (p 65)

Chapter 4:
4.1 (p 79); 4.2 (p 81); 4.3 (p 81); 4.4 (p 83); 4.5 (p 84)

Chapter 5
5.1 (p 103); 5.2 (p 104); 5.3 (p 105); 5.4 (p 105)

Chapter 6:
6.1 (p 118); 6.2 (p 119); 6.3 (p 119); 6.4 (p 121); 6.5 (p 122); 6.6 (p 123); 6.7 (p 124); 6.8 (p 125)

Chapter 7:
7.1 (p 143); 7.2 (p 143); 7.3 (p 144); 7.4 (p 145)

Chapter 8
8.1 (p 163); 8.2 (p 163); 8.3 (p 163); 8.4 (p 165)

Chapter 9
9.1 (p 179); 9.2 (p 183); 9.3 (p 184); 9.4 (p 185)

Chapter 10
10.1 (p 203); 10.2 (p 205); 10.3 (p 205)

Chapter 11
11.1 (p 219); 11.2 (p 221); 11.3 (p 222); 11.4 (p 223); 11.5 (p 224)

Chapter 12
12.1 (p 238); 12.2 (p 239); 12.3 (p 239); 12.4 (p 243); 12.5 (p 243); 12.6 (p 244); 12.7 (p 245)

Chapter 19
19.1 (p 292); 19.2 (p 293); 19.3 (p 295); 19.4 (p 296); 19.5 (p 298); 19.6 (p 299)

Chapter 21
21.1 (p 333); 21.2 (p 333); 21.3 (p 333)